My Week with Marilyn

My Week with Marilyn

Colin Clark

WEINSTEIN
BOOKS

This book is a republication of two separate works:
My Week with Marilyn (2000), first published in Great
Britain by HarperCollins, and *The Prince, the Showgirl,
and Me: The Colin Clark Diaries* (1995), first published in
Great Britain by HarperCollins and in the United States
by St. Martin's Press.

Production by Eclipse Publishing Services

ISBN: 978-1-60286-149-7
E-book ISBN: 978-1-60286-150-3
Library of Congress Control Number: 2011933864

First Edition

10 9 8 7 6 5 4 3 2 1

CONTENTS

PUBLISHER'S NOTE

In 1956, fresh out of Oxford, twenty-three-year-old Colin Clark was employed as a "gofer" on the English set of *The Prince and the Showgirl*, a film featuring Sir Laurence Olivier, Britain's preeminent classical actor, and Marilyn Monroe, Hollywood's greatest star. From the outset the production was bedeviled by problems, and the clashes between Monroe and Olivier have since entered film legend. As a lowly set assistant Clark kept a fly-on-the-wall record of the often tumultuous experience in a journal he published to great acclaim almost forty years later, in 1995, as *The Prince, the Showgirl, and Me*.

But one week was missing from the middle of that book. For nine days during the filming, Clark found himself escorting an unhappy Monroe around England in an innocent and often idyllic adventure designed to help the actress escape the pressures of working with Olivier and an often hostile cast and crew. In the process Clark earned Monroe's lasting trust and affection. From the notes Clark made shortly after the episode he wrote *My Week with Marilyn*, published in 2000, two years before his death.

Here, for the first time, *My Week with Marilyn* and *The Prince, the Showgirl, and Me* are published together in the same volume.

My Week with Marilyn

For Christopher

INTRODUCTION

All my life I have kept diaries, but this is not one of them. This is a fairy story, an interlude, an episode outside time and space which nevertheless was real. And why not? I believe in magic. My life and most people's lives are a series of little miracles – strange coincidences which spring from uncontrollable impulses and give rise to incomprehensible dreams. We spend a lot of time pretending that we are normal, but underneath the surface each one of us knows that he or she is unique.

This book sets out to describe a miracle – a few days in my life when a dream came true and my only talent was not to close my eyes. Of course I didn't realise quite what a miracle it was at the time. I had been brought up in a world of 'make believe'. My earliest memory of my parents is of remote and wonderful beings, only seen late at night, wearing full evening dress. All their friends seemed to be exotic too. Actors, artists, ballerinas and opera singers filled our house with a wonderful feeling of excitement and unreality.

And there was my older brother, Alan. Alan's imagination knew no bounds, even then. My twin sister and I were completely under his spell, and he led us into a succession of fantastical adventures and games. It was hardly surprising that by the age of twelve I had decided that 'show business' would one day be the life for me; and so it has been ever since.

I got my first job in the summer of 1956, at the age of twenty-three, working on a film called *The Sleeping Prince*, starring Laurence

Olivier and Marilyn Monroe. I had just come down from university, and I had no experience whatever. I was only employed because my parents were friends of Olivier and his wife, Vivien Leigh. The Oliviers had been frequent visitors to our home, Saltwood Castle in Kent, and they had become part of my extended family.

The news that Olivier, the best-known classical actor of his generation, was going to make a film with Marilyn Monroe, the famous Hollywood film star, caused a sensation. Marilyn was to play the part which had been taken by Vivien herself in the play by Terence Rattigan on which the film was based. Up to then she had only played strippers and chorus girls, in very limited roles. In 1955, after a terrific struggle, she renegotiated her contract with Twentieth Century-Fox and announced her intention to do more serious work. Typecasting is never easy to escape, especially in films. Her first new role had been that of a stripper (in *Bus Stop*), and the second, chosen for her by Milton Greene, her partner in the newly formed Marilyn Monroe Productions, was that of a chorus girl. The only 'serious' element was that both films were by so-called 'serious' writers. *Bus Stop* had been based on a play by William Inge, and *The Sleeping Prince* on a play by Terence Rattigan.

Filming *The Prince and the Showgirl*, as it was finally called (it was decided that the title should include a reference to Marilyn's character), went badly from the very beginning. Olivier patronised Monroe and treated her like a dumb blonde. This was exactly what she was trying to escape, and she resented it intensely. It also drastically affected her self-confidence, and as a result she constantly relied for advice on her 'dramatic coach', Paula Strasberg, whom Olivier distrusted. Paula's husband Lee Strasberg, the head of the Actors Studio in New York, was trying to control Monroe from across the Atlantic. At the same time he was extracting a huge salary for his wife, which made him very unpopular. Monroe's new husband, the playwright Arthur Miller, was treating her like a difficult child, and this also undermined her. Milton Greene was desperate to retain control of 'his' star, and was letting her take more prescription drugs than was perhaps wise. But Monroe was determined to show that she could act, despite her feelings of inadequacy when faced with Olivier and the super-professional English team that had been assembled specially for the film.

From my first day on the production as third assistant director – the lowest of the low – I kept a journal of everything that I observed. I intended to transcribe it when the film was over, but my notes became messy and hard to read, and I simply put the volume away and forgot it. Forty years later I dug it out and read it again, and it was subsequently published under the title *The Prince, the Showgirl, and Me.*

One episode, however, was not recorded in my diary.

For nine days in the middle of filming, I made no entries at all. Suddenly, and completely unexpectedly, something happened which was, to me, so dramatic and so extraordinary that it was impossible to include it in my daily chatterings. For a short time the attention of the major participants – Olivier, Greene and, above all, Marilyn – seemed to be focused on me. It was as if a spotlight had swung round, for no particular reason, and singled me out as the hero or villain of the piece.

When normal life resumed, I continued to write my diary as before. I made notes on what I felt had been the key events of those 'missing' days, but that is all. It was not until the filming was over that I could go back and write down what had happened, in the form of a letter to the friend for whom I was keeping my journal.

This, then, is the story of those missing nine days. Of course it goes much further than the letter (the text of which is reproduced as an appendix to this book), but I make no apology for that. The whole episode is still as fresh in my mind as if it had happened yesterday.

I could never have written this account while Marilyn was alive. I produce it now as a humble tribute to someone who changed my life, and whose own life I only wish I could have saved.

Tuesday, 11 September 1956

'Can't Roger handle it?' asked Milton Greene.

Milton and I were pacing up and down the small piece of new lawn outside Marilyn Monroe's dressing room at Pinewood Studios. As usual, Milton could not make up his mind.

'I'm not sure if anyone from the film crew should go near her home, Colin. Even you.'

'I rented that house for Marilyn, just as I rented yours for you,' I said. 'I hired Roger as her bodyguard, and I also hired her cook, her butler and her chauffeur. I know them all well. If we aren't very careful, everyone will just walk out. Roger is a very nice man, but Roger is a policeman. He's only used to dealing with subordinates. You can't treat servants like that. You have to behave as if they were part of the family. Believe me, Milton, I'm very familiar with these problems. My mother worries more about her cook than she does about me.'

Milton groaned. He had gone to great lengths – and considerable personal expense, he told me – to make absolutely sure that Marilyn was happy in every way. A sumptuous dressing-room suite had been built in the old make-up block at Pinewood, all beige and white, and I had taken a lease on the most beautiful house I could find – Parkside House at Englefield Green, a few miles away, which belonged to Garrett and Joan Moore, old friends of my parents. Despite all this, Marilyn did not seem to be satisfied, and Milton's pacing was distinctly uneasy.

'OK, Colin, go over to the house if you must. We can't have the servants leave. Marilyn would be mad. But whatever you do, don't let her see you. You are Sir Laurence's personal assistant, after all. And she definitely doesn't seem too keen on Sir Laurence these days.'

That was certainly true. After only three weeks of filming, a gulf had already opened between the two great stars, and everyone had started to take sides. The entire British film crew had been selected by Olivier to give him maximum support. Marilyn had brought only a small team from Hollywood – including her make-up man and her hair stylist – and they had all gone back by now. She was left with no one to support her in the studio but Paula Strasberg, her dramatic coach. Of course, she also had her new husband, the playwright Arthur Miller (their marriage – her third, his second – had taken place two weeks before they flew to England), but he had sworn not to interfere with the filming in any way.

Milton was Marilyn's partner and co-producer, but she didn't seem to be listening to him as much as she used to – probably because Miller resented the fact that Milton had once been her lover – so he needed all the allies he could get. I was only the third assistant director on the film – the person anyone can tell what to do – and as such I was hardly a threat to anybody, but Marilyn had always seemed quite sympathetic when I got yelled at, if indeed she noticed me at all. At the same time, I was Olivier's personal assistant, and I sometimes had access to him when Milton did not. So Milton had decided that he and I would be friends. On this occasion, he had probably guessed that what I really wanted was an excuse to go over to Marilyn's house; and he would have been right. After all, he spent half his time trying to stop anyone getting near Marilyn, because he knew that she was like a magnet that nobody could resist – not even a little assistant director, seven years younger than her. I should have been used to 'stars' by now. After all, Vivien Leigh and Margot Fonteyn were both family friends. But those two ladies, wonderful as they are, are both human beings. Marilyn is a true goddess, and should only be treated as such.

'I'm between a rock and a hard place, Colin,' said Milton. It was a glorious summer morning, but we had been awaiting Marilyn's arrival for over an hour, and he was getting impatient. 'Why can't Olivier accept Marilyn for what she is? You British think everyone should punch a timeclock, even stars. Olivier's disappointed because Marilyn doesn't behave like a bit-part player. Why can't he adapt? Oh, he's very polite on the surface, but Marilyn can see through that. She can sense that underneath he's ready to explode. Josh Logan* used to yell at her occasionally, but he worked with her as she was, and not as he wanted her to be. She's scared of Olivier. She has this feeling that she'll never measure up.'

'Vivien says that Olivier fell for Marilyn's charm just like everyone else when he first met her,' I said. 'She says he even thought he could have a romance with her. And Vivien is always right.'

'Oh, Marilyn can charm any man if she wants to, but when she gets mad, it's a very different story. You watch out. By the way, what the hell has happened to her this morning?'

'I thought you said she shouldn't have to punch a timeclock.'

'Yes, but when it's her own money going down the drain – and mine . . .'

'I wouldn't mind if she kept us waiting all day. Working in a film studio is hot, boring, tiring and claustrophobic. I sympathise with Marilyn a lot.'

'Yeah, but it's her job.'

At that moment Marilyn's big black car came nosing round the studio block. It was instantly surrounded by a crowd of people who seemed to appear out of thin air. The new make-up man, the wardrobe mistress, the hair stylist, the associate director Tony Bushell, the production manager, all clamouring for attention before the poor lady could even get inside the building. She already had Paula Strasberg, with her script, and ex-Detective Chief Superintendent Roger Smith, late of Scotland Yard and protective as ever, carrying her bags. No

---

* The director of *Bus Stop*, Marilyn's previous film.

wonder she fled inside like a hunted animal, taking no notice of Milton, or, of course, of me.

As soon as Marilyn had disappeared, with Milton trailing behind her, I tackled Roger. I knew I had only a few seconds in which to explain. Roger returned to Parkside House as quickly as he could after dropping Marilyn off in the mornings, and David Orton, my boss on the studio floor, would soon be wondering where I was.

'I'm coming over to the house tonight to talk to Maria and José,' I said firmly. Maria and José were the Portuguese cook and butler I had hired to look after Marilyn at Parkside House. 'Milton says it's OK.'

'Oh yes? Problems, are there?' Roger looked sceptical.

'It won't take long, but we mustn't let them get upset. They would be terribly hard to replace. We can have a drink afterwards, and maybe a bite to eat. Ask Maria to make some sandwiches.'

Roger is devoted to Marilyn. After thirty long years in the police force, this is his finest hour. He follows her everywhere like a faithful Labrador dog. I'm not sure how much use he would be in a crisis, but he is clearly very shrewd, and with a bit of luck he could avert trouble before it occurred. I expect that he could see through my ploy, just as Milton had; but Roger has no one to talk to in the evenings, and he gets lonely. He reminds me of the drill sergeants I knew when I was a pilot-officer in the RAF, so we get on very well. All of the other people around Marilyn talk in film language, which Roger hates. He and I can have a gossip in plain English.

'So you don't need to come over to collect Marilyn this evening,' I went on. (There wouldn't be enough room in the car if he did.) 'I'll ride in the front with Evans, and then he can take me back.'

Evans is Marilyn's driver. Like Roger he had been hired by me; and he is one of the stupidest men I have ever met. I don't think he even knows who Marilyn Monroe is; but he does what he is told, which is the main thing.

'Hmm,' said Roger doubtfully, but just then a shout of 'Colin!' came from inside the building and I dashed away before he could reply.

I have known the Oliviers since I was a child, and I've met all sorts of famous people with my parents. But Marilyn is different. She is wrapped in a sort of blanket of fame which both protects and attracts. Her aura is incredibly strong – strong enough to be diluted by thousands of cinema screens all over the world, and still survive. In the flesh, this star quality is almost more than one can take. When I am with her my eyes don't want to leave her. I just can't seem to see enough of her, and perhaps this is because I cannot really see her at all. It is a feeling one could easily confuse with love. No wonder she has so many fans, and has to be so careful who she meets. I suppose this is why she spends most of her time shut up in her house, and why she finds it so hard to turn up at the studio at all, let alone on time. When she does arrive, she flashes from her car to her dressing room like a blur. She seems frightened, and perhaps she's right to be. I know I must not add to those persecuting her, yet I can't resist being in her orbit. And since I am paid by Olivier to make her life easier and smoother, I have to be in the background of her life, I tell myself, if nothing more.

As soon as I went inside the studio building I was in the usual trouble.

'Colin! Where the hell have you been?' David says this every time he sees me, even if I've only been gone for ten seconds. 'Olivier wants to see you straight away. It's 10 o'clock. Marilyn's only just arrived. We'll be lucky to get one shot done before lunch,' etc., etc.

Why don't they ever realise that, like it or not, this is Marilyn's pattern, and we might as well get used to it? Olivier argues that if we didn't make a fuss she'd never turn up at all, but I'm not so sure. Marilyn wants to act. She even wants to act with Olivier. She needs to make a success of this film to prove to the world that she is a serious actress. I think she'd turn up if the pressure was off. She might even be early, but I suppose that is a risk no film company would dare to take. Olivier talks about her as if she was no more than a pin-up, with no brains at all. He seems to have nothing but contempt for her. He is convinced she can't act – just because she can't clip on a character like a suit of clothes in the way he can – and he despises her use of Paula as a dramatic coach. He can't see that Paula is only there for reassurance, not to tell Marilyn how to play the part. He only has to look at the film we've already shot to see that Marilyn is doing a very subtle job all on her own. The trouble is that he gets so frustrated by all the 'ums' and 'ahs', the missed cues and incorrect lines that he fails to recognise the flashes of brilliance when they come. Every evening the screenings of the previous day's filming remind him of the pain that he had to go through in front of and behind the camera, and he seems to take a perverse enjoyment in them. Why doesn't he get the editor to cut out all the horrors, and only show the bits that went well, however short? Imagine how exciting that would be. We all file into the viewing theatre; the lights go down; there is a thirty-second clip of Marilyn looking stunning and remembering all her lines; the lights go up again to a ripple of applause; Marilyn goes home encouraged instead of depressed; the editor is happy; Olivier is happy.

In your dreams, Colin! For some unknown psychological reason, blamed of course on technical necessity, we have to see every stumble and hesitation in giant close-up, repeated again and again, failure after failure, until we are all groaning and moaning, and Marilyn, if she has turned up, flees back to her house in shame. I just wish I could have a quiet chat with her and reassure her. But there are too many people already doing that – and patently failing.

I had only been over to Marilyn's house once since she moved in five weeks ago, and there was no point in thinking that I would get a chance to talk to her, or even to see her, if I went there again. All I wanted now was the excitement of riding in the front of the car, with this heavenly creature in the back. I wanted to feel as if I was her bodyguard, instead of Roger. I wanted to feel as if her safety depended on me. Luckily, Evans takes no notice of me whatsoever, and nor does Paula Strasberg. She has been 'coaching' Marilyn all day in the studio, but then there are sixty or so technicians there with her, not to speak of twenty other actors, and Olivier himself. In the car, Paula is only concentrating on getting Marilyn to herself for a few last minutes. She grips her arm fiercely and never stops talking, never draws breath, for the whole trip. She repeats herself again and again, pouring reassurance into Marilyn's ear: 'Marilyn, you were wonderful. You are a great, great actress. You are superb, you are divine . . .' and so on.

In the end, her praise of Marilyn's performance and acting ability gets so exaggerated that even Marilyn starts to get uneasy. It's as if Paula knows she only has this short moment in which to implant herself on Marilyn's mind for the night, and thus make herself indispensable for the following day.

Olivier, as the director of the film, naturally resents Paula's presence intensely. Paula knows nothing of the technical difficulties of making a movie, and often calls Marilyn over to give her instructions while Olivier is in the process of explaining to Marilyn what he needs, as the director. On these occasions Olivier's patience is really incredible. Nevertheless, I like Paula, and I feel sorry for her. This dumpy little woman, swathed in differing shades of brown, with her sunglasses on her head and her script in her hand, is clinging for dear life to a human tornado.

The only person who seems completely unaffected by all the hubbub is Arthur Miller, and perhaps that is why I dislike him so intensely. I must admit that he has never actually been rude to me. On the four occasions that our paths have crossed – at the airport when he and Marilyn first landed in England, on their arrival at the house I had rented for them, once at the studio and once out with the Oliviers – he has ignored me completely. And so he should. There is no one on the whole film crew more junior than I am. I am only present to make Marilyn's life, and therefore his life, run more smoothly.

And yet I don't quite think of myself as a servant. I'm an organiser, a fixer. Laurence Olivier takes me into his confidence. So does Milton Greene. But Arthur Miller takes it all for granted – his house, his servants, his driver, his wife's bodyguard, and even, so it seems to me, his wife. That is what makes me so angry. How can you take Marilyn Monroe for granted? She looks at him as if she worships him; but then, she is an actress. Vivien Leigh often gazes at Olivier like that, and it doesn't seem to do him much good. Miller just looks so damn smug. I am sure he is a great writer, but that doesn't mean that he should be so superior. Perhaps it's a combination of his horn-rimmed glasses, his high brow and his pipe. Added to all this there is a gleam in his eye which seems to say, 'I am sleeping with Marilyn Monroe, and you are not. You midget.'

All this was whirling round in my head as I jumped into the front seat of the car that evening. I had stocked up Olivier's dressing room with whisky and cigarettes, and told David that I had to go to Marilyn's house on an urgent mission, implying that I would be spying on her for Olivier. Since David is always trying to discover Marilyn's movements so that he can plan the filming schedule a little better, this seemed to him an excellent idea.

Speeding through the English countryside in the front of Marilyn Monroe's car I felt frightfully important; but as soon as we arrived at Parkside House Marilyn simply vanished inside, and that was that. Even Paula could not keep up with her. She must know that Arthur is going to take over from here on, and she followed slowly, looking very dejected, as if she had lost her child.

Roger came out of the house to meet me, grunting and chuckling, cheeks puffed out like a beardless Father Christmas, and together we went round towards the back entrance. Then, just as I had expected, Evans drove away. He had been sitting in the car since 6.30 that morning, and I'm sure that the last thing he wanted was to be given another job or errand.

'He was meant to wait and take me back to Pinewood!' I cried. 'Now I'm stuck here without a car. I'll have to walk to the village and catch a bus!'

'Don't worry,' said Roger patiently. 'As soon as they've settled down for the night' – jerking his head at the first-floor bedroom windows – 'I'll give you a lift. Come in and have your talk with

José and Maria, and then we can have a drink and a smoke in my sitting room until the coast is clear.' This was a charade that we both understood. It would give us a chance to have a gossip, and to laugh at the crazy behaviour of everyone in the film world. I can sometimes do that with Olivier, but then I have to be careful how far I go. With Roger I can say absolutely anything and he will just smile and puff at his pipe – although he will never say a word against Marilyn herself, and any mention of Arthur just has him rolling his eyes.

Talking to José and Maria just meant listening to their problems for half an hour. They both speak very little English, and naturally nobody speaks Portuguese, although I can remember a little of what I learned when I was there the year before. I simply say *'Pois'* ('Yeah, sure . . .') whenever there is pause, and it usually works. On this occasion, however, the problems seemed more serious than usual, and I was forced to fall back on my schoolboy Latin to guess what on earth was going on.

'Meez Miller,' they said – they had been introduced to 'Mr and Mrs Miller' when Arthur and Marilyn arrived, and since they had never been to the cinema in their lives, they appeared to have no idea who they were – 'Meez Miller is sleeping on the floor.' They seemed to be saying, 'Is it because we make the bed wrong? We think it is our fault. If so, we should leave.'

This seemed to me pretty egotistical reasoning even by the standards of domestic servants. I told them that I would investigate, but that I was quite sure that they were not to blame.

'This house is *"louca"*,' they said. 'Mad.' There was shouting in the middle of the night and silence in the middle of the day. Mr and Mrs Miller would not speak to them. Mrs Miller acted like she was in a dream.

I realised that it was time to be firm. 'That is no concern of yours,' I said sternly. 'Mrs Miller has a difficult job. She needs to conserve her energy very carefully. And she doesn't speak Portuguese, so she couldn't speak to you even if she wanted to. You must take no notice of her and Mr Miller. The company pays you good wages to look after Mr and Mrs Miller. We think you are the best – otherwise we could no longer ask you to stay.'

This policy worked. They both nodded nervously, and left the room as quickly as they could. I went in search of Roger.

'What's this, Roger old bean?' I asked when I had found him. 'Maria tells me that Marilyn is sleeping on the floor these days.'

Roger put a gnarled forefinger beside his nose and gave his usual chuckle. I'm never sure what this means. Sometimes he will follow it by saying, 'A nod's as good as a wink to a blind man,' which is equally confusing, if not more so.

'Trouble between Mr and Mrs M already?' I asked. 'They've only been married a few weeks.'

'I've not heard either of them complain.' Roger gave a watery leer. 'But I have heard them playing trains at all hours of the night. No doubt about that.'

'Playing trains' was Roger's euphemism for making love in all its different forms.

'Doesn't sound a very amusing way of playing trains to me – sleeping on the floor.'

'Who said anything about sleeping?' said Roger.

'Well, Maria . . .' I said.

'Maria can get it wrong. Just because there are bedclothes out there . . . What does Maria know? Marilyn's on her honeymoon. She can do what she likes. It isn't any business of ours. And now I'm going out to check the gardens for reporters in the bushes. You stay here until I get back, and then we'll go upstairs for a drink. But don't go exploring.' He had correctly read my mind. 'Arthur and Marilyn could still be downstairs, and Paula and Hedda' – Hedda Rosten, a New Yorker and former secretary of Arthur Miller, who was acting as Marilyn's 'companion' – 'are hanging around waiting for their supper, greedy things. Who would want them with them on their honeymoon, I don't know. Poor Marilyn. She's never allowed a moment's peace. No wonder she spends so much time in the bedroom.'

Another sly grin and he was gone.

'Yes, but it's her third honeymoon,' I said to his retreating back. 'She should know what to expect by now.'

When Roger got back from his rounds, it was clear that he didn't want to discuss the Millers any longer. He feels that it is disrespectful to do so, disloyal even. I'm sure that when he was in the police force loyalty to his colleagues was the most important thing in his life. Now all that loyalty goes to Marilyn. He has fallen under her spell, just like everyone else; but as a father, not a lover. One mustn't forget that somewhere there is a Mrs Roger, clucking over her knitting. I do hope she is as cosy as Roger is. When I hired him he told me that he had been married for over thirty years, and that he had a son my age. 'He's in the force now,' he said with pride.

We went upstairs to Roger's room, and he produced a bottle of Scotch and a couple of glasses. 'Here's to Marilyn Monroe Productions,' he said. Marilyn Monroe Productions paid him, but not me.

'Laurence Olivier Productions, more likely,' I replied, sitting down and lighting a cigarette.

'Roger,' I said, 'you know my job is to find out anything that might influence the progress of the film and pass it on to Olivier. So tell me, what's up?'

'Get stuffed, Colin,' said Roger amiably. 'My only job is to protect Marilyn, as you yourself told me when you hired me, and that is what I do. Why, only yesterday I caught one of those bloody reporters up a drainpipe outside Marilyn's bathroom. He'd managed to get over the fence and across the lawn, and he'd climbed the first set of pipes he saw. Another few minutes and he'd have been in Marilyn's toilet, and then she would have got a surprise!' He gave another chuckle, then started on his favourite topic: the press. What he couldn't stand was that they were so cheeky. He had spent his life catching crimi- nals – people who broke the law. Now he is confronted by a lot of men who have no respect for decent behaviour and are prepared to go to any lengths to get what they want, but who behave more like mischievous schoolboys than members of a criminal class.

'What can I do, Colin? I can't arrest them. I'm not allowed to thump them. All I can do is throw them out and wait for them to try again.' What Roger really wants is someone to make an assassination attempt on his beloved Marilyn, then he can save her in a heroic fashion. In the meantime the photographer from the *News of the World* is the enemy, and Roger has to deal with him.

When we had finished our whiskies, Roger went downstairs and reappeared with a plate of Maria's sandwiches and some bottles of beer. By 10.30 we were thoroughly relaxed, but it was getting dark outside and I still had to solve the problem of where I was going to spend the night. Roger was happy to drive me home, but I was not quite sure if he was up to it. His eyes had got very watery indeed, and his nose was alarmingly red.

'There's a spare room at the end of the corridor,' I said hopefully.

'I don't expect the bed is made up,' said Roger. 'Maria would have a fit if she found out you'd slept in it. And what would Marilyn think when you climbed into the car with me tomorrow morning?'

'I'm afraid she wouldn't even notice me. But you're right, I'd better call a taxi.' I opened the door of Roger's room and peered out. The whole house was as silent as a tomb.

'Paula and Hedda go to bed at ten,' said Roger, 'and José and Maria will be in the servants' quarters by now, so you're perfectly safe. Do you know your way down?'

'Of course I do,' I said pompously. 'I've been to this house many times before. Don't forget that the owners are great friends of my parents.' (In fact I had been there only twice before, and upstairs only once.) 'I can use the phone in the kitchen. I saw the telephone number of the local taxi company on the wall. You go to bed, I'll be fine.' I slipped out of the door and shut it firmly behind me.

It is at these rather tense moments that Mother Nature so often pays a call. The question 'Should I turn left or right?' was soon supplanted by the absolute knowledge that I had about thirty seconds in which to find a lavatory. Actually, toilets in strange houses are not that hard to locate. At the tops of stairs, in little *cul de sacs*, they often give away their presence by a gentle but insistent hiss. It did not take me long, in my desperate condition, to locate an open door with a light switch conveniently placed on the wall just inside. But when I emerged, greatly relieved, a few moments later, a new problem presented itself. The lavatory light had been extremely – absurdly, I thought – bright. The rest of the house was now in absolute pitch darkness, and I was lost. I could just make out a thin line of light under one of the doors. That might indicate that it was Roger's room, but then again it might not. If I walked in on Paula or Hedda they would certainly think the worst. They might even welcome me, and then I'd really be in trouble. My heart beating wildly, I felt my way slowly along the corridor, sliding my feet along the carpet in case I reached a step. Eventually I got to a corner, and I stopped and peered round. Still I could see nothing. 'I must wait for my eyes to get accustomed to the dark,' I decided. 'I'll stand here for a full minute with my eyes tightly shut.'

It should have been a peaceful enough solution, but after a few seconds I became aware of a very strange thing. I was not alone. I could hear breathing, and it did not seem to be mine. It sounded more like a succession of little sighs. What was going on? Had I walked into somebody's bedroom? I held my breath, but the sighing went on.

Suddenly, a door at the far end of the corridor was flung open and a shaft of brilliant light flooded the scene. There, only a few feet in front of me, was Marilyn, sitting on the carpet with her back against the wall. If I had gone on for another few feet I would have fallen right over her. Now she simply sat there, wrapped in a pink bedcover, her head turned towards me, staring straight into my eyes. She did not give the slightest sign that she could see me. Were the shadows around me too deep? Had she been sleepwalking? Or was she drugged? There were many rumours floating around the studio of the number of sleeping pills she took.

She looked strangely fragile for the first time, and my heart went out to her with a rush. This ravishingly beautiful and vulnerable woman was literally at my feet. What could I do? I held my breath. I did not move a muscle.

'Marilyn.' Arthur Miller's voice seemed to come from another world. It made me jump backwards as though I had been shot. I must have made a noise, but at least I was now safely round the corner and out of sight.

'Marilyn. Come back to bed.' His tone was insistent but strangely flat, as if it were the middle of the day.

There was a pause. Marilyn didn't answer. Her breathing never varied. Long, slow intakes and then little sighs.

Arthur's voice came nearer. 'Come on. Get up. Time to go to sleep.' There was a rustle as Marilyn's bedcover fell to the floor. I couldn't hear their footsteps on the thick carpet, but soon a door shut and the bolt of light went out.

Only then did I realise that I was shivering. I felt I was in shock. My shirt was wet through with perspiration, as if I had been under a shower.

It seemed to take me an eternity to find the stairs, and by the time I got to the kitchen I was ready to faint. My emotions were in turmoil. I had never experienced anything like this before in my life. I couldn't get Marilyn's gaze out of my head. Marilyn Monroe, staring straight at me with that amazing sort of mute appeal. I could only dream of somehow saving her – but with what, and from what, I had no idea. I stumbled into the dining room and found a bottle of brandy on the sideboard. It was full, and I took a long swig, perhaps longer than was wise. That immediately brought on a fit of coughing which threatened to wake the whole house. The only answer seemed to be another swig. Then, for the third time that night, an unwelcome light snapped on.

'We'd better get you home straight away, laddie,' said Roger grimly, his dressing-gowned figure making for the phone. 'You're not going to be in much shape for work tomorrow. Never mind,' he added. 'I don't expect Marilyn will be going in anyway. I think I heard her still awake a minute ago. Let's just hope Mr Miller doesn't ask me who was coughing in the middle of the night.' He spoke into the phone: 'Hello, taxi? Can you come and collect someone from Parkside House, Englefield Green? Five minutes? Very well. We'll be outside. Don't whatever you do ring the bell.' He turned back to me. 'Come on, laddie. You're only twenty-three. You'll be OK. You'll be in bed in a flash. Don't fall asleep in the car, mind.'

And so on and so on, until he had wedged me unsteadily in the back of the car, taken a pound out of my wallet for the driver, and told him where to go.

When I finally got to bed I was exhausted, but I could not sleep. That image of Marilyn simply would not leave my mind. She seemed to be addressing me directly, like a figure in a dream, as if her spirit was calling out to mine.

WEDNESDAY, 12 SEPTEMBER

I expected to have a terrible hangover the next morning, but when the alarm went off I was still feeling strangely excited. It took a few minutes before reality set in. It was six o'clock in the morning and I was meant to be at Pinewood Studios, ten miles away, at 6.45.

If my car had been outside all would have been well. At this hour of the morning it only took fifteen minutes to get there. But I did not have my car, and although Marilyn never turned up at the studio on time, Olivier always arrived at seven o'clock sharp. Tony and Anne Bushell, with whom I was staying at Runnymede House, which they had rented for the duration of the filming, would not be getting up for another hour. They were kind and generous people, but they would not like to be woken at 6.30 a.m. and asked for a lift. Tony is the associate producer on the film, and he does not arrive on the set until nine. Only the actors need to get there so early, in order that they can be made up and put into their costumes before shooting starts.

I dressed quickly and went out into the morning air to seek inspiration. The events of last night now seemed like a crazy dream. It was almost as if they hadn't happened at all. I certainly could not give them as an excuse for being late for work. But then, to my delight, I noticed that there were two cars in the drive outside the house – Tony's Jaguar, and an elderly MG. That must belong to Anne's son Ned, I thought. He sometimes came down for the night. Desperate times call for desperate measures. I went back inside the house and went up to the spare room. Sure enough, there was Ned, very sound asleep.

'Ned,' I whispered in his ear. 'I need to borrow your car for a few hours. Is that OK?'

Ned snored on. He is my own age, and he must have had a weary night.

I picked up his trousers from the floor and took his car keys out of the pocket. There was no time to explain. I found a piece of paper on the desk and wrote: 'Sorry about the car – back soon. Colin,' and left.

'We don't have this car registered to you, sir,' the guard said when I arrived at the main gate of the studios. 'No car that isn't registered is allowed in. We can't be too careful now Miss Monroe is here. These reporters try all sorts of tricks.'

'I'm not a reporter, you fool. I'm assistant director on the film.'

'Sorry, sir. Just doing my job.'

Cursing, I had to leave the car on the grass verge and run down the long drive to the studio. The MG had not been as fast as my Lancia, and I was late.

'What happened to you, boy?' asked Olivier as I panted into his dressing room.

'My car broke down. I'll have to sort it out at lunchtime.' I didn't dare mention what had really happened. 'I don't think Marilyn will be in early,' I said. 'Roger told me she had a pretty disturbed night.'

'We'll have a pretty disturbed *day* if she doesn't show up. We shot all the simple stuff yesterday because she was so woolly. When is she going to recover her composure and start to work?'

'She's on her honeymoon, I suppose. Maybe that's affecting her.'

'Oh, nonsense, she's not a schoolgirl. And Arthur's getting fed up too. He told me he needs a holiday already.' Olivier grimaced. 'The trouble is that she's so damn moody, and she stays up most of the night. I pity Arthur. I wouldn't sleep with Marilyn for a million dollars, I can assure you of that.'

Nor her with you, I thought, but I said nothing.

Just before lunch, to everyone's surprise, and my great relief,

Marilyn did show up after all. The usual bunch of people materialised out of thin air to pester the poor lady, but I only had eyes for Evans, the chauffeur. I did not have time to worry about whether Marilyn had seen me the night before or not, but I did most urgently need to get the MG back to Ned. Even so, I was anxious to avoid Marilyn's direct gaze. She wears very dark glasses when she first arrives at the studio, and one can never be quite sure how much she can see. By the time she was ready to start work, I imagined, she would be thinking of nothing but her lines.

'Where have you been?' asked David Orton suspiciously as I slipped back onto the stage an hour later, Evans having driven me back from Runnymede House.

'Tummy upset,' I said.

He glowered, but I was home.

Filming that afternoon followed the now-familiar pattern. We all wait around the set under the 'work' lights for Marilyn to appear. Every quarter of an hour, Olivier tells David to go to Marilyn's dressing room to ask when she will be ready. David is a professional of the old school. He believes in a chain of command.

'Colin!' he shouts.

'Yes, David?'

'Go to Miss Monroe's dressing room and ask when she will be ready.'

This of course is her portable dressing room, right there on the studio floor. From the outside, the thing looks like a caravan on a building site. Inside it is all soft lights and beige fabrics, like Parkside House.

I tap on the thin metal door. The make-up man or the wardrobe lady answers my knock. 'Not yet,' they whisper. It is as if we are all waiting for someone to give birth – and in a way, I suppose we are.

Finally, and without any warning, the doors fly open and Marilyn appears, looking absolutely gorgeous in the incredible white costume designed for her to wear in her role as the chorus girl Elsie Marina by 'Bumble' Dawson. Her head is held high, she has a little smile on her lips, her huge eyes are open wide, and her gaze is fixed upon the set. Marilyn is ready. Marilyn is going to do it now, or die in the attempt.

A shout from David. (David has, and needs, a very loud voice, as there are over fifty impatient people present.)

'Ready, studio!'

The film lights come on, one after another, with a series of terrific 'clunks'.

Marilyn looks startled. Paula, ever present an inch from her elbow, whispers something in her ear. Marilyn hesitates for a split second . . . and is lost.

Instead of going straight to her marks in front of the camera, she deflects to her 'recliner' positioned nearby. Paula, the make-up man, the hair stylist and the wardrobe lady all follow and re-surround her. Now she has to steel herself all over again, only this time the studio lights are burning away and we are poised to start work. If Marilyn loses her nerve completely, a scarlet flush, which she cannot control, spreads over her neck and cheeks, and then she has to go back to her dressing room and lie down. That means that the dress has to come off, and the wig has to come off, and it will be two hours before we can start the whole process again. It really is a miracle that anything ever gets done.

That afternoon it was clear that Marilyn was even more distressed than usual. By four o'clock she had left the set for the second time, and Olivier decided to call it a day. When I went into his dressing room to sort out the scripts – and the whisky and cigarettes – he was in an urgent discussion with Milton Greene as to what the cause of Marilyn's distraction could be.

'Don't you know anything, Colin?' Olivier asked me. 'You hired her bodyguard. Can't you find out from him what's going on?'

'I know she and Arthur had an argument last night.'

'We all know that,' said Milton. 'She rang me at one a.m. to ask for more pills. I know I promised Arthur that I wouldn't involve him with filming problems, but I'm going to telephone him now and see if he'll tell me what's up.'

'You'd better wait outside, Colin,' said Olivier. 'But don't go away.'

When they called me in again five minutes later, both men were looking pale.

'It seems that Arthur Miller has decided to go to Paris tomorrow,' said Olivier stiffly. 'Evidently he has to see a literary agent there. Milton says this is the very worst thing for Marilyn. She has a horror of being deserted, even for a day. Both her previous husbands did it, and it terrifies her. She's driving me absolutely crazy, but I suppose she's giving Arthur a hard time too, so I can't say I blame him.'

'Marilyn is still in the studio,' I said. 'Perhaps she's too upset to go home.'

'Oh, God,' said Milton. 'Still in the studio at this time? I'd better go and see what she needs.'

He dashed out of the room, but he was back in under thirty seconds, looking very grim.

'Paula won't let me in. She says Marilyn won't see anyone, and she shut the door in my face.'

'Colin,' said Olivier, his voice like a spade in gravel, 'go across to Mrs Strasberg and ask her very politely whether Miss Monroe intends to come to the studio and work tomorrow. Don't go as my assistant. Say David needs to know.'

This was pretty high-risk stuff. A direct question. Usually Marilyn and Paula are already in the car back to Parkside before the rest of us have left the set. And of course they never answer the phone once they are home. Now, for the first time, they were still in our domain, at our mercy, as it were.

I marched across the thirty feet or so separating the suites of the two great stars and knocked on the door.

No reply. Cowardice means dismissal. Knock again!

The door opened a crack and Paula's eye appeared. She gazed at me for a full five seconds, in disbelief. Even from the little I could see of her, I could tell that she was in the grip of strong emotions.

'Come in,' she croaked, standing aside. I edged past her, and she closed the door firmly behind me.

She was alone in the pretty little sitting room that acted as a foyer to the *sanctum sanctorum* where Marilyn actually got dressed.

'Go in.' She closed her eyes and pointed to the door. 'Go in.'

'Go in?' I didn't understand what she meant. 'Go in where?' I felt like Alice through the looking glass. I'd never even been allowed in this reception room before, at least not when Marilyn was in it. This was holy ground. This was too much.

'Go in.' Paula pointed to the door again. 'Go in!'

The inner room seemed to be in pitch darkness. I took two steps inside and stopped.

'Colin.' Marilyn's voice was no more than a whisper, but every word was completely clear.

'Yes?'

'Shut the door.'

I closed the door behind me, and held my breath.

There was a long pause. I could see nothing. I felt as if I had dropped off the edge of the world and was falling through space. All I could hear was a succession of little sighs. The same sighs that I had heard last night.

'Colin?'

'Yes?' I found myself whispering too, I wasn't sure why.

'What were you doing in my house last night? Did they send you to spy on me?'

'Oh, no, Marilyn . . .' What was I thinking of? This was the greatest film star in the world. 'Oh, no, Miss Monroe. I came over to talk to the servants. I hired them for you, you see, when I found the house for you, you see, and they are always complaining about something, and I thought that if I went over and listened, they would calm down. And then I stayed and had a sandwich with Roger, you see, and when I came out of his room I got lost. I'm so sorry,' I ended in a rush.

Pause. As my eyes grew accustomed to the lack of light, I could just make out the figure of Marilyn in a white bathrobe, lying on a sofa against the wall. She had taken off her blonde Elsie Marina wig and she looked very frail.

'Colin?'

'Yes, Miss Monroe?'

'What is your job on the picture?'

'I'm the third assistant director. What they call a "gofer". I have to go for this and go for that, whenever I'm told. Anyone can boss me around. I really hardly have a job at all.'

'Don't you work for Sir Laurence as well? I always see you round him. He seems to talk to you more than most of the others. Do you calm him down too, like you do the servants?' Marilyn chuckled.

'Oh, heavens, no. It's just that he's a friend of my parents, so I've known him for ages – since I was a child. I suppose I'm the only one who isn't frightened of him, that's all.'

Another long pause, while I struggled for breath.

The room was so still that I thought Marilyn might have fallen asleep. What an incredible contrast to the whirlwind that normally surrounded her. I wondered how often she managed to find solitude like that.

'Colin?'

'Yes?'

'Are you a spy? A spy for Sir Laurence? Tell me the truth.'

'I'm not a spy, Marilyn,' I said, plucking up all my courage. 'But it's my job to report to Sir Laurence anything that will help him to get this movie made as quickly as possible. I'm sure you want that too. The sooner it's over, the sooner you can go home to America. I'm sure you and Mr Miller are both looking forward to that. And now Sir Laurence has sent me to ask you if you are going to come into the studios tomorrow, and that's why I'm here,' I finished lamely, in case she thought I had just barged in.

'Mr Miller is flying to Paris tomorrow to see his agent,' Marilyn said coldly. 'He may even go back to New York for a few days. I think I'll stay home and see him go.'

'Oh, of course, Miss Monroe. I quite understand. And so will Sir Laurence, I'm sure. Of course, of course, of course.' What a relief to be told outright, for a change. And perhaps with Arthur Miller out of the way, she might concentrate more on making the film. And on me! I knew I was being a complete fool, but I did have her total attention right at that moment, and the excitement in me rose.

'How old are you, Colin?'

'Twenty-five.' It was only a small lie, but I felt bad immediately. 'Nearly.'

There was another long pause. I seemed to have been in that room for hours. I began to wonder if Olivier and Milton Greene would still be at the studio when I got out. I hoped they wouldn't think that I had forgotten about them and gone home. They would certainly be very impatient. Everything to do with Marilyn seemed to take an incredibly long time, even though she was always in a rush.

'Colin.' Marilyn spoke so quietly that I had to step forward to hear her.

'Colin, whose side are you on?'

'Oh, yours, Miss Monroe. I promise you I'm on your side and I always will be.'

Marilyn sighed. 'Will you be coming to work tomorrow?'

'Well, yes. I come to work every day.' I didn't understand the question, but I was saved by a sharp tap on the door.

'Marilyn,' said Paula in honeyed tones, 'it's really time we went home.'

She opened the door wide, catching me standing on one leg in the middle of the room.

'Colin has to finish his work now,' she said. 'Don't you, Colin? Thanks for stopping by.'

She was like a mother hen fussing over her chick. She could hardly regard me as a wolf, but then again I wasn't exactly a baby chicken either. Marilyn gave another sigh. My interview was over.

As soon as I was out in the cold stone corridor of the studio, I found myself gasping for air. My first instinct was to rush along to Olivier's dressing room and report the whole thing. I felt incredibly pleased with myself. I'd asked Marilyn exactly what Olivier wanted to know, and I'd got an answer. Even better, I felt that I had established a rapport with Marilyn which might come in useful later on.

But wait one minute! Things weren't quite that simple now. Whose side was I on? Olivier was my boss. He was also, in some respects, an old friend. Uncle Larry. 'Boy', he called me most of the time. And Vivien was my heroine of all time. She was by far the most beautiful woman I had ever seen.

But Marilyn was different again. She was prettier than Vivien, younger, of course, and more vulnerable.

And she had appealed to me directly.

'Colin, whose side are you on?'

'Yours,' I had said. I could never go back on that. I marched down the corridor and knocked on Olivier's door.

'Come in.'

'Miss Monroe says she will not be coming to the studio tomorrow. Mr Miller is going to Paris and she wishes to spend the morning with him.'

'Did she tell you this herself?' Milton was incredulous.

'Yes.'

'Is that all she said?'

'Yes.'

Both men looked at me with curiosity. For the first time ever, they were actually taking notice of what I said. I have Marilyn to thank for that, I thought, as I turned and went out. I know whose side I'm on now.

THURSDAY, 13 SEPTEMBER

All film crews take a pride in being cynical. The more well-known the stars they work with, the more the crew effects an air of studied indifference whenever the famous person appears. The team working on *The Prince and the Showgirl* is even more professional than most. They have been hand-picked by Olivier and his production manager Teddy Joseph so that they will not ogle Miss Monroe, or try to catch her eye. At the same time, they have strong views about the actors and actresses they work with, and there is a rigid pecking order which all crews observe.

Minor actors, and even major ones in supporting roles, are totally ignored.

British stars in British films, like Anthony Steel or Maureen Swanson, who are both working on other films at Pinewood at the moment, are treated as complete equals – just as if they were also technicians, merely doing a different job.

Great British stage actors, like Dame Sybil Thorndike, who is playing the Queen Dowager, the mother of Olivier's character the Regent of Carpathia, are given exaggerated courtesy, as if they were honoured visitors to the set and not participants. The Oliviers, Laurence and Vivien, are a special case, treated like royalty and spoken of in hushed tones. Olivier is always referred to as 'Sir', although not to his face. Lady Olivier is called 'Vivien', even to her face – but, oh, with what respect and awe.

Big Hollywood stars are treated with complete nonchalance, but each one is given an approval rating in the endless gossip which takes place while the crew is waiting for them to appear. Marilyn is different altogether. She is now so famous, and it is so tempting to look at her, that everyone avoids her gaze as if she had the evil eye. I am not sure if she is too happy about this. She obviously does not have much self-confidence, and I think she prefers a group of men to applaud and smile when she walks into a room, rather than to look away.

Whatever they may pretend they are doing, however, every man and woman in Studio A is keeping one eye on Marilyn every moment she is there. They can't resist, and endless Marilyn stories, Marilyn rumours and Marilyn jokes make the rounds. On the mornings when she does not show up, the crew get slack and sit around with glum faces, like children who have not been invited to a party.

This morning, for lack of anything else to amuse them, they've decided it's time to tease Colin.

'Colin is Marilyn's new boyfriend, I hear.'

'Just barges into her dressing room for a chat any time he likes, they say.'

'And how does Larry feel about that, I wonder.'

'He's jealous.'

'Of him, or of her?'

Gales of laughter.

'Look,' I said, '"Sir" simply told me to ask Miss Monroe whether she was coming to the studio today, so I knocked on her dressing-room door and asked her, and she said "No." That was all there was to it.'

'Oh? Norman [one of the hair stylists] said you were in there for ten minutes. Plenty of time for a cuddle.'

'Oh, yes. A cuddle with Paula, I suppose you mean. She was in there too. I presume Norman will confirm that.'

Jack Cardiff, the lighting cameraman, who has worked on such films as *The Red Shoes* and *The African Queen*, walked over to see what the fuss was about. Jack is the only person on the set who treats Marilyn like a chum. As a result he is the one crew member to whom she can relate, and certainly the only Englishman she trusts. In return he uses all his artistry to bring out her beauty. He clearly adores her, and because he is an artist, with no ulterior motive, she responds to him very well. The whole crew understand this and appreciate it. Jack, they can see, is the man who will save the film by putting Marilyn's radiance on the screen.

'Isn't Marilyn allowed to make friends?' said Jack. 'I wish the rest of you would be a bit more welcoming. She's a stranger here, you know, and no one is stranger than you lot. Let's get back to work.'

The truth is that the crew look at me with a good deal of suspicion. This is my first film, and I am very wet behind the ears. It was obviously Olivier himself who got me the job, and he treats me as if I was his nephew (although he often yells at me if I make a mistake). Vivien, who I have known since I was a boy, always singles me out when she visits. 'Colin, darling, are you looking after Larrykins for me?' she purrs, knowing full well that she embarrasses me as much as she pleases me. Dame Sybil also knows my parents. She treats me as if I was her grandson, and bought me a lovely thick wool scarf to keep me warm while I wait outside the studio at dawn to welcome the stars. (Come to think of it, Dame Sybil treats the whole crew as if they were her grandchildren, and would buy each one of them a woolly scarf if she could.)

Marilyn does not know my parents (thank God!), and there is no reason for her to talk to me at all. We have had a few cosy moments together (cosy for me, that is) when I have given her cues from behind the set, but otherwise she has always seemed to look straight through me as if I were a pane of glass. And so she should. The poor woman has enough on her plate without me making demands on her. I have to keep reminding myself that she is the most famous film star in the world, trying to keep up with the most famous actor in the world – and he is not the easiest man to please.

With Marilyn off the set we spent a boring day preparing to do the exterior shots, and it was not until 5.30 in the evening that I got to Olivier's dressing room to check with him before he left for home. Milton was already there, and they had obviously, from the state of the whisky bottle and the ashtray, had another of those long and intense conferences that seemed to lead nowhere at all.

'We've decided to give Marilyn another day off tomorrow,' said Olivier firmly. 'Milton says she's upset about Arthur's departure, and now she can have a long weekend to pull herself together. One rather wonders,' he continued grimly, 'if she ever asks herself why so many people need a break from her presence.'

'That's not fair, Larry. Perhaps she needs a break from us,' said Milton. He is never malicious about anyone, except possibly Paula, and he'd certainly never dare even to think unkind thoughts about Marilyn.

'Quite so, dear boy,' said Olivier. 'Well, let us say that she can rest, and take a little time to learn her lines.'

I was wondering what on earth Marilyn would do in that big house, all alone with Paula for a long weekend, when the phone rang. Milton happened to be standing next to it, and he picked it up. He practically lives on the telephone, so whenever it rings he always assumes it will be for him. And it usually is, often from the USA.

'Milton Greene. Oh, Roger. Everything OK? Whaddya want?'

Suddenly his face seemed to crumple a little. 'Yes. He's here.' He looked at me.

'It's for you.'

'For me?'

Olivier nearly exploded. 'Who is Roger? What the hell's going on?'

I took the phone. 'What's the matter, Roger?'

'Colin.' Roger sounded very formal. 'Miss Monroe wants you to come via Parkside House on your way home this evening.'

'Me? Why me? Is Marilyn OK?' I asked.

Giggle. 'I'm OK,' said Marilyn's voice cheerfully. 'In fact I'm standing right here!'

If Milton had had false teeth he would have swallowed them.

Like a trained dog, he had caught the unmistakable inflexion of his mistress's voice, and his mouth froze in terror.

'Who the fuck is on the bloody telephone?' roared Olivier, naturally furious at being excluded.

'It's Marilyn,' whispered Milton.

'MARILYN?'

'Monroe.'

'Yes, I know who Marilyn is, for God's sake.'

I heard Marilyn giggle again at the other end of the line.

'But what is my star doing phoning my third assistant director in my dressing room?'

'That's my boy,' said Marilyn. 'See you later, Colin. OK?'

'Very well, Miss Monroe. If you say so.'

Mercifully she hung up before I got fired.

'Miss Monroe was just ringing to tell me that she will not be coming to the studio tomorrow.'

'We knew that,' spluttered Olivier. 'And why is she telling you, and not me?'

'Well, you sent me into her dressing room to ask that question yesterday, so I assume she thinks you want me to be the messenger about that sort of thing.'

'Hmph! Well, what else did she say?'

'Nothing.'

'Colin, I heard her say something else.'

'She heard your voice in the background, asking who was on the phone.'

As always, Olivier forgot that he had just roared and swore.

'What did she say?' It was Milton's turn now, and he was pleading. Goodness knows why he is so scared of Marilyn. She had sounded very jolly to me.

'She asked me to pass on the message to Sir Laurence. That was all.'

'Oh, my God, Colin, you've got to be so careful with Marilyn,' said Milton. 'She gets upset very easily, if one is the least bit over-familiar.'

He turned to Olivier. 'I don't know if Colin should talk to her any more, Larry. He's so young he could easily put his foot in it. She's not too keen on Brits right now anyway.'

Olivier's eyebrows shot up.

'Colin's very British, and he doesn't realise how important it is that Marilyn thinks we all love her.'

Milton was tripping over himself in his anxiety. He was like some feeble-minded courtier of Elizabeth I when the Spanish Armada was near. 'Off with his head,' if I was the Queen, I thought.

But Olivier got the point. 'Well done, Colin,' he said. 'Keep up the good work, and keep me informed. Now get us some more whisky, won't you, there's a good lad.' And I fled.

It was seven o'clock before I got to Parkside House. I had been seriously tempted to stop at a pub on the way, but in the end I decided that I had better not arrive smelling of whisky with an idiotic grin on my face. A good messenger needs a clear head. I parked my car round the corner of the drive and went in by the servants' entrance. Roger was sitting in the kitchen, looking rather serious.

'Miss Monroe says for you to wait in the drawing room,' he said gruffly, and took me through. 'Sit down, I would.'

Nothing happened for a very long time. I got up and prowled round the room, looking at it carefully for the first time. The French windows gave out onto a garden in full bloom, complementing the flowers on the wallpaper and the curtains.

Had Marilyn ever sat in it, I wondered. There was no evidence that she had. Roger said that she and Arthur spent most of their time upstairs, which I suppose meant in the bedroom. I had seen that when I inspected the house before renting it. It was part of a large suite which included a little sitting room so that they could eat up there whenever they wanted complete privacy – which was probably always, I thought. After all, they were on their honeymoon. Even though they were both quite old, this must still count for something. But I couldn't imagine what they talked about together. They seemed such different types. The attraction of opposites, I supposed. And now Arthur had gone off to Paris on his own. That didn't seem a very good sign.

The door to the hall opened, and Paula Strasberg put her head in.

'Oh, hi, Colin,' she said without much enthusiasm, and went away without asking what I was doing there, which seemed a little strange. A little later Hedda Rosten walked in from the garden. She is meant to be Marilyn's companion, but I have never seen them together. She is a middle-aged American lady with a nice face, but she drinks quite a lot, and she smokes, which Marilyn does not. Now she looked at me closely and opened her mouth as if to speak, but she evidently decided not to say anything, so I just smiled and she went out.

By now I was beginning to feel like a fish in a bowl. What on earth was I doing in Marilyn Monroe and Arthur Miller's house at eight o'clock on a Thursday evening? Marilyn had told me that she wasn't coming to the studio next day. She had tomorrow and all weekend to get a message to Olivier. Had she lost faith in Milton Greene to communicate with her director? Was I being put to some test? Why had those two ladies come in to have a look at me? Were they going to report back to Marilyn, I wondered, or were they just curious?

By this time I had been waiting for over an hour. It was just getting dark, and I was beginning to feel annoyed. I'll have that glass of whisky after all, I thought, and I went across to the tray with the bottles and the ice.

'Have a drink, Colin.'

Marilyn had come into the room without me hearing her.

'Oh, no. I'm sorry, Miss Monroe. I was just checking to see if you have everything you need.'

'I think so. I've only been in this room once, on the day we arrived from New York. It's very pretty in here, isn't it? Go ahead and have a drink if you want. Do you drink a lot, Colin? You don't look old enough to drink.'

'I'm really quite old, Miss Monroe,' I protested.

She was standing by the window in the half-light, wearing light silk trousers and a brown silk shirt which emphasised the fabulous

Monroe bust. I had to admit that she looked absolutely stunning, but just for a minute the unworthy thought entered my head that perhaps she had delayed her entrance on purpose until the light had grown dim.

'Are you frightened of me, Colin?'

Terrified, I thought.

'No, I'm not.'

'Good, because I like you. You don't seem to want anything from me' – 'Umm,' I thought – 'and I want you to help me. Will you help me?'

'Well, I'll do anything I can, but I'm very unimportant. It's only because I'm Sir Laurence's personal assistant that I can talk to the cameraman and people like that. I'm really just a messenger, you see, more than anything else.'

'But you can see what's going on, can't you Colin? You can see both sides.'

Marilyn walked over to the sofa and sat down, stretching out her legs on the cushions beside her.

'Sit down and tell me everything that's going on.' She pointed to an armchair by her feet, and reluctantly I perched on the edge.

'Come on, Colin,' Marilyn laughed. 'I thought you said you weren't scared. Relax and let it out. Tell you what – let's have some dinner. I'm starved. Aren't you? I'll ask them to bring a tray of food.' Suddenly she seemed to get flustered. 'Or are you meant to be having dinner with someone else? Oh, gee, I'm sorry. Am I interrupting something?' Marilyn opened her eyes very wide and parted her lips, almost causing me to faint. 'There's not a Mrs Colin is there, waiting for you at home?'

'No, there's no Mrs Colin. And I am very hungry, but I'd like to make a phone call. I'm staying with the associate producer, Tony Bushell, and his wife, and they'll be expecting me for dinner.'

'Go right ahead and call,' said Marilyn. 'I'll go to the kitchen and see what they have.'

There was a telephone on the desk by the window. I dialled Tony's number.

'Bushell,' he barked. It had been many years since he was in the army, but he had acted as an officer in so many films about the war that he had permanently adopted a military manner.

'It's me,' I said. 'I can't come for dinner tonight.'

'Anne will be furious. The food is practically on the table. Where are you?'

'I'm at Parkside.' It was dangerous to tell him too much. Like David and almost everyone else at the studio, Tony was my boss. Marilyn Monroe had become 'the enemy' to him as soon as it was clear that she, unlike him, would not slavishly obey Olivier's every command. Nevertheless, being at Parkside was the one excuse that he could not ignore.

'At Parkside? What the hell are you doing at Parkside? Have the servants threatened to walk out? Are you going to cook Miss Monroe's dinner?'

'Not exactly . . .' I was stuck. I couldn't say that Marilyn was giving me messages for Olivier. Tony would have insisted that they should go via him. And he would certainly have rung Milton Greene and reported the situation immediately. I felt I was getting on really well with Marilyn, and I did not want Milton turning up to protect his investment – which he would have done at the speed of light.

'Miss Monroe has some large packages . . .' to my horror I saw Marilyn come back into the room. I made an agonised face. '. . . which she wants to be sent to America . . .' Marilyn started to giggle. '. . . and I am waiting to collect them.'

'Can't Roger handle it?' Tony asked, just as Milton had two days earlier. 'Oh well, if you're stuck, you're stuck. She keeps everyone waiting. I'll explain to Anne,' and he hung up, grumbling.

'Now, Colin,' said Marilyn, sitting down on the sofa again. 'What is going on?'

Oh, all right then, what the hell!

'I'll tell you what is going on,' I said, going back to my armchair: 'We are all trying to make a film which absolutely should not be made. That is why it is such agony for everyone. Agony for you – we can all see that – and agony for Laurence Olivier too. You are a great film star who needs to prove that you can act. Olivier is a great actor who wants to be a film star. For some reason somebody has chosen a script where you play an American chorus girl, which is the sort of part you've played before and does not challenge you at all, and Olivier plays a stuffy old man, which is the opposite of what he wants to be. The whole thing is based on a play which I saw a few years ago in the theatre, with Olivier and Vivien Leigh, and it wasn't that good even then. It was a comedy of manners, and those never translate too well to the screen. I suppose somebody hoped it would be like one of those Spencer Tracy-Katharine Hepburn movies, but our script is stifled by all that old-fashioned dialogue, and all the costumes and the sets. It's such a pity, because you and Olivier both deserve roles you can get your teeth into.'

Marilyn was staring at me with surprise.

'They told me this was a great script – and I wanted to act with Olivier, so people would take me seriously. This was the only way to get him to agree to act with me.'

'Well, I think you were taken for a ride.'

'Gee, Colin, you really care, don't you? What are we going to do?'

This was, of course, the question which all of us had been asking ourselves ever since filming began, and I didn't have the answer any more than anyone else. Luckily I was saved from having to reply by the entrance of Maria and José, each carrying a large silver tray. They did not seem the least bit surprised to see me sitting there, which rather reassured me. They simply set down the food on the coffee table and waited.

'I'll have a Coke,' said Marilyn.

José looked at me.

'*Duas Colas. Frescos se fash favor.*'

'Ooh, do you speak the same language as them?' Marilyn was greatly impressed.

'It's Portuguese. I've been to Portugal a few times.'

'Ooh.'

There was a pause.

I looked at Marilyn across the table – and for the first time I realised what was going on. Marilyn was lonely. She needed someone to chat to, someone who would make no demands, someone who didn't expect her to be great or grand or clever or sexy, but just to be whatever she felt she wanted to be. Most of the time, I suddenly realised, she was incredibly tense. It was almost impossible for her to relax. Now, because I was so much younger than her, she felt that I would not judge her, and she probably wouldn't care if I did.

Marilyn began to tuck into a large bowl of chicken mayonnaise, and it was obvious that she was extremely hungry. Those pills of hers probably suppress her appetite, I thought, as well as wake her up. Since she slept so late in the morning, this might well be her first meal of the day.

José returned with four bottles of Coca-Cola, two glasses and a bowl of ice.

'*Obrigado,*' I said.

'Ooh,' said Marilyn. She seemed to get more cheerful with each mouthful of food. 'Why couldn't you tell Mr Bushell you were here on a visit? What would he say?'

'He would explode, and kick me out of his house. He's a wonderful man, really, but he's totally blinded by his loyalty to Sir Laurence. If you are not 100 per cent loyal to Sir Laurence – as most of the film crew are, I must admit – you are the enemy as far as Mr Bushell is concerned.'

Marilyn chuckled. 'So I'm the enemy, am I? Well, don't worry, I won't give you away. After all, it's not as if we were having an affair.' More chuckles. 'But what are we going to do about the film?'

'There is nothing that can be done at this stage. It's too late to do anything but try to finish it, and make it as big a success as possible. Then go on to something better, I guess.'

'I thought I could do a great job,' said Marilyn, 'but every time I walk into that studio I get the creeps. Paula is the only person I feel I can trust. Except for you, maybe?'

She swivelled her body round on the sofa until her face was beneath mine, and looked up at me. Her eyes were so wide that I felt I was gazing down into a beautiful swimming pool, but before I could do anything about it there was a tap at the door, and someone walked in.

'Yeah?' said Marilyn, without moving a muscle.

'There is a telephone call for you, ma'am,' said Roger impassively. 'I think it is from abroad.'

Marilyn got up with a jolt.

'Gee,' she said. That vague blurred look was back in her eyes, and her shoulders had curved in. 'Well, goodnight, Colin. It was so nice of you to come over. I'd love it if you could come by tomorrow evening so we could continue our chat.' She shot out of the room like a frightened rabbit.

'You'll be leaving now, I expect,' said Roger, waiting by the door.

'Yes. Time to go,' I said, as nonchalantly as I could, and strolled out to my car without my feet touching the ground, as far as I could tell.

'Goodnight, Roger.'

'Humph.'

FRIDAY, 14 SEPTEMBER

Tony and Anne were asleep by the time I got back to Runnymede House, and I left before they woke up the next morning. It was not until 9.30 a.m. that the reverberations from the previous night began in earnest.

'Tony wants you to go to Sir Laurence's dressing room right away,' said David. 'And by the way he's roaring and stamping, you'd better brace yourself for a row. What were you up to last night, I wonder.'

'Nothing, I promise you. I can't think what it's about. I just missed dinner, that's all.'

'Ah, now. Missed dinner.' David squeezed up his face in an effort to look cunning. 'I wonder why?'

'I don't care if he is fucking her sideways,' I heard Olivier say as I walked into his room. 'Perhaps it will calm her down.'

(Olivier's language is always terrible. Jack Cardiff told me that when he first said 'fuck' in front of Marilyn, she opened her eyes very wide and said, 'Gee, do they have that word in England too?')

'Ah, Colin,' Olivier went on, without a pause. 'Tony tells me you spent last night with Marilyn. Did you learn anything?'

'Spent last night with Marilyn!' I said indignantly. 'I spent last night in Tony's house. I just went over to Parkside to do an errand for her, and stayed for a chat. And what I learned is that she is not nearly as dumb as she looks.'

'And dinner,' interrupted Tony. 'You stayed for dinner too?'

'Marilyn was having chicken salad and she offered me some too, that's all.'

'What is more, I thought I heard her chuckle when you were on the phone. Marilyn doesn't usually chuckle. What was that all about?'

'Chuckling sounds good to me,' said Olivier.

'Yes, but Larry, this is a very sensitive situation,' said Tony. 'Colin is young and inexperienced. He might say something which would upset the whole apple cart. It took a year of secret planning to get Monroe over here, and one chance remark from Colin, even if he didn't know what he was doing, might send her and Arthur scurrying back to America.'

'Arthur's probably on his way back to America already,' I said. 'And I haven't made any chance remarks yet.'

'Perhaps,' said Olivier, 'if Colin is as nice and diplomatic as he can possibly be, Marilyn will be more likely to stay.' He gave me what looked almost like a leer.

'Miss Monroe simply treats me like a chum. Is there anything wrong with that?' I protested. 'She thinks I'm just a schoolboy.'

'Miss Monroe can be very manipulative if she wants to be,' said Tony. 'She had Laurence eating out of the palm of her hand in New York, and now she treats him as if he didn't exist. You must be very careful indeed, Colin. She is a very dangerous lady. Very ambitious, and very ruthless too. You know she had another dramatic coach before Paula Strasberg, and when she got fed up with her she just dropped her like a hot potato – after pretending that she relied on her for many years. She is not afraid to use people in order to get what she wants. Don't believe anything she says. Those great big eyes are really weapons.'

Was Tony afraid that I'd upset Marilyn, or that Marilyn would hurt me?

'I don't exactly see how she could use me to further her career,' I said. 'I don't have any power over her one way or another. I just go over to Parkside to run errands. But I think last night she was lonely, with Arthur gone away, and she simply wanted to chat to someone who didn't boss her around. Paula is too sycophantic, and Hedda gets tipsy in the evenings. Anyway, I'll probably never get invited over again.'

'Well if you do, be very careful,' chorused the two men.

'And I presume you will be coming back to Runnymede House for dinner tonight,' added Tony, menacingly.

Somewhere in my mind I could hear Marilyn's voice saying, 'I'd love it if you could come by tomorrow evening,' as she had rushed to answer the phone, but she was probably only being polite.

'I'll be back for dinner tonight, I promise.'

Film sets are like pressure cookers – sealed, airless and incredibly hot. There are endless unexplained delays. Rumours go round the crew in a matter of seconds. By the time I got back to my normal post by David's side, I had become the main object of attention again.

'Arthur hasn't been gone long then, Colin,' somebody called.

'What are you talking about?' I said, blushing furiously.

'Mrs Miller coming in today, is she? Or is she too tired?'

A chorus of cheers.

'Can't Marilyn show a little friendship without you clowns jumping to conclusions?'

'Oh, it's "Marilyn" now, is it?'

'That's the first time I've heard it called "showing a little friend-ship".' Etc. etc.

Richard Wattis, the actor who is playing Mr Northbrook of the Foreign Office, came over to give me some advice. Dicky is what you might call a confirmed bachelor, so I could guess what he was going to say.

'Have you heard of a flower called the Venus fly trap, Colin? Well, you are the fly. You think you can just buzz around, minding your own business, when suddenly a heady scent attracts you, and "Snap!" that's the end of you. Believe me, she is a very dangerous woman. I'm an actor. I know.'

'Oh, phooey to the lot of you,' I said. 'She is just a pretty girl who has got a bit out of her depth. Just imagine the pressure she is under, especially with you lot following her every move.'

'Give Marilyn a break,' said Jack Cardiff, coming to my rescue again. 'She's doing the best she can. You are all far too quick to gang up against her. She's the most beautiful woman I've ever photographed,' he said to me. 'And a very lovely person too.'

Finally, Olivier walked in, and everyone shut up and began to work.

As soon as we broke for lunch, however, it was Milton Greene's turn. For the first time he was waiting for me, rather than for Olivier, in the dressing-room corridor.

'Colin, I must talk to you very seriously.'

'Oh, goodness, not now, Milton. Sir Laurence is getting awfully irritated by all this. What on earth is the matter? I haven't done anything wrong.'

'I had a call from Arthur Miller in Paris last night. He was quite upset.'

'Arthur Miller! He doesn't even know who I am.'

'He does now. It seems he called Marilyn late last night, and she took a long time to come to the phone. When he asked her why, she said she had been saying goodbye to you.'

'Oh, she is naughty. I suppose she was cross with him for going away and decided to make him jealous. It wasn't late, it was about nine o'clock.'

'Ten-thirty, according to Arthur.'

How time had flown, to be sure.

'He's on French time. They're one hour ahead,' I said, thinking fast.

'That's not the point,' said Milton. 'Arthur wanted to know what you were doing there at all. And I couldn't tell him. What *were* you doing there? Tell me the truth.'

'I wasn't doing *anything*! Such a lot of fuss over absolutely nothing. Miss Monroe asked me to come over so she could give me a message for Sir Laurence. She kept me waiting for an hour or so, then she offered me some chicken salad, and then I left. That's all.'

'And what was Miss Monroe's important message for Sir Laurence which you had to deliver?'

'Well, it was just that she wasn't coming to the studio today.' It did sound a little lame.

'Something that Olivier already knew, right? In fact, it was Sir Laurence who told Marilyn that she needn't come in.'

'Well, er, yes. That's true, I suppose. I thought it was a little odd.'

'*Thought*? You didn't think at all, did you? If you'd "thought", you would have realised that you can't even go near someone as important as Marilyn Monroe without upsetting someone else. In this case, her husband. And me.'

Milton suddenly got friendly.

'Now, Colin, please don't go over to see Marilyn again. Or even talk to her without informing me first. She is completely, totally, off-limits to you and everyone else on the crew. Got that? I like you, Colin, but if this happens again I'll have to tell Sir Laurence that you must be banned from the studios completely. Sorry, but that's the way it is. I'm going over to have dinner with Marilyn myself this evening, and I'll explain the situation to her, so you don't need to call on her. She told Arthur that she might see you again tonight, and clearly that must not happen, tonight or any other night. OK?'

'OK, Milton. But I still think you're making a mountain out of a molehill.'

It had been fun while it lasted, but I did not want to lose my job. Nothing had happened, but I felt desperately sorry for Marilyn. The poor lady was completely trapped by her own fame. An innocent from California, trapped by all those crafty New Yorkers – a golden goose shut in a golden cage and forced to lay golden eggs for them all to enjoy. Arthur was the wicked king who kept her locked up in his castle. Milton was the magician who made sure she did what she was told. Paula was the corrupt courtier who poured endless soothing words into her ears, to fool her into thinking that she was really the one with the power. The rest of us – including Olivier, although he didn't realise it – were just part of the scenery. All the trappings of being a great star were a total sham – literally, in the case of this film, nothing but a façade. Now the princess had tried to tell the world she was a prisoner. That was the real message Marilyn wanted to give me. And, naturally, that was exactly what all those greedy men did not want anyone to find out. No wonder Milton had tried so hard to warn me off.

I wanted desperately to save her, but what could I do? I couldn't tell the police. I couldn't tell a newspaper. No showbiz journalist would want to believe me – and anyway, they were all in on the plot. They were much too frightened of the establishment to rock the boat. Marilyn was like a prize cow, to be shipped from show to show, primped and polished and prodded while the audiences jeered and cheered. If she took one tiny step of independence, the sky would fall in. 'She is a dangerous, manipulative woman,' they would say, like Tony. 'You can't trust her an inch.'

Olivier was still in his dressing room when Milton left, and in desperation I decided to try to discuss the problem with him. Olivier is a human being, I thought, a wonderful, loyal and sensible man. Perhaps if I explained the matter properly . . .

'Forget it, Colin,' he said before I could even speak. 'This thing is bigger than all of us. That's why I hate Hollywood so much. The studios there are so powerful that everyone is scared. It's just a great big money-making machine. They call it a dream factory. It is a factory; but not about dreams, just about money. Power, sex, glamour – those things just dazzle the public and conceal the truth. And girls like Marilyn are trying to exploit it, just as it is exploiting them. It's a war. No quarter given on either side. Believe me, you have to be pretty tough to get one tenth of the distance Marilyn has got. Now she has become the most famous star of them all. She took on the Hollywood bosses, and with Milton's help, she won quite a victory. For a while she even thought she was free. But who really controls her? MCA, the biggest Hollywood agency. Who pays for this film? Warner Brothers. Who does she still have a contract with? Twentieth Century-Fox. She just can't work without Hollywood's help and Hollywood's approval. Of course she'd like to have you as a chum, but it's too late for that. There are no chums in Hollywood. Just thank God that it isn't like that over here yet. Now go home to dinner with Tony and Anne. They are genuinely fond of you, you know.'

'Thanks, Larry,' I said, and went home with a heavy heart.

Saturday, 15 September

It was an absolutely glorious summer morning, and for once I did not have to get up at six a.m. to go to the studio. When I finally came downstairs, Anne Bushell was in the kitchen preparing lunch. She watched dubiously as I helped myself to cornflakes and milk.

'Tony tells me you've had quite an exciting week,' she said finally.

'It's been blown up out of all proportion,' I said. 'Do you really think it's such a dreadful sin to make friends with Marilyn? She doesn't have many friends, and Arthur's gone away and she's lonely.'

'That's where the danger lies, I suppose, Colin. You do have a bit of a reputation for chasing the ladies. Didn't I hear Tony talking about a girl in the wardrobe department? And some ballerina in London?'

'Oh, Anne, surely it's not a crime to admire beautiful women? I'm not having an affair with anybody, you know.' Anne was very attractive herself.

'Well, Marilyn is not just *any* beautiful woman, is she? There's a lot of money riding on her, you know. There's this film, and poor Larry's reputation as a director as well. And don't forget that she's on her honeymoon. That's definitely not the time for her to start making new young male friends. I heard that she had a terrible row with Arthur the other night. I hope it wasn't about you.'

'Of course not. Perhaps Marilyn doesn't like the way Arthur looks at her — as if she was a prize that he'd won in a raffle. She seems rather scared of him to me. She treats him like a very strict father whom she adores but can never quite please. Why he's gone to Paris

I can't imagine. It may have been pre-arranged – they would be over in Europe anyway, and all that – but the rumour is that he's going back to New York before he returns here.'

'Oh, poor girl,' said Anne. 'She must be miserable.'

Just then I heard the noise of a car, and I went out to see who had come to visit. To my surprise there was Roger's elderly black Wolsey crawling up the gravel drive. Had he bought it when he retired from the police, I wondered. His faithful steed.

Tony had heard the arrival too, and strode out from behind the house to investigate.

'What's the problem, Roger?' he barked. Tony liked a problem. His military manner gave everyone the impression that he could cope in an emergency. In fact he was just an actor, and he always missed the point.

'No problem at all, Mr Bushell,' said Roger. 'I've just come over to take Colin out to lunch.'

'Now, Roger, you're not taking him back to Miss Monroe's house, are you?' said Tony severely. 'That would be very much frowned on indeed.'

'Definitely not,' said Roger. 'I'm not here to take Colin back to Miss Monroe's house. I promise you that.'

'Oh well, that's all right, then. Just for a moment I thought she might have sent you over to collect him.'

'No,' said Roger. 'No, she didn't. Colin, why don't you hop in? It's time we were off.'

'Where to, Roger?' I asked, climbing into the front seat. 'Where on earth are we going?'

'Never you mind. Just shut the door, would you?' He scrunched the Wolsey into first gear.

Tony peered nosily through the rear window, but we were already on the move.

'Wait a minute! What's under that rug in the back seat? I thought I saw it move.'

'That's my little dog, sir,' said Roger over his shoulder. 'We're going to take her for a walk in Windsor Great Park.'

We lurched off round the corner of the drive, leaving Tony standing on the lawn scratching his head.

'Why have you left Miss Monroe alone, Roger?' I asked. 'I thought I told you never to do so.'

'Surpri-hise!'

Marilyn's blonde head suddenly erupted in the rear-view mirror like a jack-in-a-box, giving me partial heart failure.

'Marilyn! What on earth are you doing here?'

Peals of giggles. 'Well, that's better. It's "Marilyn" at last. I'm fed up with that "Miss Monroe" stuff. It sounds so pompous. And anyway, I don't want to be Miss Monroe today. I just want to be me. Roger and I thought we'd come over and give you a surprise. Aren't you pleased to see me?'

'Of course, I'm thrilled to bits. It's just that yesterday, er, everyone seemed very cross that I'd gone over to Parkside at all, and that I was interfering with your life and the film and all that.'

'Oh, nonsense,' said Marilyn. 'Don't you take any notice of those old spoilsports. It's a lovely summer day, and Roger and I decided to go out for an adventure, didn't we, Roger?'

'Hmm,' said Roger. He slowed the car to a halt, with two wheels on the grass verge. 'Now, where are we going?'

I swivelled round and stared into Marilyn's very naughty eyes.

'Yes, but Milton said that if I ever spoke to you again he would have me sacked and banned from the studio.'

Marilyn frowned. 'I used to have another coach before Paula. You wouldn't believe how often she was banned from the set. But she never went. No one can sack you, Colin – except me, of course.' Another giggle. 'You're quite safe.'

'What the . . . ?'

Unheard by us, Tony had come padding down the drive to investigate, and was now staring into the back seat, his face contorted with rage.

Marilyn screamed and buried herself under the rug. Roger let out the clutch with a jolt, and the car flapped off again like an old black crow.

'Wait!' shouted Tony. 'Colin! I want a word with you!' But this time Roger's police training stood him in good stead. No one was going to kidnap Marilyn Monroe while he was at the wheel, not even Mr Bushell.

'Phew! That was a close one.' Marilyn emerged from the rug looking even more dishevelled and cheeky than before. 'Do you think he saw me?'

'I'm quite sure he did,' I said. 'He'll be on the phone to Sir Laurence already.'

'Ooh. What do you think Sir Laurence will say?'

'He'll think it over for a minute, and then he'll laugh out loud and tell Tony not to tell anyone else, to keep it a secret.'

'You know Sir Laurence pretty well, don't you, Colin?'

'Yes, I do, and he's a great man. But I realise that he probably doesn't look like one to you at the moment.'

'Oh, I don't know about that. He's just so terribly severe. He treats me like a schoolgirl, not an actress.'

'That's just his manner. He can see you're an actress every time he looks at the previous day's film. We all can.'

'I hate to interrupt,' said Roger, 'but where are we going?'

'Anywhere,' said Marilyn. 'It's Saturday, and I want to be free. How about that Windsor Park you mentioned to Mr Bushell? Do you think he'll follow us and spy? Hey, it doesn't matter. We've got Roger. We can go wherever we want.'

'Windsor Great Park it is, then,' said Roger. A few minutes later he swung the car down a long avenue of trees. 'It's right here.'

Soon we reached a pair of tall iron gates with a little gatehouse beside them. Roger stopped, got out and knocked. A man came to the door and Roger chatted to him for a few moments, then showed him what I presume was some sort of pass.

'I don't like being on my own in the back,' said Marilyn. 'I feel like the Queen. Come and join me.' I squashed into the Wolsey's less than commodious rear seat beside her. 'That's it. You said you weren't scared of me. Snuggle up. This is fun.'

Roger got back behind the wheel, and sighed at the now vacant front seat beside him as the man opened the gates.

'We're off to see Her Majesty now,' he said. 'You two just behave yourselves in the back seat.'

'Ooh,' said Marilyn, 'Mr Bushell can't follow us here.' And she gave my arm a squeeze.

This was all going much too fast for me. I felt as if I was the one who had been kidnapped. I mean, it was incredibly exhilarating to be in the back seat of a smelly black Wolsey with Marilyn Monroe, speeding through the back entrance to Windsor Castle – but what would happen next? I wasn't even wearing a jacket. Where could we go? What could I do? After this, how could I go back to working on the film as third assistant director? All the normal, everyday rules seemed to have been chucked out of the window. Roger was the only sensible person in Marilyn's whole entourage, and now he seemed to be in on some sort of plot. I could probably be sued for breach of contract, or alienation of affection, or something. Maybe the studio would have me bumped off. I was responsible, they would say, for the abduction of their million-dollar film star, the most famous woman in the world. What if we crashed and she was killed?

'Stop the car, Roger,' I said. 'Let's get out and think. There's no one around. Let's have a little stroll in the fresh air.'

Roger drew in to the side of the road and Marilyn and I got out. She still had hold of my arm, I noticed.

'I'll stay here on guard,' said Roger. 'Why don't you two walk down to that little stream and cool off?'

'Great idea,' said Marilyn, releasing her grip and bending down to pull off her shoes. She was wearing a short white wool dress instead of her usual trousers, and she presented, as she must well have been aware, an extremely attractive rear end.

'Come on, Colin.' She swayed off down the slope, her bare feet crinkling the grass. 'Don't be stuffy. Take your shoes off. It's great.'

By the time we reached the stream, we were out of breath and very hot, and it seemed a good idea to wade straight in. 'I think this is the most lovely thing I've ever felt in my life,' said Marilyn, serious at last. 'What do you think, Colin? Can't you feel it?' She held out both her hands and grasped mine. 'I feel so alive. For the first time I feel like I was part of nature. Can't you feel it, Colin? I'm sure you can feel it too.'

Frankly, I felt as if I was going to drown, although the water was only two inches deep.

'I can feel it, Marilyn,' I mumbled.

But she wasn't listening to me.

'Why do I take all those pills? Why do I worry about what all those men think? Why do I let myself get pushed around? This is how I ought to feel, every day of my life. This is the real me . . . isn't it, Colin?'

My feet had grown cold by now, and I led her to the bank and sat down.

'No, Marilyn. Alas, it's not the real you. It's just a beautiful, beautiful illusion. You are a star. A great star.' I was beginning to sound like Paula Strasberg, but it was true. 'You can't escape that. You have to perform. Millions of people love you and admire you. You can't ignore them. You can't run away. Let's just have a super fun day, a day that we will never forget, and then we must go back to real life.'

'Only one day?'

'Well . . . perhaps a weekend?'

'Or a week?'

'We'll see.'

Marilyn brightened. 'OK. So how shall we spend our day?'

'Let's go to Windsor Castle. Her Majesty might be in. Then we could go across to my old school, Eton College. There's a little tea shop where they give you the most scrumptious food. Then maybe we could have a swim in the river before we go home.'

'That sounds great. Let's go. Do you think Roger will mind if we treat him like a chauffeur?'

I gazed into her eyes. 'He'd do anything for you, Marilyn, as you know.'

Roger obviously knew the road to Windsor Castle well. 'I used to work here,' he said. 'Looking after the Family.'

He parked on the slope leading to the main gate and marched up to the guardhouse, with Marilyn and me a few steps behind. He was obviously glad to be back in charge.

There were two large uniformed policemen blocking the archway, and although they did not know Roger personally, it was quite clear that like recognised like at about twenty feet.

'Detective Chief Superintendent Smith,' said Roger. 'I'm escorting this lady and gentleman for the day, and they wish to see round the castle. Is there any way in which you can assist?'

'Do they know anyone here, sir? We need to write down a contact name in the book. Otherwise one of us would need to be with them at all times, and they might not want that, sir.'

Marilyn was clutching my hand in a rather desperate fashion, and I sensed that she was scared stiff that they would recognise her – and at the same time terrified that they would not.

'My godfather works here,' I said. 'I used to visit him quite often when I was at school. He's the librarian. He's called Sir Owen Morshead. Maybe you could call him.'

Eyebrows shot up all round. I was wearing a white shirt, grey flannel trousers and sandals, not exactly the dress of a typical castle visitor. We all went inside the guardhouse, and the policeman dialled a number.

'Sir Owen? Main gate here, sir. I have a young gentleman, name of –?'

'Clark. Colin Clark.'

'Name of Clark here, sir, would like a word with you, sir.' He handed the phone to me.

'Colin, is that you? What are you doing here?' Owen Morshead is an eccentric scholar with a wonderful sense of humour. He has an equally delightful wife called Paquita, and together they are like a breath of fresh air in royal circles.

'I'm working on a film nearby, and I thought I would bring my, er, friend, my lady friend' – I grinned at Marilyn – 'over for you to meet her.'

'How delightful,' said Owen. 'I'm expecting some visitors in a short time, so it would be nice if you could come right now. Do bring her up at once. Just follow the road up the hill until you see another policeman outside my door. He'll direct you.'

'I think I'll just wait at the gate,' said Roger. 'You'll be safe enough in the castle, Miss Monroe.'

'Ssh!' said Marilyn with a broad wink and a wiggle, which made the two policemen's eyes pop out, and off we set.

News spreads fast, and at the next police post three or four men came tumbling out to see if it was true. In fact they were so intent on gazing at my 'lady friend' that I had to push them out of the way so that we could get through the library door.

Once inside we were in another world. Sir Owen Morshead did not look as if he had ever been to the cinema in his life.

'How charming, how charming. You are pretty, my dear. I'm sure you and Colin have so much in common. Well, this is my humble den.' His arm swept round the Royal Library, room after room lined with books and pictures. The tables were covered with books, all the chairs had books piled on top of them, and there were even stacks of books on the floor.

Owen gave a hoot of laughter. 'It looks rather dull and dusty, doesn't it?' he said, but Marilyn was in awe.

'Oh, Sir Owen' – you never quite knew whether she would remember a name or not – 'I love books,' she said in a childlike whisper. 'Have you read them all?'

'Luckily one doesn't have to do that.' Owen was enjoying himself immensely. 'A lot of them just have pictures.' He took a large portfolio from a shelf and opened it. 'These are all by an artist called Holbein.'

'Ooh, what a beautiful lady,' said Marilyn, looking over his shoulder. 'Who is she?'

'She was the daughter of one of the King's courtiers, four hundred years ago.'

'Imagine, four hundred years ago, and she still looks great. Gee. How many of these have you got?'

'Eighty-nine. And these,' said Owen, taking out another folder of drawings, 'are all by an Italian artist called Leonardo da Vinci.'

'Wait a minute!' cried Marilyn. 'I've heard of him.' You never knew with Marilyn. 'Didn't he paint that picture of the lady with the funny smile? You know the one I mean, Colin.'

'The *Mona Lisa*.'

'Yeah, that's her. Have you got that here too?'

'Alas, no,' said Owen, sighing. 'That one got away. But enough of all this art. I mustn't bore you with my hobby.'

'You aren't boring me, Sir Owen,' whispered Marilyn. 'I love it here. I could sit here for hours.'

'Let's go and look at the part of the castle where the Queen lives. She's not here at the moment, but she will be very sorry to have missed you.'

'Really?' said Marilyn in total amazement.

'Oh, yes,' said Owen. 'Why, she was only saying to me the other day, what must it be like to be the most famous woman in the world?'

So, you could never tell with Owen either.

'Now this,' he went on 'is the White Drawing Room. Very pretty, isn't it? And that is a portrait of King George the Third. He was the one who was silly enough to lose our American colonies two hundred years ago. And that is his wife, and those are his children.'

'Oh, they're gorgeous,' said Marilyn, completely unable to figure out whether Owen had recognised her or not.

We were almost having to run in order to keep up with him as he strode through one huge chamber after another.

'And this the Green Drawing Room. A lovely view of Windsor

Great Park out of the windows, isn't it? But you've been there already, haven't you?'

That gatekeeper had probably telephoned him and warned him of our arrival – like all royal courtiers, Owen had a network of spies.

'And this is the Crimson Drawing Room. It is a little opulent, I suppose.' Even Owen could not resist showing off. There weren't many rival monarchs left to impress, but Hollywood film stars were the next best thing.

Marilyn was stunned. 'You mean Her Majesty actually lives here, in these rooms?!'

'Well, she has her own private apartment where she sleeps, but this is where she entertains.'

'Gee!' said Marilyn.

'If it all seems a little overwhelming,' said Owen with great glee, 'let's look at something a little smaller.' He led us along a very wide, grand corridor lined with pictures, then through a small door, and down a staircase.

'Now, what do you think of this?' We were in a plain stone room, completely filled by an enormous dolls' house furnished and decorated like a tiny mansion. Everything imaginable was inside – beds, chairs, baths, basins, taps, table lamps, rugs, chandeliers, all accurate down to the tiniest detail, and all exactly to scale. There were cars in the garage, lawnmowers on the grass, pots and pans and food in the kitchen, even a little Singer sewing machine on the nursery table.

Marilyn clasped her hands in rapture and dropped to her knees. She looked so young and so innocent that my heart nearly broke. Owen, too, did not take his eyes off her as for nearly a minute she simply radiated joy. Then she stood up, squared her shoulders and looked straight ahead. 'I sure never had a dolls' house like that when I was a kid. Why, most people I knew didn't even have a house that size. But I guess if you're a queen . . .'

'And now I'm sure you must be longing to get on your way,' Owen said. One of the first things a courtier learns is how to stop guests staying for too long. 'But I'll tell Her Majesty you were here. I believe you are due to meet her next month.' (She was, at the Royal premiere of the film *The Battle of the River Plate*.)

'So you do know who I am,' said Marilyn.

'Of course I do, dear girl. And I'm very flattered that my godson brought you to see me. You're every bit as lovely as your photographs.' This wasn't quite true at that moment, I thought. Marilyn looked like a waif. 'Now, goodbye, goodbye. I mustn't keep you,' and we were popped out of another little door, into the sunshine.

'Wow!' said Marilyn. 'You've got quite a godfather, Colin. Do you think he's like that with the Queen?'

'Identical,' I said. 'That's why she likes him.'

When we got back to the main gate, a crowd had gathered. Despite Roger's protests, the two policemen had told their friends who the visitor was, and they had told their friends, etc. At first I thought Marilyn would be nervous, but she was clearly thrilled. She must have been feeling a bit unhappy at being incognito to her public for so long.

'Shall I be "*her*"?' she asked.

Without waiting for an answer, she jumped up on a step and struck a pose. Her hip went out, her shoulders went back, her famous bosom was thrust forward. She pouted her lips and opened her eyes very wide, and there, suddenly, was the image the whole world knew. Instinctively the audience started to applaud. Several of them had cameras, and for a few minutes Marilyn gave them all the poses they required. Considering that she had hardly any make-up on, and had not done her hair, it was an incredible performance.

But I felt distinctly uneasy. What was I doing with this Hollywood star? A moment ago I had been squeezing her hand as if she was a girlfriend. If I didn't watch out, I was going to make a complete fool of myself. I would never have dared to take liberties like that with Vivien Leigh – and I knew her much better than Marilyn, who I hardly knew at all. I found myself skulking at the edge of the group, feeling about two feet tall and wishing I was dead.

Finally Roger decided the crowd was getting too big, and gave a signal to the policemen. They pushed the onlookers to one side and made a path for us, although people were still frantically pushing forward to catch another glimpse, as if some goddess had come down from heaven into their midst.

'Who are you?' One man challenged me as I tried to squeeze into the back of the car.

'Oh, I'm no one,' I said. 'I'm just working on the film with Miss Monroe.'

'You must never say you're no one,' said Marilyn very seriously when the door had shut. 'You are *you*. Anyway, it's me who should be asking that question. Who do I think I am? Marilyn Monroe?' And she burst into giggles. 'I'm hungry, Colin. Where are we going to eat?'

We went to an olde-worlde tea shop in Eton High Street called The Cockpit, all black beams and inglenook fireplaces and little old ladies eating scones. I had thought of going to the Old House Hotel, which has excellent food, but someone would certainly have recognised Marilyn, and I couldn't face that again. I had just been reminded how quickly Marilyn could attract a crowd. I suppose I was getting possessive – and the truth was that I preferred being with Marilyn when she was frail, and not playing the great star. Now she looked like a schoolgirl as she tucked into a large pile of egg and cress sandwiches, and sipped coffee out of a mug. My heart went out to her again.

'What are we going to do next, Colin? I haven't felt so hungry in ages. Boy, these sandwiches are really good. Pretty fattening too, I guess, but what the heck. I feel as if I was being taken out on a treat. Did you ever get taken here by your mom and dad? Now I can imagine exactly how you felt.'

'Let's go and have a look at my school,' I said. 'I haven't been back there since I was eighteen.'

'That long, huh? But don't forget about the swim. You promised a swim.'

'We haven't got any swimming costumes,' I protested. (Just imagine what a crowd that could involve. There'd be a riot.)

'Oh, phooey,' said Marilyn. 'You can wear your pants. After all, it isn't every day that you get a chance to go swimming with Marilyn Monroe.' She hooted with giggles again, making the old ladies at the nearby tables give us disapproving looks.

'Roger,' I said, 'there's a clothes shop across the road. Could you pop across and buy a couple of towels and a pair of swimming trunks for me? I'll pay you back for all this when we get home.'

'If we get home in one piece,' muttered Roger. He clearly thought that swimming was a very bad idea, but he went anyway, coming back into the tea shop a few minutes later with a brown paper parcel which he put disapprovingly under his seat.

'This is such fun,' said Marilyn. 'I'm so excited. Let's go.'

'A bit more culture first,' I said. 'It will warm us up.'

'Ooh,' said Marilyn.

Roger drove us off, and stopped by Eton School yard. We all went inside.

'It all looks awfully old,' said Marilyn. 'And a little bit dusty too, if I may say so.'

'It is old,' I said. 'Over five hundred years. That statue is of the founder of the school, King Henry the Sixth. When we were students, if we didn't work hard enough we would be beaten with a bundle of sticks. It was called being swiped, and it took place in that room over there. Our trousers would be pulled down, and we would be whipped until the blood ran down our legs. The legend was that if a boy could break away, climb the railings and touch the foot of the statue before he was caught he would get the royal pardon, and wouldn't be swiped.'

'Gosh. I'm not sure I like this nobility stuff. Were you ever beaten, Colin?'

'I was beaten quite often with a cane, Marilyn, but I was never swiped.'

'Poor Colin. I had a very unhappy time as a kid, but I was never beaten like that. Let's get out of here before they catch us. Race you back to the car,' and she ran off across the quadrangle like a gazelle, with me in pursuit.

The day had become hot and sultry. Roger had left the car in the shade, but the temperature in the back of the old Wolsey was now tropical. I showed Roger where to turn off the main road in order to get within a reasonable distance of the river. The track was more bumpy than I remembered, and Marilyn held on to me for dear life, so by the time the car stopped, we were glued together with perspiration. It was with huge relief that we dashed across the grass to the water's edge and prepared to plunge in.

'This is the only place where there's sand to walk on,' I said. 'That's why it's the nicest place for a dip. I've swum here, many, many times, even at the risk of being beaten. But watch out, Marilyn. The water's cold.'

'That's just what I need!' cried Marilyn. 'A cold bath. But why isn't there anyone else here?'

'All the boys have gone home for the summer holidays.'

I take a long time to get undressed (or dressed, for that matter). For some reason, I always think I have to be neat. By the time I had got my new trunks on, Marilyn and I having taken separate bushes behind which to change, I had already heard the splash of Marilyn jumping into the water. When I finally emerged, her smiling blonde head was bobbing about on the surface of the Thames. As I waded in to join her, I could hear her singing to herself, and laughing out loud.

'Oh, I'm so happy. I really feel that this is happening to me, and no one else.' She stared at me, laughed again, stared again, and then suddenly looked serious. 'Colin,' she called, 'I've got something in my eye. Would you help me get it out?'

Laboriously I waded towards her through the icy water, my hands held high above my head, and peered down into her huge eyes. Marilyn put out her arms, clasped them behind my head, pulled my head to hers and kissed me full on the lips.

It took about a hundredth of a second before I realised what was going on, and then another hundredth before I realised that Marilyn was naked, at least from the waist up. The sensation of her lips and bosom pressed against mine, combined with the icy water, nearly caused me to pass out.

'Phew! That was great,' gasped Marilyn. 'That's the first time I've ever kissed anyone younger than me. Shall we do it again?'

'Later, Marilyn darling.' I was in a panic. 'What if a boat comes past? And anyway, we'll freeze. You wait here for a second while I get the towels. If you come out like that and someone sees you, we'll get arrested.'

'Oh, nonsense,' said Marilyn, wading out with me. 'Roger will fix it. Now, Colin, it's nothing you haven't seen before.'

It was true that I had indeed once seen her in the nude when I accidentally barged into her dressing room unannounced, but that did not mean that I could keep my eyes off her now. Her beautiful body was simply glowing with health and vitality, and she reminded me of one of those adorable young ladies who sit on clouds in paintings by Tiepolo. I reached the bank before her, grabbed one of the towels and wrapped it round as much of her as I could. Then I picked up the other one to hide the all too obvious evidence of the powerful attraction which I felt.

'Oh, Colin,' giggled Marilyn. 'And you an old Etonian.' She threw back her head and laughed, because that was what she had said when I had burst in on her before, and she knew it had caught me out. 'That was great. I'm not used to being kissed, you know. The men in my life don't seem to have time. They either jump straight on top of me, or want me to jump straight on top of them.'

Roger was sleeping peacefully under a tree when we got back to the car, and he viewed our tousled appearance and wet clothes with obvious disapproval. 'Time to go home, I'd say.'

'I suppose it is,' said Marilyn. Suddenly she looked depressed. She got into the car and hunched down in the back seat, like a child who knows it is going to be punished.

The drive back to Parkside House took twenty minutes. I held her hand, but she didn't speak again. For some reason I felt desperately guilty, but there was nothing I could say. It was time to be grown up again.

Sure enough, when we arrived there were two cars parked in the drive, and when we went in, two men waiting in the hall. One was Milton Greene. The other was Marilyn's lawyer, Irving Stein.

'Hello, Irving. Hello, Milt,' said Marilyn sweetly. 'Roger can drive you home now, Colin. And if you' – looking at her lawyer and her co-producer – 'hurt one hair of his head, or get him fired off this picture, I'll be very, very upset. Understand?'

'Yes, Marilyn,' they both gulped.

'*Very* upset.' And she vanished upstairs.

'Perhaps we could just have a word with you, Mr Clark, before you leave,' said Stein.

'I suppose so,' I said warily. They looked like the enemy to me.

'Have you heard of the legal term "enticement"? Miss Monroe is legally contracted to us, as you know. Anyone who entices her not to fulfil her contractual obligations to us could be held responsible under the law. And this includes her personal relationships.'

Milton looked wretched, like one of the Lost Boys in *Peter Pan*, but Stein was clearly in charge.

'Every single minute that I have spent with Miss Monroe has been at her invitation,' I replied. 'And what is more, we have never been out of the presence of Detective Chief Superintendent Roger Smith of Scotland Yard. You could hardly ask for a more reliable chaperone than that. Catch you later, Milton. Come on, Roger, I thought you were going to give me a lift. Mustn't keep you waiting . . .' And I was gone.

I asked Roger to drop me at the pub near Runnymede House, and I had dinner there. I could not face explaining what had happened to anyone. Tony would most definitely not have understood.

When I did get to bed, I could not sleep. The image of Marilyn seemed to be dancing round my head – laughing, weeping, waving, sighing – twice lifesize. I remembered the kiss, but I couldn't seem to remember feeling it. I was immensely exhilarated, but at the same time desperately sad. When I did finally pass out, I dreamed that I was swimming in a stormy sea, towards a life raft that I could see and even feel, but never quite grasp.

Sunday, 16 September

'Well well. Who's been a naughty boy, then?'

Next morning, at Runnymede House, Anne Bushell was positively flirtatious. 'Tony nearly had an apoplectic fit when he saw Marilyn in the back of Roger's car.'

'Me too.'

'Oh, so you didn't know she was going to be there? It wasn't all a cunning plot?'

'If it was, I wasn't in on it, I can assure you. It was just a sudden whim of Marilyn's. She wanted to escape that stuffy house, and all those people telling her what to do. She can be tremendous fun, you know.'

'I'll bet she can,' said Anne.

I ignored the innuendo.

'What did you two do together, exactly?'

'We went to Windsor Castle and met my godfather – he's the Royal Librarian. We had lunch at a tea shop and then we visited Eton College.'

'That all sounds very nice and cultural, but it doesn't quite explain your appearance when you got in last night.'

I had gone straight up to my room, but Anne always noticed everything.

'You looked as if you'd been swimming to me. Can Marilyn swim?'

'Well, er . . . yes, she can, actually, very well, and you see, it was so frightfully hot, so we went for a dip in the river at a little spot I knew from when I was a schoolboy.'

'Quite,' said Anne. 'I'd better not ask what you used for swimming costumes.'

I was temporarily saved from this line of questioning by the telephone ringing in the hall.

Predictably, it was Milton Greene. 'Hey, Colin, I wonder if I could drop over for a chat. Everything's fine. Don't worry, I'm not going to scold you. I just think we should talk – man to man.'

'Anne, is it all right if Milton comes over? . . . OK, Milton,' I said wearily. 'Come over, but Anne's going to give us lunch at one o'clock, so you'll have to be gone by then.'

'Take him out into the garden,' said Anne after I'd hung up. 'Perhaps the English countryside will help him to calm down.'

Ten minutes later, Milton drove up.

'Let's walk down to the river's edge,' I said. 'This place is called Runnymede. Do you know why Runnymede is famous?'

'No,' said Milton.

'Runnymede is the island on the River Thames where King John was forced to sign the Magna Carta on 15 June 1215. Every English schoolboy knows that. That's 741 years ago, Milton, and the Magna Carta is still the foundation of the British Constitution today. Among other things, it guaranteed every man the right to a fair trial. The barons had to capture London before the King would agree to sign it. I only mention this because I want to put my little trip with Marilyn into perspective.'

'Hey, Colin, I'm not mad at you. Not mad at all. I've just come over to give you a word of advice. I'm entirely on your side. I just don't want you to get hurt, that's all.'

Oh, sure, I thought. Except you wouldn't mind if I broke every bone in my body falling off a cliff.

'How kind of you, Milton.'

'You see, I've known Marilyn for a very long time – it must be seven years now – and I understand where she's coming from. I fell in love with her just like you did. She was living with a powerful Hollywood agent called Johnny Hyde and I was a photographer for *Life* magazine, and she and I had a ten-day romance. That's the trouble with Marilyn, and there's no way I can break this to you gently, Colin. Marilyn has a romance with anybody who happens to take her fancy. I know you put her on a pedestal. We all do. But it's a mistake to fall in love with her. She'll only break your heart. You've obviously had a great time together. Now leave it at that. Get out before you get burned.'

'Finished, Milton?'

'Hey, don't get mad. I'm sorry I had to tell you this, but it's for your own good.'

'Firstly,' I said, 'Marilyn may have "a romance", as you put it, with the man in the moon for all I care, but she isn't having one with me. It is possible to spend the day together and have a lot of fun without romance, you know.'

Milton looked doubtful. 'She said you kissed her.'

'Secondly, I have not fallen in love with Marilyn. I don't know about Hollywood, but in England we take a little longer than a day to fall in love. And thirdly, I have not put Marilyn on a pedestal, or anywhere else. To me she is just a beautiful, funny, rather sad lady whose company I enjoy enormously. Of course I realise that she's also the most famous film star in the world. Nor have I forgotten that she's on her honeymoon, and that her husband is a well-known writer. But she is under tremendous pressure. She's trying to give a great performance in a very difficult film. Her co-star is being horrid to her. She doesn't know who she can trust.'

Milton frowned.

'Now her husband has left her for ten days, I can't imagine why. So she jolly well deserves a day off, and if she chooses to spend it with me, I just count myself incredibly lucky, and I certainly won't refuse.'

'Did she say anything about me? Or the filming?'

'Nothing. Not a word. She did not utter one word of complaint the whole day. We went to see my godfather . . .'

'Yeah, I heard. Gee, I'd sure like to see those pictures. Those Holbein drawings are probably the greatest portraits in the world. I'm a portrait photographer, don't forget.'

'Maybe we can go over there one day. Then Marilyn and I went out to lunch – always with Roger by our side – and then we went to look at my old school. Marilyn was more interested in culture than romance.'

'And then you went for a swim. She said you went for a swim, and kissed in the water.'

Poor Marilyn, I thought. She's like a little girl. Why does she tell Milton everything, as if he was her father? 'Daddy, Daddy, I kissed Colin.' She's trying to rebel, I suppose.

'Well, she's home now,' I said, 'safe and sound. Perhaps a little fresh air and exercise will have done her good. I hope Sir Laurence realises that I've been working hard for him all weekend. We've still got a film to make.'

'Marilyn had forgotten that she'd promised to go over her lines with Paula Strasberg this afternoon, so they're doing that now. Paula said Marilyn was very nervous, and asked for some pills.'

'Pills? What the hell does she need pills for?'

'Colin, you don't understand.'

'I understand, all right. She's scared – of Paula and you, as well as Olivier. You're all meant to be working with her, not against her. And I think she's hooked on those pills. She can never be herself. None of you want her to be herself. You want her to be "Marilyn Monroe, Hollywood sex goddess", because that's where the money is. Just imagine how difficult it is for her. Even in the movie, she can't be "Elsie Marina, the showgirl" – she has to be "Marilyn Monroe, the Hollywood sex goddess, acting Elsie Marina, the showgirl". That's why she has such difficulty with her part, and can't remember her lines. Underneath it all she's just a lonely, simple child, who deserves to be happy, just like any child. But you lot stretch her until she's about to break. And one day she will break, and where will you be then? Long gone, and making a fuss of someone else, I'll bet.'

'Hey – so you are in love with her, Colin!'

I could only groan.

To do him justice, Milton seemed genuinely upset by my attack on his motives. He paced up and down that beautiful island on the Thames just as King John must have paced over seven hundred years ago, and told me the whole history of his relationship with Marilyn. After their short affair they had become friends. Marilyn was a victim of the old studio system, whereby actors got trapped in long-term contracts from which they could never escape, no matter how famous they became. The studios would dictate the roles they played, ruthlessly typecasting them to exploit their fame. The studios squeezed every possible dollar out of their films, while still paying the star the tiny salary they had originally signed for. Milton had persuaded Marilyn to rebel. By clever manipulation, and with the help of his lawyer friend Irving Stein, Milton had enabled Marilyn to escape from her contract with Twentieth Century-Fox, and to ensure that when she re-signed it – not even Marilyn, it seems, can operate without a contract – it was on much better terms. From then on Marilyn could decide which films she did or didn't make, and even make a film entirely on her own. *The Prince and the Showgirl* was the first film being made by Marilyn Monroe Productions, of which Milton was an equal partner.

'Well, not quite equal, Colin,' Milton admitted. 'Fifty-one per cent to her, and 49 per cent to me. But heck, 49 per cent of Marilyn Monroe can't be bad, can it?'

'I'd like 1 per cent,' I said.

Milton grinned ruefully.

'Marilyn's hard to pin down. It's like owning 49 per cent of a dream. It doesn't mean very much. I think you do own 1 per cent of her right now, Colin, and it's probably worth more than my 49 per cent. The trouble is, for how long?'

Milton suddenly sat down on the grass and put his head in his hands. 'I'm not sure I can go on for much longer, but I've got no choice. I've got every single penny I ever earned invested in Marilyn, and she simply doesn't understand what that means. I've been paying her living expenses for over a year now – her apartment, her staff, her shopping, her doctors – it adds up to thousands of dollars. Twentieth Century-Fox won't release any money until she starts working for them again, so I have to pay. Don't get me wrong. Marilyn doesn't ask for lots of cash; she just never gives it a thought. She's not interested in money, actually. She's only interested in her career. But she loves to be generous, and that can cost a lot. And Arthur needs money, and Lee Strasberg needs money, and they both treat Marilyn like a bank. Now, Warner Brothers have put up the cash for this film, but when I start taking some of my investment back, Marilyn thinks I'm swindling her. I'm sure she's been put up to that by Arthur. He's definitely not on my side, Colin. He's looking out for himself. But Marilyn worships him, you know.'

'I certainly don't worship him,' I said. 'I think he's too vain. I don't think he loves Marilyn as much as she thinks, either. Not in the way she deserves to be loved, anyway.'

'You're right. He's a bigger damn prima donna than she is. Now he's behaving like he'd had some awful surprise. He must already have known what life with Marilyn would be like. When he first met her she was Elia Kazan's mistress, and she was very mixed up. Then he saw her when she was filming *Bus Stop* with Josh Logan. She'd phone him for hours on end, and it can't have been hard to see how nervous she got when she had to give a performance. I think he just liked the image of himself as the man who captured the most famous woman in the world. It made him as famous as her. He wants to control her, and that makes him try to turn her against me. And now he's gone running off to Paris, and from there he's going to New York, as if he was fed up with Marilyn after only four weeks. I'd much rather Marilyn ran off with you, believe me.'

'Me too. But that's not going to happen, Milton, I can assure you, so you can relax.'

'Paula's after Marilyn's money too. Well, it's not really Paula, it's Lee. Paula is a very unstable lady – which is sort of a pity, since

Marilyn depends on her for her stability. Paula's a frustrated actress. She has no self-confidence at all. She pours all her hopes and fears into Marilyn – like a typical Jewish mother, I suppose. That feeds into Marilyn's insecurity, and Lee takes advantage of it. Lee wants to be a great impresario, and Marilyn is his passport to the fame he thinks he deserves. He's charging a fortune for Paula to be here. More than anyone else. Much more than me. Why is everybody in the film business a frustrated something or other, who thinks they deserve to be paid thousands of dollars a week?'

'I don't think Olivier is that frustrated,' I said. 'Except perhaps in bed. And I don't think he's that interested in money, either.'

'No, basically Olivier is one of the good guys. He's just out of his depth. He doesn't have any idea what's going on in Marilyn's head. He treats her like a silly little blonde, even though he can see in the dailies that she's really very good – better than he is, I'd say. Olivier is an old-fashioned actor with a great reputation. Marilyn thought that if she acted with him she'd be taken seriously at last. That's why she wanted to buy the rights to *The Sleeping Prince* – so she could tempt Olivier with a script she knew he liked. After all, he'd done it onstage, and with his wife. Imagine if little Marilyn could steal a part from the great Vivien Leigh, and maybe seduce Laurence Olivier as well. I must admit I thought she was crazy, but she brought it off – almost.'

'Poor Marilyn. She must be disappointed. She couldn't seduce Olivier, so she ended up with me.'

'You're making her happy right now, Colin. But, as I said, for how long? Nobody makes Marilyn happy for very long, and that's the truth.'

At one o'clock Tony came to tell me that lunch was ready, and Milton left. Tony was in a terrible sulk, so it was an uncomfortable meal. I felt sad that I had disobeyed his orders, especially as I was a guest in his home, but I had no regrets. Looking back on it, Saturday had been the happiest day of my life.

MONDAY, 17 SEPTEMBER

Back in the studio on Monday morning, things were even more depressing than usual. Marilyn didn't show up, and when I called the house as usual at nine a.m., Roger could tell me nothing. She was still in bed. He didn't know why. I was sure she had taken too many pills. Milton and Paula were regaining control. They would rather have a beautiful corpse than a free spirit, I said to myself, gnashing my teeth; but there was absolutely nothing I could do. I had served my purpose and been dismissed.

Milton turned up at the studio at eleven o'clock, and went straight into conference with Olivier. He looked grim and tired, and I don't suppose any conclusion was reached. I was convinced that the crew must be thinking of me as an upstart, someone who had had the cheek to fly too high, and had got his wings burned as a result. But I could not take my mind off what might be going on at Parkside House. Marilyn was certainly dreadfully confused, and probably desperately unhappy. I knew she liked to work, if she could. She wanted to finish the film. What could she be doing all afternoon? That house was like a prison, like an asylum. I should never have let her go back there. By lunchtime, I was really worried.

'Colin is really worried!'

Dicky Wattis always seemed to know exactly what I was thinking. He is old – at least he seems old to me* – and thin and

* He was forty-three.

very perspicacious. 'Frankly, my dear, I couldn't care less if Marilyn Monroe dropped dead,' he said sniffily. 'She's giving the rest of us actors a simply dreadful time, keeping us waiting for hours in these stuffy costumes.' Dicky had to wear a uniform with gold braid up to his throat. The only things he seemed to like were the white silk stockings and patent leather slippers that went with it. 'If the film can't be finished, the insurance company will pay us off and we can all go home.'

'She's trying her best, Dicky,' I said. It was dangerous to show any support for Marilyn on that set, but I couldn't resist it. Thank goodness, no one seemed to know about our excursion on Saturday. Olivier must have sworn Tony to secrecy, because he had been literally bursting to tell someone last night.

'It's all those people around her,' I went on. 'Roger tells me she was fine yesterday. They scare her to death, and then she thinks she needs those pills.'

'She's Marilyn Monroe, dear,' said Dicky. 'That's her life. Pills, booze, sex, publicity. What a way to carry on. I only wish I could be the same.'

'Oh, Dicky. How can you say that? She's really very confused. It's like the script of this film. She doesn't have enough love in her life.'

'Nor do I, dear,' said Dicky, laughing. 'Nor do we all. Don't you worry, Colin. Marilyn will survive. She's tougher than you think.'

But the life of the studio, which normally made me feel so excited and important, seemed unbearably tedious now. I could hardly wait for the day to end. At five o'clock I rang Roger again, but he made it clear that I was not allowed to come over to Parkside House that night.

'Sorry, no can do. No visitors allowed. She's gone into hibernation. Maria's left two trays of food outside her room, but she hasn't touched them. Milton and Paula have both had long conversations with her keyhole, but the door stays locked. But she's in there, all right. I've just been up to check, and I think I can hear her snoring.'

'I'm getting worried, Roger. You said she was so well yesterday.

Maybe she's ill. Maybe she's dying in there. Shouldn't you call a doctor?'

'I'm not in charge, Colin. Milton thinks she's OK. Evidently she's done this before, and she doesn't like her bedroom door being broken down by the fire brigade. Milton says let her sleep, so that's what I do.'

'But Roger . . .'

'Don't fret, Colin. I'll go up and check again this evening, I promise.'

Olivier was not at all sympathetic when I went to his dressing room after filming stopped.

'She's the stupidest, most self-indulgent little tart I've ever come across. What the hell's she playing at now? Tony says you took her out for the day on Saturday. What went wrong? Why can't she turn up for work? I don't want the details. I don't care if you made love all afternoon. I just want to know one thing: can you get her to come to the studio tomorrow morning? Is she going to finish this film or not?'

'Marilyn and I had a lovely, innocent day in the country,' I said. 'But as soon as we got back, Paula got hold of her and frightened the life out of her, and then Marilyn took those pills. It was her way of re-exerting her control. I suppose Milton and Paula felt I'd threatened their influence. Now they won't let me near her, or even talk to her. I doubt if she'll be in tomorrow, but I can tell you one thing for certain: she is determined to finish the film. She told me so very seriously. In fact that was the only thing she said about her work the whole day. Otherwise she just decided to take a day off . . .'

'With you,' said Olivier grumpily.

'. . . and I happened to be around for her to take it with.'

'Well, if you should happen to "be around" again, try to persuade her to come to work. She wants to be thought of as a professional actress. She'll never be that, of course, but if she turned up at the studio at all it would be a start.'

Dinner with Tony and Anne that evening was even more sombre than before. Olivier had obviously told Tony not to be angry with me, but I'm sure he felt I had let the side down. The trouble was that, as usual, Tony did not really understand what was going on.

When I went upstairs to bed, Roger still hadn't telephoned, and I didn't dare call him from the phone in the hall, with Tony glowering at me and Anne listening to every word. I must have finally nodded off, because when I heard the scrunching of tyres on the gravel outside the house, my clock said 1.30. Then I heard Milton's voice calling from the garden.

'Colin!' He was standing on the lawn waving a torch. 'Colin!'

I opened the window as quietly as I could. Tony was a heavy sleeper, but Anne was not.

'What's the matter?'

'It's Marilyn.'

Life seems more dramatic in the middle of the night.

'Is she dead?'

'No, for heaven's sake, but she's not well. She said she wanted to see you right away. Get your clothes on and come down. She may be in a coma.'

There seemed to be a contradiction in there somewhere.

'What can I do?'

'I don't know,' said Milton, 'but it's worth a try. Otherwise I'll have to call a doctor. Hurry up!'

A doctor! That sounded bad. I pulled on a pair of trousers and a sweater, and crept down to the hall. I didn't dare to turn on a light, and in my haste I had several near-fatal accidents on the slippery oak stairs. What Tony would say if he caught me I did not even dare imagine. Outside, Milton was waiting in his car with the lights off.

'Get in,' he said. 'There's not a moment to lose.'

'No fear. I'm not being trapped at Parkside again,' I said. 'I'll follow you in my car.'

When we got to Parkside House, there was the same little huddle of people in nightclothes and blankets which I remembered from air-raids in the war. Paula was clucking like a hen, Hedda was wild-eyed, and Roger very grave.

'I think we should break down the door,' said Roger, clearly fearing the worst.

'Not yet, not yet,' said Milton peevishly. A new door would cost a lot of money, and breaking in on Marilyn might upset her even more. Hovering in the background I could see Maria. She'll give notice tomorrow morning, I thought, especially if we break down the door.

'Colin should go up straight away,' said Paula. 'After all, she asked for him by name.'

'That was an hour ago,' said Roger grimly, 'and we've heard nothing since.'

'She's probably just sound asleep,' I said, 'and I doubt very much if she wants me to wake her up. But if it's the only way to get you all back to bed, I suppose I'll have to try.'

We trooped upstairs onto the landing, into the same corridor where I had first encountered Marilyn sitting on the floor – what a long time ago that seemed – and up to the bedroom door.

Tap. Tap. Tap.

'Marilyn? It's me. Are you awake?'

Silence.

Tap. Tap. Tap.

'Marilyn. Wake up!' The trouble was that I couldn't think of a reason why she should. 'It's Colin. I've come to see if you're all right.'

Silence.

'I think we should break it down.' Poor Roger seemed out of his depth. He was hoping this was 'a police matter', so he could take charge.

'It's two in the morning,' I said. 'Wouldn't Marilyn normally be asleep at this hour?'

'She slept all day,' said Paula.

What nobody dared say, but everyone thought, was that perhaps Marilyn had taken one too many pills.

'Let's go back down to the hall,' I said. 'Please, all of you just wait here until I say so. Roger, come outside with me, and bring a torch.'

They were so tired by this time that they did what they were told.

'I saw a long ladder in the garage, Roger,' I said. 'It's quite warm tonight, so the bedroom window will probably be open. I'm going to climb up and take a look inside before we do anything drastic.'

We found the ladder, and Roger pointed out which window was Marilyn's. It was slightly open, as I had guessed.

'As soon as I'm inside, you take the ladder away – I don't want Marilyn to know how I got in. She must think that her door wasn't properly locked, or I'll be out of a job. As it is I'm taking a terrible risk simply to calm down all those old women.' (He didn't seem to realise that that included him.) 'Then you go back to Marilyn's bedroom door – alone, please – and wait, in silence, until I open it from the inside. The others have got to wait down in the hall. I won't let the whole crowd barge in and disturb her. Especially not Milton. He might give her another pill.'

Roger held the ladder while I climbed up, carefully lifted the wide sash window and scrambled in. 'Go!' I whispered to him once I was safely inside, and shut the window behind me.

Like all great beauties, Lady Moore, the owner of the house, had installed blackout curtains an inch thick, and the bedroom was in total darkness. It took quite a bit of fumbling before I found the right cord and let in the moonlight. It took a full minute for my eyes to adjust enough for me to make out the silhouette of the enormous double bed against the far wall. I could also see three doors, although which one concealed Roger, and which went to a bathroom or dressing room, I could not remember.

'Marilyn,' I whispered. 'It's Colin.' I didn't want her to wake up and think she was about to be raped by some mad fan (or by me, for that matter).

'Marilyn, it's me. Wake up.' I approached the bed, stumbled over something, and sat down heavily on the corner of the mattress.

Now I could hear steady breathing, which was a huge relief, and I could also smell that wonderful warm, moist scent which beautiful ladies give off when they sleep. I put out a hand and patted the bed.

Sure enough, the last pat hit skin. Marilyn seemed to be lying on her tummy across the width of the bed.

'Mmm . . .' I heard.

'I'm so sorry,' I said. 'It's Colin. I just wanted to make sure you're OK.'

'Hi, Colin. I thought you'd come. Get in.'

'Marilyn, everyone in the house is very worried. You wouldn't answer your door, and they thought you might be ill.'

'Oh, phooey,' said Marilyn, with a sleepy chuckle. 'Get in.'

'Wait,' I said.

I got up and went to door number one. It opened, so that wasn't the one. The next one was the same. The third door was locked tight, but there was no key. 'Roger,' I hissed through the keyhole. 'Are you out there?'

'What's going on? Is Miss Monroe all right? Why don't you open the door?'

'I can't find the key. Marilyn's fine. She's just asleep.'

'How do you know? Maybe she's passed out. Turn on the light. Better let me in.'

You must be joking.

'There's no key,' I said again. 'Marilyn woke up long enough to say "Hello." She's absolutely fine. Tell everyone to go to bed and leave her alone. They mustn't come back until they're called. I'll stay in here until morning. I can sleep on the sofa. Marilyn asked me to stay, so I'll stay. I'm not leaving her at the mercy of that lot in the hall. Now off you go, Roger. See you at breakfast.'

Roger snorted. He was meant to protect Marilyn, after all.

'Off you go, Roger, and goodnight.'

By the time I got back to the bed Marilyn was unconscious again, and this time my gentle pat could not rouse her. I sat down on the bed, and suddenly I felt very tired. What on earth was I doing there? I certainly could not take advantage of a sleeping Marilyn Monroe; but half of that huge bed was empty, and my eyelids were beginning to droop. If I could first take a little nap, perhaps I could work out what was best. Slowly, cautiously, I leaned forward onto the satin sheets, and fell absolutely fast asleep.

'Oh! Colin! What are you doing here?'

I woke slowly, to find myself lying face down on a very soft and sweet-smelling eiderdown quilt which I could not identify. 'What am I doing where?' I rolled my head around and stared. Marilyn was hunched up in the far corner of the bed, wrapped in the same pink coverlet which I had seen in the corridor, and lit by a small lamp on the table beside her.

'Colin? It's the middle of the night, isn't it? How did you get in here? I thought I locked the door.'

She didn't look scared but she did look a bit frantic, and I expect I did too.

'Oh, Miss Monroe,' I said (frown from Marilyn). I flailed around in the quilt in an effort to sit up on what was a dangerously soft mattress. 'Oh, Marilyn, I'm so sorry to disturb you. You see, Milton and Paula and Roger were worried that you might be ill. You weren't answering when they called.' I couldn't say that they thought she might have taken too many pills. 'And they said that they heard you call my name . . .'

'I must have been dreaming, I guess,' said Marilyn coyly.

'So they came and asked me to help, and I got in through the window,' I added lamely.

'The window?' Marilyn looked baffled. 'The window? Is there a balcony? Hey, it's like Shakespeare, isn't it? What's the name of that play? *Romeo and Juliet.* How romantic. But I'm not sick. What made them think that?'

'I haven't the faintest idea, Marilyn. If you ask me, I think they fuss over you far too much. You always seem fine to me.'

Marilyn gave a little smile and slowly closed her eyes, as if she were waiting for something.

'It's time for me to leave,' I thought, but that presented a problem. The only door to the outside world was firmly locked. I couldn't just slip away, and I did not feel it would be polite to start crashing around looking for the key as if I were trying to escape. How on earth had I got myself into this crazy situation? I was trapped in the bedroom of the most beautiful woman in the world, and there was nothing I could do. I cursed my stupidity in allowing myself to be fooled by all those panicky film people. But Marilyn was not asleep.

'I am fine, Colin, especially when I'm with you. I do see a lot of doctors, though.' Her voice was dreamy, almost as if she was talking to herself. 'Mostly sort of psychoanalysts, I guess. They're always telling me to explore my past.'

'Your past, Marilyn? Did you have a very terrible childhood?'

Marilyn gazed at the ceiling, and her great big eyes seemed to be unable to focus.

'Not terrible, Colin. Nobody beat me like they did you. It was just that nobody seemed to stay around for long. You know what I mean?'

'I don't believe in exploring the past too much, Marilyn.'

The bed seemed too wide for such an intimate conversation. I leaned towards her and came perilously close to doing a somersault. 'I believe in exploring the future. What is going to happen next? That's the important thing, isn't it?'

'You mean between us?'

'Oh, no, Marilyn.' I leaned back quickly. 'I didn't mean . . . I mean . . . I meant . . . in the future.'

There was another long pause.

Now Marilyn leaned towards me. 'Do you love me, Colin?'

How is it that beautiful women can throw me completely off balance just when I think I am being smooth and wise and completely in control? Every time Marilyn looked me straight in the eyes I seemed to lose my grip on reality. I was certainly at the mercy of a powerful emotion, but was it love? And what sort of love? Love, passion? Love, sex? Love, romance? Love, marriage? I didn't know what language we were talking.

'Yes, I love you, Marilyn,' I said desperately, 'but I love you like I love the wind, or the waves, or the earth under my feet, or the sun coming out from behind a cloud. I wouldn't know how to love you as a person. If I loved you as a person, then I would want to possess you. But that would be impossible. I could never even dream of possessing you. Perhaps no man can, or should even try. You are like a beautiful force of nature, Marilyn, forever out of reach.'

'But Colin, I don't want to be out of reach. I want to be touched. I want to be hugged. I want to feel strong arms around me. I want to be loved like an ordinary girl, in an ordinary bed. What's wrong with that?'

'There's nothing wrong, Marilyn. It's just not the way things are. You are a goddess to millions and millions of people. Like an ancient Greek goddess, you can come down to earth every now and then, but you always remain out of reach to human men.'

'I'm not Greek,' said Marilyn, clearly confused.

'Don't be upset. A goddess is a wonderful, glorious thing to be. It means that you are one of the most special beings in the whole world, and whatever those awful teachers and psychoanalysts say, you have achieved that all by yourself. You should be incredibly proud.'

Marilyn sighed.

'A whole film crew is dependent on your slightest whim. Great actors and actresses are waiting for your cue. Thousands of fans all over the world are laughing when you laugh and crying when you cry. Of course it's a very big responsibility. Of course you feel a tremendous lot of pressure. All goddesses do. But there is nothing that you can do to change what you are.'

Marilyn giggled, and edged closer across the bed.

'Sometimes I feel like a little child lost in a storm. Where can I hide?'

'You're not lost in a storm, Marilyn. You *are* the storm! You must never look for somewhere to hide. A good goddess crashes around making everyone else wonder where they can hide.'

'Oh, Colin, you are funny.' Marilyn began to smile again at last. 'But I'm a person, too.'

'Of course you are, Marilyn,' I said gently. 'You are a very lovely person. And you've got Mr Miller to take care of that very lovely person.

Every goddess should have a dashing and handsome god to take care of her and remind her that she is also a woman. Any minute now he will be roaring out of the clouds to claim you, and he won't be a bit amused to find the court jester in his place. He'll probably throw a thunderbolt at me.'

'I won't let him hurt you.'

I couldn't help grimacing.

'Yes you will, Marilyn; and you'll hurt me too. But it will have been worth it.'

Marilyn sighed again and closed her eyes. Suddenly she looked very tired. I knew very well that I should tiptoe away and leave her to go back to sleep, but I seemed to have lost the use of my legs. I could only sit and gaze at this beautiful creature who seemed so innocent and yet wielded so much power.

'Colin,' she whispered, 'I have to tell you something. There is a part of me that is very ugly. Something which comes from being so ambitious, I guess. Something to do with all the things I've done – not bad things, but selfish things. I've slept with too many men, that's for sure. And I've been unfaithful so often I couldn't remember. Somehow sex didn't seem that important when I was a kid. But now I want people to respect me and to be faithful to me, and they never are. I want to find someone to love me – ugliness and beauty and all. But people only see the glamour and fall in love with that, and then when they see the ugly side they run away. That's what Arthur has done now. Before he left for Paris he wrote a note saying that he was disappointed in me. I saw it on his desk. I think he meant for me to see it. And then you came along and we had such fun and now I'm all confused. Why is life so complicated, Colin? Arthur says I don't think enough, but it seems I'm only happy when I don't think.'

'I'm sorry,' I said, 'but I'm not going to say "Poor Marilyn." You have talents and advantages most people only dream about. You just don't have anyone to help you use them properly. Like all ambitious people, you need to grow all the time – grow as an actress, and grow as a person too. And growing is painful, no doubt about it. Growing pains, they are called. But you don't want to stand still. You can't bear to sit back and think, "I'm Marilyn Monroe, and it's enough to go from one brainless Hollywood movie to the next." If you could do that, you wouldn't be here now. You wouldn't have married a famous writer, or read *The Brothers Karamazov*, or agreed to act with Laurence Olivier. You'd be driving a pink Cadillac in Beverly Hills, and having lunch with your agent every day, and counting the money in the bank.'

Marilyn opened her eyes. 'What makes me always want more, Colin? Do you think I'm being too greedy? Perhaps it's because when I was young I never had enough.' She sighed again.

'I never really knew my mom and dad. I was brought up in other people's homes mostly, but I did have a sort of auntie called Grace, who took care of me sometimes, and she was always telling me that I could be a great actress. "Norma Jean," she'd say, "one day you are going to be as famous as Jean Harlow," and she'd take me to the beauty parlour and get them to do my hair real nice. And she worked in movies too, so I always believed her.

'At one of the schools I went to, the other kids all called me "the mouse", 'cos I was so dowdy. My hair was brown then, too. I still feel like a mouse sometimes, running around in a film star's body. But then my bosom began to grow and I dyed my hair blonde. Some guy took my picture, and all the boys began to make a big fuss and try to make out with me. I didn't know any better, I guess. I used to have a lot of terrible pain every month – I still do – and I thought it was God punishing me for knowing about sex so young.

'I got married when I was sixteen. Poor Jimmie. He didn't really want to get married at all. He did it for a favour. Otherwise I would have had to go back to the orphanage. Grace couldn't take care of me any longer, you see. And I didn't know who I really was yet. I thought if I got married I'd be someone. I'd look after my husband and my house and I'd be someone.

'But it didn't work out like that at all. After a few months, Jim hardly came home at night, and when he did we had nothing to talk about. Then he went off to the war and I began to work as a model. Most marriages seem to break up in the end, don't they, Colin? Mine just fell apart. And I was unfaithful pretty often, I guess. Somehow it seemed natural to sleep with the photographer. I always did. Like giving them a reward for taking beautiful pictures. But modelling was fun. It was putting on an act. I always tried my very best, and I did good. When Jimmie came back he couldn't stand it. We got a divorce in Las Vegas about the same time as my first movie test. That was great. I just loved going in front of the movie cameras. Somehow it felt just right. But, boy, what a lot of men there are in the film business – and they all think you've got to sleep with them.'

'And did you, Marilyn?'

'Quite a lot. Too many. I didn't feel bad at the time. I was only a dumb kid. But I feel bad now. I feel guilty now.'

'I understand, Marilyn. But you mustn't feel guilty for the past. Everyone understands what it's like. I'm sure Arthur understands.'

'Joe didn't understand. He didn't like it at all. He married me, but I don't think he ever forgave me for what I did before I met him. That's not fair, is it?'

'Joe DiMaggio, you mean?'

'Yeah. He was great in so many ways. So strong. So sure of himself. I really tried to be a good wife to him, but by that time my work was starting to get better than his, and he had been so famous and all, and he couldn't stand that either. He got so jealous of everything. I guess I couldn't just change in the way he wanted me to. Then Arthur came along, and he was different. Arthur was always different from all the rest. Why, he wouldn't even sleep with me on the first date. He treated me like I was a real person. He was so wise. He didn't speak much – well, nor did Joe – but somehow you knew how smart he was just from looking at him. And he was so sexy. I really fell in love with Arthur, and I still am. But now I feel I've let him down. I must have, or he wouldn't have run away, would he Colin?'

'You and Arthur are hardly the typical honeymoon couple, you know,' I said. 'You are under incredible pressure to give a great performance in a very difficult film. You have to put all your efforts into your work, whether you like it or not. You've got Milton and Paula pestering you morning, noon and night. I don't expect Arthur had any idea what you would both have to go through. Right now he's running away from the whole bloody showbiz circus, not from you.'

Marilyn was looking so miserable that I couldn't resist stretching out my hand and holding hers. She didn't seem to notice for a moment, and then, suddenly, she gripped it with all her strength.

'Do you think so, Colin? Do you really think so?'

'Of course I do. In fact, I know that's what it is. He told Olivier that the pressure this film created was driving him crazy. He didn't say that *you* were driving him crazy.'

'But I saw the note on his desk. It said I wasn't the angel he'd thought I was. It made out that he was disappointed in me.'

'If Arthur really thought he was marrying an angel, he must have been nuts. Did he want a fantasy, or did he want a real person? He knew that you were the most famous film star in the world. Did he think you'd gone straight to where you were from heaven? Of course not. As you say, Arthur is a writer. Those notes he writes are just an author scribbling down random thoughts as they come to him. I've seen the way he looks at you. He understands you. He's proud of you. He adores you. It's just that he had no idea – no one has any idea – how much work is involved in making a film like this.'

Marilyn's voice was only just above a whisper. 'You don't think he's going to leave me, then? You think he'll come back?'

'I'm sure of it. And now it's time I left and you went back to sleep.'

'Oh, don't go away, Colin. I can't stand it if you go too.'

Marilyn opened up her swimming-pool eyes again and held onto my hand as if her life depended on it.

'Please stay, Colin.'

'All right, I'll stay. On one condition – that you come into the studio on time tomorrow morning. That will surprise everybody. That will show them all what you're made of. That will show them that you are a great, great star. That when things look bad you can rise above it and give the performance of your life.'

'Oh, Colin. You make it all sound fun.'

'Will you do it, Marilyn? Just once? Not for me – for yourself. We won't warn Paula or Milton or anyone. We'll just go. I'll set the alarm for seven o'clock. That gives us another four hours of sleep.'

Marilyn giggled. 'Four hours! Aren't we going to make love, Colin? Will that give us enough time?'

'Oh, Marilyn, you are a naughty girl,' I said sternly. 'We are not going to make love, OK? It's bad enough me being here. You've got to be able to tell your husband that we didn't even think about sex – that it never even crossed your mind. You've got to be able to say that with your hand on your heart. Otherwise he jolly well will leave you forever. And you don't want that.'

Marilyn sighed. 'I guess so,' she said.

I gave her hand a squeeze. 'Just out of interest, though, would you have liked to make love?'

'Kinda.'

'Me too. But now we're going to sleep.'

'I tell you what, we'll spoon.'

'Spoon?'

'Yeah, I used to do this with Johnny – Johnny Hyde – when he was sick. Pull off your trousers and get into the bed, Colin. Now lie very straight, with your face towards the edge. Hey, it's good that you're thin like Johnny.'

Marilyn turned off the light and lay down behind me. I could feel her stretching out her face towards the back of my neck, until her body ran the whole length of mine. This is getting dangerous, I thought. One thing could lead to another in the dark. But Marilyn was clearly enjoying herself, being in control.

'Now slowly bring your knees up, Colin, and curl your back forwards.'

As I did so I could feel Marilyn doing the same, until I was completely enveloped in a soft embrace.

'See?' said Marilyn. 'Like a spoon!'

I breathed out at last. 'Goodnight,' I said. 'Sleep well.'

'Mmm,' said Marilyn. 'This is great. I will.'

Tuesday, 18 September

For the first two minutes, I was feeling so wonderful that I could not even imagine falling asleep. The next thing I knew, an alarm clock was going off on the other side of the bed, and sunlight was streaming into the room. To my amazement I could hear singing and splashing coming from the bathroom.

> 'I found a dream, I laid in your arms the whole
> night through,
> I'm yours, no matter what others may say or
> do . . .'

Marilyn was rehearsing the beautiful little waltz written by Richard Addinsell for the film – 'The Sleeping Prince Waltz'. So she can get up in the morning after all, I thought, if she wants to.

Then, as I clambered over the quilt to silence the clock, it dawned on me that I could be in serious trouble. I had just spent the night in bed with someone else's wife, and there were five witnesses right here in the house. I retrieved my grey flannel trousers from the floor and went into the dressing room. At least there was a sofa in there, even though it was rather short. I went back into the bedroom for a couple of pillows and that fancy pink coverlet and arranged them in careful disarray, to make it look as if I had spent the night as far away from Marilyn as possible. Only Maria would see it, I thought, so I must make sure she would notice. I might need her to give evidence later – I was not sure to whom. I put an ashtray and a glass on the floor by the sofa, as well as a pile of books.

'Marilyn,' I called. 'I'm going to the studio. See you there soon. OK?'

Marilyn came out of the bathroom in her white towelling robe.

'Hey, Colin, you look a bit messed up. What will Sir Laurence say? I slept great. I'm really going to show him what I can do today. Wait a minute, you need the key to escape.'

She laughed and went to her dressing table.

'There you are. Tell Roger I'll be down in ten minutes. See you later.'

It was already a quarter to seven.

''Bye, Marilyn. You are a star.'

I tore downstairs, almost crashing into Roger in the hall.

'Miss Monroe will be leaving in ten minutes,' I gasped.

Roger looked grim.

'Don't worry, Roger. She's feeling great.'

'I'll bet she is.'

'Now, Roger, don't jump to conclusions. I slept in the dressing room. See you at the studio. And please, put on a cheerful face. We can't have her losing her nerve now.'

'Morning, Evans,' I called cheerily as I roared off down the drive.

I managed to get to the studios just one minute before Sir Laurence's brown Bentley came round the corner of the dressing-room wing.

'Morning, boy! Is make-up ready?'

'I'll check, Sir Laurence.'

Olivier stopped and stared.

'You look a bit rough this morning. Anything up?'

'Everything is fine, I think, Sir Laurence.'

'Good. Well, let me know when Marilyn arrives. That is, if she does arrive at all. Any clues?'

'Oh, I think she will arrive this morning.'

Olivier gave me a piercing look.

'I really hope so,' I said to myself. You could never be absolutely sure with Marilyn.

'High time, too.'

He went into his dressing room and shut the door, while I went in search of the make-up man. Ten minutes later, to my huge relief, Marilyn's car appeared, Evans impassive at the wheel. Out got Roger. Out got Paula, out got Marilyn.

'Good morning, Colin.'

'Good morning, Miss Monroe. It's a lovely day.' I couldn't resist a grin.

'Yes, isn't it Colin!' and she grinned right at me, to Paula and Roger's obvious alarm.

'Make-up is waiting in your dressing room. I'll be back in an hour.'

'All right. See you then.'

I rushed along to Olivier's dressing room bursting with pride.

'Miss Monroe has arrived, Sir Laurence. She's being made up now.'

'What? At 7.15? Why, she's almost on time. What the hell brought that about? Colin, were you involved in this?'

Olivier glowered, and then gave a roar of laughter.

'You spent the night with her, didn't you? No wonder you look so scruffy. Oh dear, what will I tell K and Jane [my parents]?'

'Nothing improper happened, Larry, I promise.'

'I don't care if it did. At least you got her to the studio on time. That's all that matters. Now, let's settle down and try to make a film. And well done – but if I were you I'd go along to wardrobe and try to smarten up. And maybe to make-up too. And have a shower. You don't want the whole studio to know.'

Gradually the rest of the crew arrived, and one by one they nearly fainted with surprise. 'Marilyn!' 'Here already?' 'I can't believe it!' 'That's a first!' etc. The set was dressed and the lights rehung in half the normal time. David Orton kept me busier than usual on the studio floor, and I forgot all about Marilyn until her dresser came to find me two hours later.

'Miss Monroe would like a word, Colin.'

David groaned. 'At least let me know if she's ready, will you?'

'Oh, she's ready, Mr Orton,' said the dresser. 'She just wants a word with Colin first.'

'Oh she does, does she? Has Colin taken on Paula's job too, then?' He raised his eyes to heaven. 'Lord, what did I do to deserve an assistant director like this?'

When I got to Marilyn's dressing room, she was still in the inner sanctum, but fully dressed and looking radiant.

'Colin, I'm feeling a little nervous now,' she said. She gripped my fingers hard. 'What do you think?'

'Marilyn, darling,' I didn't care if Paula could hear or not. 'Think of the future. You *are* the future. Now, come on the set and show those old fogies what you can do.'

It was a wonderful day. I only had eyes for Marilyn, although I didn't speak to her again. To my great relief most of the crew simply ignored me. It was as if my new role made me someone else, and put me on a different level. Paula fussed around as usual, but Marilyn seemed to have risen above her in some way, like a swan gliding through the reeds. She remembered her lines, came in on cue, and smiled brightly at the other actors on the set. When Olivier went over to give her some direction, she looked directly into his eyes and said, 'Gee! Sure!' instead of turning to Paula halfway through.

It was not until she was back in her dressing room at the end of the day that I got a chance to spend a moment with her alone.

'You were magnificent! You did it! You showed them all!'

'I was scared. Will you come by again this evening? Please? Come after supper. I've got to spend some time with Paula. I've got to learn my lines.'

The ice beneath my feet was wafer-thin, but I could not resist those eyes.

'All right. I'll come. But I've got no excuse to spend the night this time.'

'See you later then, Colin.'

'Goodbye.'

Tony and Anne looked pretty stunned when I reappeared at Runnymede House that evening. By now they knew where I had been the night before, and I don't think they ever expected to see me again. It was as if they thought Marilyn had swallowed me up, like a snake. Anne seemed rather upset, but Tony was full of congratulations.

'I don't know how you did it, Colin, but Laurence' – Tony is the only man in the world who calls Olivier 'Laurence' – 'was absolutely delighted. At this rate we'll finish the film early. What did you do? Do you think it will last?'

'I wouldn't bet on it,' I said.

'I think we can all guess what Colin did,' said Anne tartly. 'The question is, what happens next? And what will Mr Miller say when he gets back?'

'Marilyn and I are not having an affair,' I said wearily.

'No, of course not,' said Tony bluffly. 'Just good friends, right? Anyway, you're much too young for her.'

'And much too naïve,' added Anne.

'So you'll be staying here tonight, I assume,' said Anne.

'Ah, well, I suppose, I'm not sure about that. I have to drop by Parkside after dinner, just to make sure Marilyn is all right. She absolutely insisted. But I do want to come back here to sleep – if I can.'

'Quite,' said Anne.

When I arrived at Marilyn's house again Roger was pacing up and down outside, obviously waiting to talk to me before I went in. I parked as discreetly as possible and he came across, knocking his pipe out on his shoe.

'Miss Monroe is quite upset. She's with Paula at the moment. I'd leave them to it and wait, if I was you.'

'For heaven's sake, what's the matter now?' Colin, the twenty-four-hour cure! 'She was super today. Olivier was happy, she looked happy. It was as if the sun had come out.'

'You didn't think they'd let you take her over, did you?'

'I don't want to take her over. She's not a company. She's a person. I just want to help.'

'I think you'll find she *is* a company. Marilyn Monroe Productions. That's who pays my wages, anyway. And Milton Greene was here for an hour, too. He's plotting something, that's for sure. But I don't think he'll tell Mr Miller. I think he sees Mr Miller as a bigger threat than you.'

'So he jolly well should. Mr Miller is her husband. I'm nothing more than a passing fancy. Everybody in the movie industry fusses too much about what is happening that actual minute. Nobody takes the long view. It's a wonder any film ever gets finished at all.'

'It'll certainly be a miracle if we ever finish this one.'

Roger and I went into the kitchen to wait. Poor girl, I thought. I bet Paula is confusing her all over again. But then, I suppose that if she didn't, she'd be out of a job, just like the rest of them.

It was nearly dark by the time Paula appeared.

'Hello, Colin. You'd better go up. But don't stay too long. She's very tired, and she's not feeling too well.'

When I got up to the bedroom, Marilyn was lying down in the half darkness, looking very fragile indeed.

'Oh, Colin. I'm feeling so bad.'

'What has upset you now?'

'Paula told me that Sir Laurence yelled at her that I couldn't act, and never would be a real actress. And in front of the crew. The whole film crew.'

'Today? Olivier did that today? But I was there all the time.'

I was totally incredulous. I couldn't believe Olivier would do such a thing, especially today.

'No, I guess it wasn't today,' admitted Marilyn. 'Maybe yesterday.'

Oh, that Paula really was a witch. What an unkind thing to say!

'Well, I don't believe it, Marilyn. Maybe Olivier lost his temper and Paula got it wrong.'

'You think I can act, don't you, Colin?'

I sat down heavily on the side of the bed. Here we go again. How insecure can one person be?

'No, I don't think you can act! Not in the sense Olivier means.

And thank God you can't. I'm fed up with Olivier implying that there is only one way to act – and that's his way, of course. Olivier can give great performances, but most of the time he's doing nothing more than dazzling impersonations, brilliant caricatures. He's a great stage actor. He can reach out across the footlights and hypnotise an audience into believing anything he wants. He loves to use tricks, false noses and funny wigs. He knows his craft backwards, and he carefully plans how to shock, and to seduce, and to beguile. But as soon as he has to be an ordinary person, he's dreadful. It's as if he needs some special exaggeration – a dagger, a hunchback, a false eye – in order to exist. Without them, he looks awkward and self-conscious. In his early films he was embarrassing.'

'I saw Vivien Leigh in *Gone with the Wind*,' said Marilyn. 'She was great.'

'She was great, Marilyn, because she wasn't impersonating Scarlett O'Hara in the film, she *was* Scarlett O'Hara. She knew exactly how Scarlett O'Hara would have felt. She got right inside the part. Olivier can't imagine that. He can put on a character and take it off like a suit of clothes, without any effort at all. That works fine for the stage, but you can't get away with it on film. The movie camera shows up everything. A great movie actor or actress has to *be* the part, right down into their mind. And that is what you can do, Marilyn. I don't know how, but you can do it. You are going to steal this picture away from Olivier, and he knows it. Mind you, he is a great man, and in one way I don't think he minds. I really admire him for that. He can see what you've got – I don't care what Paula says – and he's prepared to hand you the film on a plate if that will make it a success. He wouldn't do that unless he knew, deep down, that you were an actress. It's the same with Marlon Brando. Olivier admires him, but he also fears him. The problem is that neither of you acts the way he acts, and that is very hard for him to understand. And he can probably see that you are the future, which must frighten him a bit.'

'Oh, Colin. What should I do?'

'Get to the studio as early as you can, dear Marilyn. No one expects you to behave like a bit-part player, but the film can only be finished if everyone turns up. There are some lovely music sequences coming along, and you enjoy those. And there are some nice scenes where Elsie Marina takes control of the love affair, and those will suit you very well. In fact, I want you to take control of the film. Marilyn Monroe Productions and Laurence Olivier Productions – you're equal partners, aren't you? It's time you put your foot down. Forget about poor little Milton; he's just a stooge. Forget about Paula; she's only there to hold your hand, and she's scared stiff of you anyway. Even forget about Mr Miller. He can't take the heat. You'll have plenty of time to make him a good Jewish wife when you're back in the Bronx. You've got to march into that studio and take control. Lay it on the line: "This is the way I want it, and this is the way it is going to be done." '

'Gee, Colin, do you think I could? But I'm too scared. I'm scared that when I get in front of that camera I won't feel right – that I won't know what to do. I wish I had a few of those tricks of Sir Laurence's up my sleeve.'

'God forbid, Marilyn. Do you want to be a ham like Bette Davis? Of course not! You always know exactly what to do when you're in front of the camera. You are a natural. An incredible natural talent. Don't be scared. Enjoy it. Revel in it.'

'There you go again – you make it sound fun. Why do I get such bad nerves?'

'Listen, Marilyn. When I left school I went into the air force and became a pilot. I was flying single-seater jet planes every day. When I was in the plane, I was sitting so far forward that I couldn't even see the wings. And sometimes I would look out into the vast blue sky and think, "Help! What's keeping me up? Nothing but thin air. Any minute now I'm going to fall twenty thousand feet into the sea." Of course I knew all about aerodynamics and that stuff, but for a moment I would panic and my heart would stop. But then I would think, "It's not for me to worry about that. All I have to do is fly the damn plane. And that I can do, or I wouldn't be up here on my own in the first place." Then I would be back in control again; and as you can see, the plane never fell.'

Marilyn clapped her hands. 'You're right. I'm going to fly! I can fly! But first I've got to be free. Free of all those pills and doctors. Free of everyone.'

'And free of me.'

'Oh, Colin, no. Stay a little while. Lie down beside me till I fall asleep. Please. I feel I can't be alone tonight. Otherwise I'll have to take the pills. And anyway, I want you to tell me all that stuff again – about being natural, I mean. That's what I really want to be.'

'All right, Marilyn. I'll stay a little while, but for now, let's get some sleep.'

I turned the light off and lay down in that soft quilt again and closed my eyes.

I heard Marilyn giggle in the dark.

'Natural. Do you think you and I could ever be natural together, one day?'

'Perhaps, Marilyn. When the film is over, perhaps. It would be nice.'

'Mmm,' said Marilyn. She reached out, took my hand and held it. 'Natural is nice . . .'

Less than an hour later, she was awake again.

'Colin! Colin!' she cried.

I sat bolt upright in the darkness and fumbled desperately for the light. I had fallen asleep on top of the bed and, thank goodness, fully dressed. I had not even taken off my shoes.

'It hurts. It hurts.'

Marilyn lay on her back, clutching her stomach. She was as pale as a ghost.

'What's the matter?' I reached out and put my hand against her cheek. She didn't seem to have a fever. 'What's the matter?'

'It's cramp. I've got cramps. It's terrible. Oh no! Oh no! Oh no!'

'What is it, Marilyn?'

'The baby! I'm going to lose the baby.'

'The baby? What baby? Are you having a baby?' I simply could not comprehend what was going on.

For the first time since I had known her, Marilyn began to weep. I had never seen so much as the sign of a tear in the studio, even when Olivier was at his worst. I suppose I thought of her as someone whose life had been such a struggle, who had known so much pain as a child, that she would never allow herself to cry again.

'Poor Marilyn,' I said, as gently as I could. 'Tell me about the baby.'

'It was Arthur's,' Marilyn said, between sobs. 'It was for him. He didn't know. It was going to be a surprise. Then he would see that I could be a real wife, and a real mother.'

A mother – I could hardly believe it.

'How long have you been pregnant?'

'Just a few weeks, I guess. At least, my period is a couple of weeks late. And I didn't dare mention it to anyone, in case it wasn't true. Ow!' Another spasm gripped Marilyn's tummy. She was clearly in terrible pain.

'I'm going to lose the baby. Maybe it's a punishment because I've been having such a good time.'

'Nonsense, Marilyn. We didn't do anything wrong. Nothing at all. I'd better tell Roger to call a doctor right away. And he'd better tell Milton too – only you are not to take any pills. Shall I get Paula and Hedda too?'

'Don't tell them about the baby, Colin. I always have cramps when my period is due. They're used to that. This seems just much worse, that's all.'

'OK. But you'd better tell the doctor about it when he comes. I'll be right back.'

'Please come back soon, Colin. Please don't leave me alone.'

I rushed out of the room and down the corridor to Roger's bedroom, and turned on the light.

'Roger! Wake up at once. It's Miss Monroe. She's ill.'

'What's the trouble?' Roger was out of bed in a flash, and pulling on his trousers and shirt.

'You'd better call a doctor at once. She's not seriously ill, but she's in a lot of pain. The telephone operator will know the name of a local doctor who's on call at night. Try to find someone who'll come right now. Then, and only then, can you wake Paula and Hedda and send them along. And call Milton too, I suppose. In the meantime I'll be holding Marilyn's hand.'

Roger shot off downstairs to the telephone and I went back to the bedroom. Marilyn was nowhere to be seen, but there was a light under the bathroom door.

'Are you OK, Marilyn?' I called. 'Roger is talking to a doctor right now. He'll be here very soon.'

Marilyn let out a cry. 'Ooh! I'm bleeding so much.'

'Listen carefully, Marilyn, this is important. Don't lock the bathroom door. If it's already locked, as soon as you can, reach out and unlock it. Even if you have to crawl on your hands and knees. I promise I won't come in. I won't let anyone in. But you might faint, and the doctor has to be able to get in as soon as he comes.

'Oh, Colin!'

I heard a shuffling noise and some groans, and then a click as the bolt was pulled back.

'Good girl.'

Roger appeared at the bedroom door.

'The doctor's on his way. I'm going to call Paula and then Milton. Let me know if there's anything I can do.'

'Hang in there, Marilyn,' I called out. 'The doctor's on his way. Try to take it easy if you can.'

'It's not the pain, it's the baby. I should have stayed in bed for a few weeks.'

'Marilyn, if it's not to be, this time round, it's not to be. You and Arthur are just beginning. You'll have plenty of time after the film is finished. Don't upset yourself too much. What will be, will be.'

At that moment Paula hurled herself into the room, and I had to jump in front of the bathroom door to stop her from bursting in.

'Marilyn! Marilyn! My baby! What has Colin done to you?'

'Colin's done nothing, Paula,' said Marilyn through the door. 'Don't be silly. I'm just having a very bad period, that's all.'

Paula glared at me.

'We've done nothing wrong at all,' I said firmly. 'Trust me, Paula. No one is to blame. Poor Marilyn isn't ill. It's her monthly cramps, that's all. The doctor is coming just in case.'

Paula slumped down beside me on the carpet, ever the tragedienne.

'Marilyn, Marilyn. What can I do? Why isn't Arthur here? He should be by your side. Colin is a nice boy, but he isn't your husband. Oh dear, oh dear, you'll have to cancel the film now.' She sounded exactly like a typical Jewish mum.

Roger was the next person to appear at the bedroom door. 'I've telephoned Milton,' he said. 'He's on his way too. Soon we'll have the whole bloody circus here. I'll go down and wait for the doctor.'

It was not long before we heard a car drive up outside.

'The doctor's here,' I called through the door.

But it wasn't. It was Milton.

'What in God's name is going on, Colin? What have you two been up to? Where's Marilyn? Why isn't the doctor here yet? You should have called him before you called me.'

'Marilyn's in the bathroom, and she does not want anyone to go in. Repeat, *not*,' I said severely, looking at Paula, who had stood up. 'No one is to go near her until the doctor arrives. I promised Marilyn I'd personally bar the door.'

There were occasional groans coming from the other side, and Milton and Paula were both desperate to investigate further, but mercifully, at that moment another car could be heard, and soon Roger appeared with an amiable-looking elderly man.

'Now then, where is the patient? What on earth are you all doing here?'

'The patient is Miss Monroe you see, and . . .' gabbled Milton and Paula at once.

'The patient is in the bathroom here,' I said loudly. 'And all of us are now going downstairs.' I started shepherding them out like a lot of bleating sheep. 'My name is Colin Clark, doctor,' I said over my shoulder. 'The bathroom door is unlocked. We will leave Miss Monroe to you.'

And we left.

'This is Dr Connell,' I heard him say as I closed the door. 'May I come in?'

Downstairs in the hall Milton and Paula looked at each other, and me, with equal hostility.

'This is absolutely nothing to do with me,' I said. 'I was simply waiting for Marilyn to fall asleep before I went home. She'd been complaining of stomach cramps, and didn't want to be left alone. Then she said she was feeling worse, so I told Roger to call a doctor.'

There didn't seem anything else to say, so no one spoke. Soon, to my relief, we were joined by a sleepy Hedda Rosten. Hedda sometimes to get tipsy in the evenings, but she is a nice, motherly lady, and is not part of the film world. If anyone could help to calm down Marilyn, it would be Hedda.

There was an uncomfortable fifteen minutes of foot-shuffling and hand-wringing before the doctor came downstairs.

'Is Miss Monroe's husband here? No? Well, which of you is in charge?'

We all stepped forward.

The doctor raised his eyebrows. It was very late at night.

'Well, Miss Monroe is in no danger. I've given her an injection and the bleeding has stopped, and she is going to sleep. I suggest that you ladies' – he frowned at Milton and me – 'take it in turns to stay with her. She should stay in bed tomorrow for the whole day, but after that she should be fine. I'll come back to see her at lunchtime.'

There was a huge sigh of relief from us all. Paula and Hedda went upstairs immediately to inspect their charge and decide who slept where. I suspect Paula wanted to ensure that she was the first person Marilyn saw when she awoke.

'Let me walk you out to your car, doctor,' I said.

'Me too,' said Milton, anxious not to leave me alone with anyone, ever again.

'You weren't surprised to find that your patient was Miss Marilyn Monroe, doctor?' I asked as we got out into the fresh night air.

'Oh, no, Mr Clark. My wife is the head of the Sadler's Wells Ballet, so I'm used to leading ladies.'

'The head of the Sadler's Wells Ballet? I must know her then. My father is on the board of the Opera House. What's your wife's name?'

'Oh, no,' Milton groaned. 'Here we go again. Isn't there anyone you don't know, Colin?'

'She is called Ninette de Valois,' said the doctor.

'Oh, how lovely! Of course I know Ninette. I admire her enormously. What a coincidence. Do give her my love. Tell her from one of the Clark twins.'

'I will. And what are you doing here, Mr Clark, if I may ask, in Miss Monroe's house at two o'clock in the morning?'

'I'm working on the film Miss Monroe is making at Pinewood Studios, and I'm, er, a friend of Miss Monroe's as well.'

'And Miss Monroe's husband? I presume she has a husband?'

'He's in America. I think.'

'Oh, really? And how long has he been gone?'

'Oh, a week. Six days, to be exact. And the baby, doctor?'

Milton looked completely stunned.

'Oh, you know about that, do you? Well, it's true. Miss Monroe was about three weeks pregnant, I would say. Not now, of course. But she can always try again. It isn't the end of the world. I must be off. Goodnight, gentlemen.'

And he climbed into his car and drove away.

'I'd better be going too,' I said.

'Yes, Colin, you had. I told you it would end in tears.'

'My conscience is clear, Milton.' I said. 'No tears from me. I'm sad for Marilyn, of course, although I find it hard to think of her as a mum.'

'Perhaps, Colin . . .'

'I'll tell you what, Milton. I'm going to see Marilyn once more, tomorrow. Just once, I promise. After that I'll vanish back into the scenery. OK, Milton? Goodnight.'

The fairy story had ended, as dramatically as it had begun.

WEDNESDAY, 19 SEPTEMBER

'Marilyn, darling, the time has come to say goodbye.'

As I drove over to Parkside House the next day I knew exactly what I had to say. Somehow I had an image of Marilyn, reclining on a garden bench in the shade of a beech tree, wrapped in her white towelling robe. I would walk across the lawn towards her. She would be very pale, lying there with her eyes closed, very quiet but not asleep.

'Marilyn, darling . . .' I rehearsed it again. One thing was certain: she must wipe our friendship from her mind completely. I had telephoned Milton from the studio at eight a.m., and he had told me that Arthur Miller was returning that very afternoon, five days earlier than planned. He had heard of last night's happenings from Hedda, I suppose, and while I did not think she would have mentioned me, there was a very real danger that Marilyn might, just to make him jealous. Added to this, she could sometimes be mischievous. 'I kissed Colin,' she had said to Milton, just to tease him, and she had thought it highly amusing, although Milton – and I – had not. Milton had warned me that if Marilyn ever became dependent on anyone, she tended to add them to her retinue without too much thought of the consequences. She thought nothing of having two psychoanalysts, two dramatic coaches, or two Hollywood agents at the same time. She had sometimes had two lovers simultaneously in the past, as Milton himself could testify. It wasn't that she was duplicitous or cunning. It was simply that she really didn't think it was important.

She seemed incapable of comprehending the effect she had on those who surrounded her, and how much she meant to them; this even applied to her husbands, I suspect.

I had made sure that I was at the studios earlier than usual, and that I was waiting outside the dressing rooms when Olivier arrived.

'Morning, boy.' Olivier's usual greeting. 'Marilyn here yet? Is she going to surprise us again?'

'I'm afraid not, Sir Laurence. She was taken seriously ill in the middle of the night. Well, it looked serious, anyway. A doctor had to be called, and he said she must stay in bed all day.'

'Good gracious. Bed all day? That sounds bad. And what illness did the doctor diagnose?'

'It turns out that it's only a very bad period. But Marilyn was in considerable pain, and she lost a lot of blood.'

I wasn't going to mention the baby. That was something private between Marilyn and Arthur.

'I see. Josh Logan warned me about that possibility. Evidently she always needs a day off once a month. We allowed for that in the schedule. But of course we've used up all that time by now. Whatever next?'

'Milton tells me that Arthur is returning from New York this afternoon. I'm sure that will help. Marilyn told me she's going to work especially hard every day from now on, like she did yesterday, and I think she's serious. Her relationship with Arthur was a bit frantic when they first arrived, and his departure gave her a terrible shock. I think she'll concentrate on her career for a while now. At least until this film is finished.'

'I hope you're right, Colin.'

'And it's time I got out of the equation, Larry. So with your permission I'll go over to Parkside this morning and make that clear. Not that there has been anything improper between Marilyn and me, but I wouldn't want Arthur to misunderstand.'

'No, quite so. You run along. Try to find out if she'll be in tomorrow. Please assure her that we all want to finish this film as soon as possible. Personally I wish I'd never set eyes on the woman, but don't tell her that.'

What a pity it is that Olivier never let himself get to know Marilyn properly, I thought, as I drove to Parkside House. This could have been a great film, and a wonderful experience for all of us.

Marilyn was awake, Roger told me when I arrived, and the house was full of people as usual. She was in the bedroom – so much for my shaded lawn – and I did not have the courage to go in unannounced. It was nearly an hour before Paula took pity on me, and called me upstairs.

'Marilyn, it's Colin. Do you want to see him?'

That was bad. I hadn't needed an introduction yesterday.

'Sure. Oh, hi, Colin. Come on in. Now, don't say you've come to say goodbye.'

How did she read my mind so accurately? You could never tell with Marilyn.

'You're not going anywhere, are you? I've decided I want to finish the film as quickly as possible. Why, it was you who told me I must do that. And Paula is going back to the States soon to get a new permit or something, so I'll need you to hold my hand as well as Sir Laurence.'

'I'm sorry, Marilyn,' I said, taking no notice of Paula, who had sat down beside me, 'but I don't think you should even catch my eye after today, let alone hold my hand. Mr Miller is coming back this afternoon, and it's so important that he doesn't find out that we're friends, or have been friends over this past week. We both know that we did nothing wrong. We know that we just had fun and enjoyed each other's company. But Mr Miller might find that very hard to understand. He might think that while the cat was away, the mice were behaving like rats.'

Marilyn gave a weak laugh.

'I guess you're right, Colin. He never seemed to mind about that sort of thing in the old days, but he's much more intense now.'

'Marilyn, darling, you are his wife now. And I don't care what you say about the note you read on his desk – he worships you. Just as I do.'

Marilyn sighed.

'The trouble is that you never can believe how wonderful you are,' I said. 'I suppose it's because of your childhood. You assume that everything nice is going to be taken away from you in the end, so you're frightened to get your hopes up.'

'I adore Arthur, too,' said Marilyn in a whisper. 'I really do. He's so strong, and so wise. And he's a gentleman. He always treated me like a lady. I wanted to marry him from when I first saw him in Hollywood, all those years ago . . .' She paused.

'I think you're made for each other,' I lied. 'You need someone who takes you seriously. Who sees what a great person you are. No ordinary man could do that.'

Marilyn looked relieved. 'Gee, Colin. You make me feel better right away.'

'You are great, Marilyn. And you are going to have a great career, and a great life. Mind you, after this production is over you must be more careful which films you decide to make. Maybe you should take Mr Strasberg's advice. Not about your day-to-day routine, but about scripts. He knows a lot about scripts.'

Paula beamed, suddenly my ally for life. She got up and went to the door. 'I'll leave you with Colin now,' she said.

'When this picture is over,' Marilyn went on, 'I'm going to settle down and be a good wife to Arthur. I'm going to learn to make matzo-ball soup just as good as his dad's. I'm not going to make any other movies until I've shown Arthur I can look after him. He'll never want to leave me again, that's for sure.'

'So you see why it's so important that he shouldn't suspect that there was anything between us?'

'Nothing serious. He wouldn't think that, would he? That would be terrible.'

'Well, he might. So you must be very careful. You must say nothing at all.'

'Nothing?'

'Nothing. Just imagine what his reaction would be if he thought that I'd done something which had resulted in you losing his baby.'

Marilyn gasped.

'I'm sorry to be so blunt, Marilyn, and we both know that I didn't do any such thing. But just imagine. What would he say? What might he do? I know what would happen if our parts were reversed and you were my wife.'

Marilyn opened her eyes wide.

'I'd kill him.'

'Oh, Colin.' Marilyn began to sob quietly. 'I love Arthur so much. How can I show him? How can I convince him? Do you think I can ever give him a child? Do you think he wants a child? We've never discussed it. I know he'd be a wonderful father. Why, he's like a father to me. I'll never lose him. I'll make it all up to him. I'll never disappoint him again.'

'Of course you won't, Marilyn. And I don't think you ever have. He's frightened now, just as you are. You are both artists, great artists. Did you think it was going to be easy? Great artists need other artists in their lives. It takes one to understand one. But they will always clash – every now and then. A great writer like Mr Miller needs to be selfish in order to create his masterpiece. And so do you. Sure, an actor like Olivier can just walk out on the stage and play a part. But when you give a great performance, you actually *become* the person; you feel their joy and feel their pain. That is an incredible strain, but that is what makes you a star.'

'Ooh, Colin.'

Marilyn was beginning to cheer up. 'So what must I do now?'

'Give Arthur a great welcome home. No sex for a bit, though. Tell him how much you missed him. Tell him you've decided to settle down and finish the film as quickly as possible. Tell him that you won't bother him when he is writing – Milton said he had some deadline now. Ask him to come and pick you up at the studio each evening when Paula is away. Whenever Paula is here, don't let her stay with you past seven in the evening. All good, simple rules, Marilyn, and not too hard to obey.'

'Yes, sir,' said Marilyn, giving a little salute. 'Anything else?'

'Yes. Never look at me, not so much as a glance. You may be a great actress, but I'm not, and my face could easily betray what I feel.'

'What *do* you feel, Colin? Tell me.'

'I feel incredibly lucky to have been able to spend a few days in the company of the most wonderful, brave and beautiful person in the world, but . . .'

'"But"?'

'But if Arthur ever mentions my name, you've got to shrug and say, "Colin? Oh, he's just a messenger, nobody of any importance at all."'

'Oh, Colin. I couldn't say that. But I understand about Arthur.'

Marilyn stared gloomily at the quilt. Then suddenly she brightened up.

'I'll tell you what – I'll wink. No one can stop me winking at you, and you've got to wink back. When things get tough at the studio, when Sir Laurence gets mad, I'm gonna look for Colin, and wink. And you'd better watch out. Paula is going back to New York soon, so I may wink quite a lot.'

It was such a brave, childlike solution to a potentially tragic situation that I lifted Marilyn's hand up off the bed and kissed it.

'I'll wink back,' I said. 'Never fear.'

POSTSCRIPT

And so it was over. A brief flirtation between a young man of twenty-three and a beautiful married woman, who was as innocent as she was mature.

No one really seemed any the worse. Marilyn had lost the baby, of course, but I am not sure that was such a bad thing. I simply could not imagine her as a mother. There had been nobody to look after her as a child, and consequently she had no idea how to look after anyone else. Each time she had got married she had tried desperately hard to take care of her husband, but she always made a total mess of it, and they ended up looking after her. She was, I am afraid to say, just too self-obsessed.

Marilyn always said that she had an ugly side to her character, but if she had, I can honestly say that I never saw it. Confused, frightened and totally lacking in self-confidence, she had not got that sense of her own identity which is so essential for a stable life. Like many celebrities she felt that she couldn't cope with the demands that were thrust on her, and this made her quick to suspect the motives of people whom she had allowed to get too close. Luckily I never fell into that category, so we could remain chums.

Marilyn's idea that she had a dark side helped her to explain why everyone seemed to desert her in the end. She never knew whom she could trust, and this was because the answer was probably: 'No one, no one in the whole world' – all through her life.

One reason she failed to take people with her was that she had no idea of where she was going herself. Nevertheless, she got there. No one can dispute that, and, basically, she did it on her own.

Imagine how many blonde starlets were being abused by those horrible Hollywood moguls night after night – and still are, for all I know. They all faded away, but Marilyn did not. Nearly forty years after her death she is still the most famous film star in the world.

After our adventure, the filming went on as usual on the set of *The Prince and the Showgirl* at Pinewood. Marilyn became a little more punctual and, compared to her behaviour on her subsequent films, she was very professional. All the dubbing and 'post-sync' work, for instance, was completed in a couple of days, far quicker than anyone had imagined possible. Marilyn seemed to have resigned herself to finishing the movie first, and being the perfect wife to Arthur Miller later, although she never ceased to gaze at him with awe and to obey his slightest command.

She did sometimes wink at me in the studio, especially when it seemed that Laurence Olivier was about to explode. Because it could ease the tension, Olivier did not mind. Indeed, after filming had finished he took me with him into the theatre as his personal assistant. Two years later I was winking to his wife, Vivien Leigh, who had become just as unstable as Marilyn ever was, from the wings of the Burgtheater in Vienna. Perhaps I was born to wink.

After Marilyn went back to America, I never spoke to her again – but I did hear from her once, or at least I like to think so. In early 1961, a friend of mine in Olivier's office rang me in New York to say that Marilyn Monroe had telephoned the night before and left a number for me to call. He had not spoken to her himself, he said. He had just found a note on his desk. Of course, it could have been someone playing a joke. I was well known for supporting Marilyn, although this was increasingly hard to do as she became more and more unstable. The rest of Olivier's circle, including Olivier himself, actually welcomed reports of her deteriorating condition as evidence that their opinion of her had been right all along. It was only towards the end of his life that Olivier was able to relent.

When I got the message, I must admit that I hesitated. Apart from the possibility that it was a hoax, I was not sure that I could handle a distraught Marilyn on the line. She was famous for making long, rambling calls, and I knew that I would not be able to help her. It was clearly far too late to wink.

In the end, I did dial the number, and I could hear it ringing away in the Californian night. But no one replied, and I am ashamed to say that I was relieved. It was not that I had abandoned her, certainly not in my heart. It was just that by now nobody could help her.

Poor Marilyn. Time had run out.

APPENDIX

*Letter written by Colin Clark to Peter Pitt-Millward
in Portugal, 26 November 1956*

Dear Peter,

At last the filming is over and I am back in London again. You can't imagine what a relief it is not to have to get up at 6.15 a.m. and spend the day in a hot, crowded film studio with a lot of quarrelsome prima donnas. It took a total of eighteen weeks to make the movie, including two weeks for preparation, and by the end we were all heartily fed up. I thought of you every night, and not always too tenderly either, because that was when I would write my daily diary, or journal, as I promised you I would. The trouble was that I was usually very tired, and I couldn't type, or my clacking would have kept other people awake, so I wrote it by hand. My handwriting got worse and worse until finally it was virtually illegible, and the whole thing is a mess. I might transcribe it one day, but I doubt it. Who on earth would want to know the day-to-day details of how a film is made? Nevertheless, it was a great experience to work with Marilyn and Olivier. I don't think the final film will be any better than my diary, but they are both 'wonderful people to know'. I am going on working with Olivier in a few weeks' time – this time in the theatre – and although I will probably never see Marilyn again,

I will certainly never forget her. Well, even you are one of her fans, and you've never seen any of her films.

The thing about Marilyn is that she is a mixture. She can be sweet and funny and innocent; she can be a tough and ambitious go-getter; she can be totally lacking in self-confidence; and she can do a pretty fair impression of Ophelia after Hamlet has gone. Since she is also an excellent actress in her own way – not like Olivier, of course, but I think she is *better* than him in this film – you will realise that she is a pretty hard lady to pin down.

Poor old Olivier did not appreciate this at all. All he saw was a Hollywood blonde who was always late, didn't learn her lines and refused to listen to his directions. I think that when he first met her, and agreed to do the film, he thought he could have an affair with her. But after a few weeks on the set, he would gladly have strangled her with his bare hands. Marilyn is more astute than she looks, and she was well aware of how Olivier and his hand-picked English crew felt about her. She had her own supporters whom she brought from the USA – her partner Milton Greene, Lee and Paula Strasberg, a secretary called Hedda, and her new husband, Arthur Miller. They certainly were not the team I would have picked . . . They are all Jewish – as are her lawyer, her agent and her publicity men – while Marilyn is a typical California blonde; so how they can understand the way her mind works, goodness knows.

No wonder the poor woman often looks so confused!

When Marilyn first arrived, I wasn't much bothered about her. After all, I know Vivien Leigh pretty well, and Marilyn had stolen Vivien's part in the film and all my loyalty was to the Oliviers. But I found myself being seduced by Marilyn's image; her aura is very powerful indeed. Gradually, just working on the film wasn't enough. I was determined to get to know her more directly – although, given that as third assistant director I was the most unimportant person on the whole production, that looked very unlikely. However, it was not impossible. When I was working in the office it was me who had hired Marilyn's servants, and her bodyguard (ex-Scotland Yard), and rented the house she was living in, so one evening I invented an excuse and went over there to try my luck. Imagine my surprise when I did meet the great star – but not at all in the circumstances which I expected. I was so absolutely stunned that I stopped writing my diary for a whole week, and when I started again I changed the dates in case anyone got their hands on it. I seriously thought that I might be sued or bumped off. It is hard to imagine, but there is so much money riding on Miss Monroe's pretty blonde head that people get very, very ruthless.

What actually happened was that after a few drinks with Roger (the ex-cop) I went out for a pee and stumbled right into Marilyn, sitting on the floor in a dark corridor outside her bedroom door. Whether she had had a row with Arthur Miller or not I don't know. She simply stared at me and said nothing, so I backtracked as fast as I could and hoped I'd got away with it. If she had made a stink about it the following day, I would certainly have been fired. That she did not do, but it turned out that she *had* remembered, and after filming she called me into her dressing room and asked me if I was a spy. Luckily I could absolutely swear that I was not, and I must say that I felt jolly sorry for her, too. She hasn't got many (any?) real friends, and Miller had told her that he was going away to Paris and New York for the following ten days. And they are meant to be on their honeymoon. I was so grateful to Marilyn that she hadn't said a word to anyone about my foolish escapade that I swore my undying loyalty there and then – which was a little rash, since Laurence Olivier is my boss.

I did not tell anyone what had happened, and I thought that was the end of it, but the next day Marilyn actually telephoned me in Olivier's dressing room. She had not been in to work as she was seeing Miller off, and she asked me to go via her house again on the way home. I assumed she had more messages for Olivier or something. She found it very hard to talk to him directly by that time. Even so, I didn't tell Olivier where I was going, in case he thought

I was plotting something behind his back. Then, when I did get to the house, Marilyn asked me to stay for supper, and I could see that she was just lonely and wanted someone to chat to. I am six years younger than her, and I suppose I was one of the few people around who wasn't trying to get something from her.

Anyway, we were getting along famously when Miller – yes, I know, he's her husband – had to ring from Paris. Marilyn immediately looked hunched and defensive, and I left toot sweet.

Marilyn did not come in to the studio the next day – Olivier had given her a day off – but everyone seemed to know I had had supper with her. Olivier thought it was frightfully funny. He absolutely takes my loyalty for granted, and so he should. Milton Greene, as Marilyn's partner, had a complete fit. To make matters worse, Marilyn had told Miller I was there when he rang – to make him jealous, I suppose – and the upshot was that I was forbidden ever to talk to Marilyn again, on pain of death. Sad, I thought, but what's a boy to do! However, as I was soon to learn, you can't get involved with Marilyn without getting involved with Marilyn. The following day was Saturday. I was staying with a very kind couple, called Tony and Anne Bushell, who are great friends of Olivier. Tony is Associate Director on the movie, and as such does not approve of Marilyn at all. Just before lunch, Roger, the cop, turned up in his old car and announced that he had come to take me out. As we drove away, Marilyn jumped out from under a rug on the back seat, nearly giving me a heart attack, to say nothing of Tony Bushell. She was bored of her stuffy house, she said, and she wanted an adventure.

So I took her to Windsor Castle and we saw my godfather, Owen Morshead, who is librarian there. He gave us the grand tour, which Marilyn seemed to enjoy, and then we went and had a look at Eton. It was a glorious sunny day, and Marilyn could not have been jollier or more natural, but I felt rather apprehensive nonetheless. After all, she is the most famous film star in the world. Once she did demonstrate her power. 'Shall I be "*her*", Colin?' she asked as we left Windsor Castle, and she gave her famous wiggle. Immediately she was recognised, and a crowd began to gather, until we had to get into the car and flee.

When we got home, Marilyn's lawyer was waiting for me, full of dire threats, but Marilyn rose to her full height and told him that if he lifted a little finger against me it would be him who got fired, not me. Even so, I kept my head down on Sunday. Everyone was talking as if Marilyn and I were having an affair, which was jolly flattering but complete nonsense. Milton Greene came over and gave me a long lecture about the dangers of getting involved – he seems to think Marilyn Monroe is *his property* – and I agreed to stop. Monday was just a normal day at the studio. Marilyn did not appear, and I thought it was all over.

But in the middle of the night, there was little Milton again, outside my bedroom window. Would I get dressed and go back to Marilyn's house at once? She had locked herself in her room and did not respond to anyone. 'Why should she?' I thought, but I suppose I was flattered to be asked to help. I went over and joined the little group of sheep bleating outside her door, but to no avail. Finally, I had an idea. I went outside to the garage with Roger-the-cop and found a ladder. I put this against the wall under Marilyn's window and climbed up and in. All I meant to do was open her bedroom door from the inside so that her female companions could get in and check on her health. I could hear her sleeping, so at least she was alive. But she had taken the key out of the lock, so I couldn't get out without waking her up and being caught *in flagrante*. I went back to the window but Roger and the ladder had gone, so there was nothing to do but take a nap and wait until dawn, when I could find the key and escape. An hour later, however, Marilyn woke up. There's no doubt she was pretty startled at first, especially as she clearly remembered locking the door. I managed to calm her down, and then she suddenly decided that it was like *Romeo and Juliet* – me coming in by the balcony – and was very sweet and kind. She said she did not want to be left alone, so I spent the rest of the night there (No – I behaved impeccably) and I persuaded her to come in really early to the studio the next day. This she did, which went down very well with Olivier and the crew, and I was a bit of a hero.

On the next night, I had decided that I better not sleep there again, but then Marilyn really did feel ill, so I said I'd stay until she fell asleep – she has a lot of trouble sleeping and often takes pills, like you – and then she got terrible cramps, and I had to wake the whole house up and call a doctor. (Can you imagine, he turned out to be the husband of Ninette de Valois, the head of the Sadler's Wells Ballet, who I know quite well. What a coincidence.) It seemed that Marilyn was not in any danger, so I fled. I mean, after two nights, people might have easily got the wrong impression and thought that I'd done something to make Marilyn ill. And it is not as if Marilyn was just a little wardrobe girl or something. Apart from anything else, she is MARRIED, and sure enough Arthur Miller came scurrying back from New York the next day, four days earlier than planned. I had to keep my head down as much as I possibly could for the next week, and go back to being the little messenger boy whom everyone could shout at. But what an adventure it had been.

I've told you all this in lieu of the diary, because if it had been in the diary it would have been the best bit, if you see what I mean. It probably looks like a lot of crazy nonsense to someone so far away, but please keep it until I come out next time so that I can take it back and put it with the journal, however scruffy that is. I might want to write it all properly one day.

As ever,
Colin

The Prince, the Showgirl, and Me

For Christopher and Helena, with love

PREFACE

In 1943, when I was ten years old, my boarding school decided that my class should see *Gone with the Wind*. Film shows were a monthly treat then, and we had already seen several stirring black-and-white wartime epics, but *Gone with the Wind* was different. It was in colour, it was very long, and it contained some gruesome scenes of wounded soldiers, the sort of thing which was obviously never included in British films of the time. Our teacher took great trouble to explain to us that the film was just an illusion, made up of clever special effects. Nevertheless, watching it in that bare school hall had a dramatic effect on all of us.

At about the same time my father, Kenneth Clark, had been made controller of home publicity at the Ministry of Information. This meant that he was responsible for extricating British actors and actresses from the armed forces so that they could work in patriotic films. He made frequent visits to the studios around London to see how they were getting on, and I persuaded him to let me come too. His principal ally was Alexander Korda, who was the most powerful British producer at the time, and whom my father had persuaded to join in the 'war effort'. Through him my father and mother met all the stars of the film world. Laurence Olivier and Vivien Leigh became their close friends, and William Walton, who was composing the music for Olivier's *Henry V*, was made my godfather to replace the original one who had killed by a bomb. Another Hungarian producer, Gabriel Pascal, had managed to persuade George Bernard

Shaw to let him have the film rights to all his plays. He came to our house in Hampstead with a beautiful young American actress called Irene Worth, and promised to buy me a pair of white peacocks if I would act for him, offering me the part of Ptolemy in his production of Shaw's *Caesar and Cleopatra* (with Vivien Leigh). My parents said no, but I was not the least bit disappointed: I knew that I could never be an actor, and I also knew that those white peacocks were as much a product of Pascal's imagination as *Caesar and Cleopatra* was of Shaw's.

I had become completely fascinated by the concept of a fictional idea being made into a real film, which is in itself an illusion. It is a fascination which I have never lost. At the age of twelve I explained this to my father, and told him of my determination to be a film director. My only worry was that all the directors I had met were fat and ugly. To my surprise he took me seriously. Although he was involved in all the performing arts – opera, ballet and theatre as well as film – his main love was painting. He pointed out that painting contains the same elements of illusion and reality as film, and that Michael Powell and David Lean were both successful directors, and they were thin.

From then on, a visit to a film set was like a dream fulfilled. I saw Noël Coward in a tank of oily black water making *In Which We Serve*; I saw Vivien Leigh being carried on a very wobbly litter in front of a plaster Sphinx on the set of *Caesar and Cleopatra*; I saw her again in *Anna Karenina* – she had offered me the role of her son, again refused; and many more. I was not in love with the magic of film the way many children are with theatre or ballet: I was in love with the way in which that magic was made.

When I got to Eton in 1946 it became clear that I had chosen a pretty eccentric path. 'Art' did not then have the respectable connotations that it does today. My family, though wealthy enough, was as far from the typical 'hunting, shooting and fishing' set as it was possible to be. None of my more conventional contemporaries had ever heard of an art historian, and I was forced to describe my father as a professor (he had been Slade Professor of Fine Art at Oxford). My friends could not understand me at all – many still can't – and as if to underline the difference between us, I chose to be a pilot in the RAF during my National Service rather than to go into the Guards, and then to get a job as a keeper at London Zoo rather than work in a merchant bank.

In the summer of 1952, while on vacation from Oxford, I went on a motoring tour of Europe and found myself stranded in a little palace in the mountains of north Portugal. It belonged to an Englishman called Peter Pitt-Millward, and apart from his occasional guests, I had no one else with whom to converse for over two months. To make things worse, I fell passionately in love with someone who could speak nothing but Portuguese. I could not even confide in Peter about this as he was also in love – with the same person. So I started to keep a daily journal in which I could explore my emotions, and my loneliness. This feeling of isolation persisted throughout the remainder of my time at university.

By the time I got the job on *The Prince and the Showgirl* in 1956, my diary had become a firm friend. However tired I was, I could not sleep before I had written down some of the things that had happened during the day, and confided some of the opinions that I had not dared to express to anyone, scribbling away in an old ledger which I kept wrapped up in my pyjamas. I did not always get things right, and as I never expected anyone else to read what I had written, I had no need to be what we now call 'politically correct'. Even so, in this published version of my diary for June to November 1956, I have cut very little out. I was a well-brought-up boy, and when you see 'f—' in this book, it is because I wrote 'f—' in my diary.

When the filming of *The Prince and the Showgirl* was over, it was many, many years before I dared to read my diary of that time again, just as it was many, many years before I could bring myself to see the film in a cinema. Even now I have trouble seeing past the pain and anxiety in Marilyn Monroe's eyes.

This book is really all about Marilyn. For five months, whether she turned up or not, she dominated our every waking thought. I was the least important person in the whole studio, but I was in a wonderful position from which to observe. The Third Assistant Director is really a kind of superior messenger boy. I got to meet everyone and go everywhere, unencumbered by responsibilities which might tie me down, or narrow my viewpoint. No one can feel threatened by a 3rd Ast Dir (except perhaps the 'extras', who he has to keep under control), and most of the people involved in making the film felt they could be more open with me than with a possible rival. When the filming was completed I was almost the only person who was still on speaking terms with everyone else. That alone probably makes this diary unique.

The Prince and the Showgirl
Cast List

ELSIE MARINA	*Marilyn Monroe*
THE REGENT OF CARPATHIA	*Laurence Olivier*
THE QUEEN DOWAGER	*Sybil Thorndike*
MR NORTHBROOK	*Richard Wattis*
THE KING OF CARPATHIA	*Jeremy Spenser*
MAJOR DOMO	*Paul Hardwick*
MAISIE SPRINGFIELD	*Jean Kent*
LADY SUNNINGDALE	*Maxine Audley*
FANNY	*Daphne Anderson*
BETTY	*Vera Day*
MAGGIE	*Gillian Owen*
FOREIGN OFFICE MINISTER	*David Horne*
THEATRE DRESSER	*Gladys Henson*
HOFFMAN	*Esmond Knight*
LADIES-IN-WAITING	*Rosamund Greenwood*
	Margot Lister
VALETS	*Dennis Edwards*
	Andrea Melandrinos

PRODUCTION CREW

PRODUCER AND DIRECTOR	*Laurence Olivier*
EXECUTIVE IN CHARGE OF PRODUCTION	*Hugh Perceval*
EXECUTIVE PRODUCER	*Milton Greene*
ASSOCIATE DIRECTOR	*Anthony Bushell*
FIRST ASSISTANT DIRECTOR	*David Orton*
DIRECTOR OF PHOTOGRAPHY	*Jack Cardiff*
PRODUCTION DESIGNER	*Roger Furse*
PRODUCTION MANAGER	*Teddy Joseph*
ART DIRECTION	*Carmen Dillon*
EDITOR	*Jack Harris*
CONTINUITY	*Elaine Schreyck*
CAMERA OPERATOR	*Denys Coop*
SOUND RECORDISTS	*John Mitchell*
	Gordon McCallum
LADIES' COSTUMES	*Beatrice Dawson*
MAKE-UP	*Toni Sforzini*
HAIRDRESSING	*Gordon Bond*
SET DRESSER	*Dario Simoni*
SCREENPLAY	*Terence Rattigan*
MUSIC COMPOSED BY	*Richard Addinsell*
DANCES ARRANGED BY	*William Chappell*

THE DIARIES

SUNDAY, 3 JUNE 1956

Now that University is behind me, I'm going to get a job – a real job on a real film. At 9 a.m. tomorrow I will be at Laurence Olivier's film company to offer my services on his next production. The papers say it will star Marilyn Monroe, so it should be exciting.

Two weeks ago, Larry and Vivien came down to stay at Saltwood* for the weekend. Mama told Vivien that I wanted to be a film director. I was mortified, but Vivien just gave a great purr and said 'Larry will give Colin a job, won't you Larry darling!' I could see Larry groan under his breath. 'Go and see Hugh Perceval at 146 Piccadilly,' he said. 'He might have something.'

So that is where I have an appointment in the morning. And every night I am going to write this diary. It could be fun to look back on, when I am old and famous!

MONDAY, 4 JUNE

This is going to be really hard. I know absolutely nothing about making films. I'm totally ignorant. Did I really think they were actually shooting a film in Piccadilly?

* Saltwood Castle in Kent, my parents' home.

At 10 a.m. I turned up at the office of Laurence Olivier Productions, punctual and sober.

The offices themselves are very few. A large luxurious reception area with sofas, a secretary's office at the far end, and Mr Perceval's office leading off that. It is clearly the ground floor of what was once a private house. The secretary, friendly but detached – would I wait. Mr Perceval was on the phone. Soon I was ushered in, anxious now. There didn't seem to be enough going on. Mr P is a tall, thin, gloomy man with black-rim spectacles. His sparse black hair is brushed back and he has a black moustache. He puffs a pipe continually.

'Yes. What do you want?' (No introductions whatever.)

'I want a job on the Marilyn Monroe film.'

'Oh, ho, you do? What as?'

'Anything.'

I suppose he could see that I was a complete fool and he softened a little.

'Well. We don't start filming for eight weeks. You really should come back then. At the moment we have no more offices than you can see here, and no jobs. I only have my chauffeur and my secretary. I am afraid I misunderstood Laurence. I thought you were coming to interview me about the film.'

Blind panic set in. I must say something.

'Can I wait here until there is a job?'

'For eight weeks??'

'In the waiting room – in case something comes up?'

'Grmph.' Very gloomy, and bored now. 'It's a free country, I suppose. But I'm telling you, it's going to be eight weeks. And then I can't promise anything.'

Gets up and opens door.

'Good day.'

I went out and sat down on one of the sofas in the waiting room. The secretary gave me a very cold look. She's quite pretty, but is certainly not flirtatious.

I just didn't know what to do. I had expected huge offices, even

studios, lots of work going on – willing hands needed in every department, and a bit like the London Zoo when I turned up there and
asked for a job as a keeper in '53 (and got one!*).

So I just sat and waited.

At lunchtime I was saved by a friendly face. Gilman, Larry and
Vivien's chauffeur came in, brash and cockney as ever.

"'Ullo Colin. What you doin' 'ere?'

I explained.

'Hmm. There's no work here. I've got to get his nibs' lunch.
Come and have a drink in the pub.'

I went gratefully (but only ½ of bitter). Gilman told me what
was going on. He was on loan to Perceval. Every morning he did
errands, for Perceval or for Larry, and then came back here to get
Perceval's lunch. This never varied: two cheese rolls and a Guinness.

'You won't get work from him, Colin. Miserable bugger.'

'Well, I've got nothing else in the world to do but wait, so I might
as well wait.'

'OK. Good luck. We can always have a pint together at lunchtime.'

We went back with Mr P's sandwiches and drink and Gilman
sped off in the Bentley. I waited until 6 p.m., when they all packed
up and left.

'Night all,' said Mr P gloomily, without a glance at me. I had a
large brandy and water in the pub. I'll be back in the office tomorrow.

TUESDAY, 5 JUNE

I was there at 8.30. The secretary arrived at 8.55. Mr P punctually at
nine. He just gave me a grim stare as he came in. Then he gets on
the phone and stays there most of the day. He never smiles and he
never raises his voice. The secretary gets the calls for him and then
taps away at the typewriter. She is polite but not friendly. She treats

* In the tropical bird house.

me like a client. I wonder if she knows that 'M and D'* are friends of Larry and Vivien?

She went to lunch at 12.30 with her handbag and gloves. Gilman arrived at 12.45. Then we went to the pub, and got back with Mr P's lunch at 1.15. I wonder if this is a regular situation. Maybe I can make something out of it. Mr P grumbles at the delay but Gilman is irrepressible.

Vivien had told me why she had hired Gilman. He was a relief driver, sent along when their old chauffeur was ill. On the first day, as he drove her and Larry down Bond Street, he suddenly slammed on the brakes. 'Cor. Look, what a lovely waistcoat!' he cried, pointing to a very exclusive man's-shop window. Vivien adores that sort of unspoilt character and hired him on the spot. Needless to say he now worships both of them, and is fanatically loyal. He is a Barnardo boy and very tough, so Larry probably thinks he is a good bodyguard for Vivien too. He certainly is a good pal to me and saves my life when he appears.

I get a bit nervous in my role as the invisible man. But I was more relaxed there today, and so was the secretary.

Now I've got to use my head.

WEDNESDAY, 6 JUNE

Yes. There is a pattern, and it should be possible to exploit it.

I am completely ignored all morning, but as there is no door between the waiting room and the secretary's office, I hear quite a lot. Also, she often leaves Mr P's door open when she is in there with him.

Today I didn't go to the pub with Gillers. I just gave him a wink which he picked up immediately. This meant Mr P was alone for 45 minutes. During this time, he keeps on working and the phones keep ringing.

---

* My shorthand way of describing my parents. Five years previously they had told me to stop calling them 'Mum and Dad' and to address them as 'Mama and Papa'.

He has three lines. I just ignored them, but after five minutes
he opened his door and glared at the empty secretary's desk. Then he
slammed his door shut again. Two minutes of phone ringing later,
he opened it again and glared some more, this time at me.

'You still here? Well you might as well answer the phone. Don't
think you've got a job, though. There's no chance of that at all.'

He slammed out.

Phone rings. Mr P answers. Next phone rings.

'Hello. Is that Laurence Olivier Productions?'

'Yes. Can I help you.'

'Is Sir Laurence there?'

'No, I'm afraid he's in America until the end of the week.'

'Oh. Thank you. I'll ring next week.'

'Any message?'

'No thank you.'

Click. Mr P's door opens.

'How did you know that Sir Laurence is in America until the end
of the week?'

'I heard him tell my mother.'

'Hmph. Why didn't you put the call through to me?' (There is a
buzzer on each phone.)

'There didn't seem to be a need to bother you. But if you want
every single call . . .'

'Hmph.'

Door slams again. Phone rings.

'Laurence Olivier Productions.' I'm chirpy now!

'Is Mr Perceval there?'

'Certainly. Whom shall I say is calling?'

'The *Daily Mirror*.'

'Hold on please.' Click. Bzzz. 'Yes?'

'The *Daily Mirror* for you.'

'Hmph.'

I put through about eight calls, and I was beginning to enjoy it
when the secretary (Vanessa) came back at 1.30. She didn't look very

happy at first, but I had left her a note of all calls and messages, so she began to smile again.

Finally Gillers returned with Mr P's rolls and Guinness. He was 20 minutes late and he gave me another terrific wink, which I was frightened that Mr P saw, but he gave no sign.

I had hoped to go back to the pub for my lunch with Gillers, but Mr P sent him straight down to Notley.* So I had to go alone. I had a large pink gin with my sandwich, and sure enough no one addressed a word to me all afternoon.

But it doesn't matter. At least I have a role to play from 12.30 to 1.30. I must make the most of it.

FRIDAY, 8 JUNE

By now Mr P takes it for granted that I am on duty at lunchtime. Only one week here and already I am part of the furniture.

Being efficient is the easy part. Suppressing one's ego completely for hours at a time is really hard. Gilman phoned in to say he was staying with Vivien all day, and what Vivien wants, Vivien gets; no question of that.

I went round to the pub and got two cheese rolls and a Guinness *before* Vanessa left at 12.30. Then at 12.45 I walked silently into Mr P's office and put it on his desk. Mr P was on the phone – a long-distance call to America (he must have got someone out of bed). He puffed at his pipe and gave me a mournful stare over the top of his hornrim glasses. I think he realises I'm going to win in the end! I crept out and shut the door without a word from either of us.

When Vanessa came back, I left. 'See you Monday,' I said. '8.30 sharp.' She just laughed, but in a friendly way. I'll bet she reports every word I say to Mr P. At the same time, her private life is obviously more important to her than her job – unlike Mr P, or me for that matter. So she is really a non-combatant.

* Notley Abbey, Laurence Olivier and Vivien Leigh's home in Buckinghamshire.

After lunch I got in the car and came down here to Saltwood for a break.

'How is the new job?' asked Mama.

'Very good.'

'Settling in nicely? It was kind of Larry to give it to you.'

But she is too shrewd to be convinced. Actually I don't think she believes either of her sons can get a good job or ever will.

I told Celly* the minimum. She is incredibly sympathetic as usual, but she leads such a busy life that I didn't think I could quite explain my 'wait eight weeks' policy. It does sound a bit hopeless when looked at from down here, but I am committed to it.

MONDAY, II JUNE

I was surprised to find myself glad to be back at 146 Piccadilly at 8.30 this morning.

Vanessa turned up at 8.55 with another girl. Are there to be two secretaries from now on? Mr P has moved faster than I thought, hence the mournful stare. My heart went to my boots, but incredibly, at 12.30 they both went out together for lunch. By this time I had already rushed out to the pub and got Mr P's two cheese rolls and Guinness. If Gilman had turned up I would have explained, but luckily he didn't, so I was alone as usual. Vanessa and her companion regard me with complete indifference and don't seem to be bothered by Mr P either. They chattered away all morning as if he hardly mattered, except for phone calls and typing. I think he is scared of them. When I took his lunch in at 12.45 he didn't even look up. 'War of nerves'. However, by 1 p.m. he needed help.

'I need to find the telephone number of someone called Noël Coward.'

He pronounced the name very carefully as if I was an idiot.

'It won't be in the telephone book. You will have to call X, and

---

* My twin sister Colette.

he will know the number of Y, and Y should know Mr Coward's number. He will give it to you if you say you are calling for me.'

'Yes, Mr Perceval.'

I rang Saltwood.

'Oh Col, how lovely to hear you.' (I had only been gone 14 hours.) 'Mama, this is urgent. I need Noël Coward's phone number in England, right away.'

'How exciting.' I could hear Mama looking at her voluminous card index. 'Here it is.'

Straight into Mr P's office with the number on a piece of paper. No time to check it. I put it on his desk: NOËL COWARD and the number. 'Hmph.' Dark look. 'That was very quick.' Grudgingly: 'Good.'

Ah, these tiny triumphs! And it must have been the right number or he would certainly have complained.

I stayed late to savour my success and try to glean something from the girls' gossip. Absolutely nothing.

But Mr P said 'Goodnight Colin' as he went out.

TUESDAY, 12 JUNE

At 11 o'clock, a boring morning was interrupted by much kerfuffle outside.

Then in strode Larry. He was taken aback to see me (probably couldn't recognise me at first) but managed 'Hello, dear boy' before disappearing into Mr P's office. I expect his first question was 'Who the hell's that?' and the second 'What the hell's he doing here?'

A few seconds later in comes Vivien, followed by a grinning Gilman. (He will have briefed her after Larry left the car. Vivien is *never* caught off guard!)

'Colin, darling.'

Vivien comes up so close to me that our noses are almost touching. She gives a pleading look: 'Please look after my darling Larry for me, will you?'

She flutters her eyelids, gives a small quick confidential smile and sweeps off into Mr P's office, ignoring the two girls. I am left standing in the middle of the reception room, as if struck by lightning. Vivien does pack about 100,000 volts, and she completely stuns me. The two secretaries are equally dumbfounded.

After 10 minutes, Vivien reappears, kisses me on both cheeks, with her lips pointing at my ears, and goes off with Gilman. Larry stays about an hour. As he goes out he says: 'Do find this dear boy something to do, Hughie.'

Then a very charming and sincere goodbye to each secretary before he and Mr P go off for lunch at the Ivy.

After five minutes, the girls had recovered their composure and went out to lunch, again together, leaving me to answer the phones and take messages. They now regard me as a convenient fixture, but I wonder what they would have done if I didn't exist. The same I expect.

When Mr P comes back he says: 'I might have a job for you tomorrow, Colin. (Colin!!) Just one day's work, mind. Nothing permanent, you hear. No chance of that. So be in early in the morning.'

Hasn't he noticed that I am always here first? Maybe it's part of his 'Keep Colin in his place' strategy. Anyway I've refused a really good party tonight. I hope my virtue is rewarded.

WEDNESDAY, 13 JUNE

Work at last.

I arrived at 8.30 and Mr P came in almost immediately. Vanessa too. (She must have been warned!)

'Come straight in, Colin.'

Mr P had a problem.

MM's publicity man is coming to London tomorrow. He wants to see the house MM is going to stay in while she is in England for the filming. Mr P hates publicity men and thinks this one is fussing much too early. Naturally no one has started to look at houses yet.

Mr P wants me to find a suitable house today. It must be no more than 40 minutes' drive from Pinewood Studios and no more than 40 minutes' drive from central London. Minimum three double bedrooms and three bathrooms plus ample servants' quarters. It must be surrounded by gardens and well off a main road. It must be ultra-luxurious. Price no object.

'Check the estate agents. You can have one of these phone lines all morning. Report back to me by 5 p.m. I'm putting my trust in you. Don't let me down.'

My mind was racing. I walked out of the offices and went and sat in the car. 40 minutes was about 20 miles. I didn't even know where Pinewood Studios were. I got out the AA map, found Pinewood and made a rough 20-mile arc around it. Ah-hah. Ascot. I walked down Piccadilly to the St James's Club.

'Morning Mr Colin.'

'Morning Lockhart. Mr Cotes-Preedy in yet?'

'Not yet, but he's always in by noon.'

'Good.'

Enough time for a hearty breakfast. Last year Tim R* and I had rented a tiny cottage from Mr Cotes-Preedy's wife. They lived in the big house, Tibbs Farm, opposite Ascot Racecourse. It was up a long drive and was exactly what Mr P had specified. Mrs C-P is a splendid lady – much older than her husband and looking like a macaw, but somehow attractive and even sexy. They were both very fond of money, like all the Ascot crowd.

After breakfast, I still had a long wait, and I made a lot more phone calls. I'm going to try to pull off a stunt. If I don't do something to surprise Mr P I'll be sitting in that waiting room forever.

By the time Mr C-P arrived I was all fired up. Mr C-P is a lawyer. He was surprised to see me but he did remember me – he's seen me occasionally in the bar. I put the proposition to him in stages.

'Rent the main house? Out of the question. Mrs C-P would

* Tim Rathbone, with whom I had been at Eton and Oxford. Elected Conservative MP for Lewes in 1974.

never agree . . . £100 per week!!! For 18 weeks? Famous film star?'
He simply shot to the phone to call Mrs C-P and came back all
smiles.

Copious drinks bought for everyone in the bar. (Only one for me.)
Some more frantic phone calls, lunch, and back to Mr P by 3 p.m.

Raised eyebrows. 'Hmph. Hmph. Hmph.' But he didn't dare call
my bluff.

'Have you got a car?'

'Yes.'

'You are to be at the Savoy Hotel at 9 a.m. tomorrow and ask
for Mr Arthur P. Jacobs.* He's MM's publicity man and he has to
approve the house. Take him to see it in your car and then bring
him back here to me.'

I left and came straight home. I rang Mr C-P to confirm that Mrs
C-P would be ready for us, and then washed the car, inside and out.

Now I can't sleep because of my gamble, but, to be honest, I
haven't that much to lose. Just an awful lot to gain.

THURSDAY, 14 JUNE

I got to the Savoy at 8.45 a.m. At nine I went in and told the concierge.
He looked up Jacobs and said he had a wake-up call booked for
10 a.m. (!) so I went back and sat in the car until eleven, then checked
again. 'Yes, he had been called at 10 a.m.,' and 'Don't bother me
again, you serf,' implied.

At 11.30, APJ emerged. Close-cropped black hair, pugnacious,
bad tempered, puffy face. Naturally no apology – not even good
morning or hello. He looked at my car with great disgust and got in.

He was carrying one copy of every single newspaper you can
buy, and these he proceeded to read until we were on the A4 by the
airport. Then quite suddenly he wound down his window and threw
the whole lot out. I could see them in my mirror, blowing all over

* Arthur P. Jacobs (1918–73) later became a producer. His films included *Dr Dolittle*
(1967) and *Planet of the Apes* (1968).

the road, blinding other drivers. It seemed to me the single most anti-social act I had ever seen. I couldn't resist a protest.

'In England we do not normally behave like that,' I said icily.

'Whadja talking about?'

'Throwing all those newspapers out of the window. They caused a terrible mess.'

'I'd finished with them.'

Nothing more to say.

I can't believe everyone does that in America. He's just a totally egocentric and insensitive boor, and that's that.

But I soon had my revenge. The passenger seat back on the Bristol rests on two chrome 'cams'. If I corner too fast to the left it slips off these cams, and falls back flat. The first corner I came to off the A4 was a left-hander. I was grinding my teeth with rage and consequently driving faster than normal. Suffice it to say that for a fraction of a second Mr Jacobs thought that he was falling through the bottom of the car onto the road. Of course I stopped and helped him to sit up again, with many sincere apologies. But he looked pale, and at last he actually noticed who I was for a fleeting moment.

We were very late for Mrs C-P at Tibbs, but the house is exactly as I remembered it. Thick gold Wilton, heavy curtains, eau-de-nil bathrooms etc. surrounded by dark foliage. Mrs C-P all charm and very excited: 'Your friends were here,' she said to me but APJ, unremittingly odious, took no notice.

After 20 minutes we drove back to Piccadilly. No lunch of course. I suppose APJ had had a healthy breakfast at the Savoy, but I'd had nothing since seven and I was in a bad temper.

'Well?' said Mr P, after giving APJ a patently false show of comradeship.

'Not bad, I suppose,' said APJ – just as I thought he would – and shut Mr P's office door in my face. I went out for lunch and made another phone call.

At 5 p.m. I wandered back in. It was now or never. Luckily it was now.

Mr P's office door was open. 'They want to see you right away,' said Vanessa. 'I'm afraid they're rather angry.'

'Good,' I said and marched in. APJ was in a corner, his face black with rage. 'Colin,' said Mr P, very growly, 'Have you seen this?' He held out the *Evening Standard*.

Headline: 'This is the house Marilyn Monroe will live in while in England blah blah.' Picture of Tibbs Farm.

'Yes, I have.'

'There is only one person who could have given the papers this story.'

'You must have given it to them before I even saw the house,' said APJ through clenched teeth.

'Of course I gave it to them.'

'Well now you've ruined everything. It was the perfect house, but once the press know of it, it is out of the question. Couldn't you have realised it had to stay a secret?'

'It wasn't the perfect house this morning.'

Mr P: 'Colin. What's going on?' He is a shrewd old bean. He knows that I like and admire him. He can't stand APJ and can see that I can't stand him either. Suddenly I saw it cross his mind, 'Maybe I can trust Colin after all.'

'When you told me to get a house for MM yesterday, I took the precaution of finding two. I showed Mr Jacobs the least good first. Now the press will always think that MM is staying there and we can rent the second house for her to live in. The second house is much better. It belongs to a Lord. I can take Mr Jacobs to see it now, or tomorrow morning, if he'd like. It is only a couple of miles from the first house, but it is much more elegant.'

Mr P: 'And what are we going to say to the owners of the first house?'

'I thought perhaps the production team could use it.'

'What do you know about production teams?'

Before I could admit to total ignorance, APJ suddenly recovered his composure. 'Hey, Milton and Amy could use it. It would be perfect. Near the studio, near Marilyn.' Now he was the PR man, selling it to us. I suppose that in Hollywood people like him have to jump backward somersaults every day.

Mr P: 'OK, that's settled then. Arrange for both houses to be rented from 9 July, for four months. By the way, how much are they?'

'£100 per week, each.'

Mr P's eyebrows went up. Then he brightened. 'Well, it comes out of Marilyn Monroe Productions' budget.'

'Don't you want to see the other house?' (I was really proud of it.)

'Nah, no need, we trust you boy.' Arthur had completely changed sides, and probably did not fancy another trip in the Bristol. Mr P nodded towards the door, and I left. Soon APJ left too. 'See you, kid,' to me. 'Bye, sweetheart,' to the secretaries. Then Mr P: 'See you tomorrow, Colin.' Just a hint of a smile.

I call that victory.

FRIDAY, 15 JUNE

And a victory it is.

On Monday I start working on the staff of LOP Ltd, at £8.10s. per week, as Mr P's assistant. When I came in this morning, Mr P called me into his office and actually gave a grin. Somehow Arthur Jacobs had persuaded himself that the whole house business was *his* triumph and had gone away (to Paris) happy. Mr P loathes him – quite rightly, he's a bullying shit – and sees it as *his* success, a problem neatly solved by a member of his staff (!).

'Never trust that Hollywood crowd, Colin. The better you are, the more likely they are to stab you in the back.'

The secretaries already knew of my appointment and offered friendly congratulations. I've been living in their office for two weeks only now am I officially one of them. It means that I can share the gossip with Vanessa, which will be useful as well as fun.

Gilman bounded in and gave a whoop of delight. 'You can get his lunch now – official!'

It did seem rather wasteful for Sir Laurence and Lady Olivier's Bentley and chauffeur to be sent in every day just to get Mr P a cheese roll. The pub is only 100 yards away, but that's showbiz.

It seems that as from Monday there will be another LOP production office at Pinewood. They will have the job of hiring all the personnel and facilities needed to make the film, and the Pinewood accounts office will pay people too – including me. Mr P promised to take me down to look over the studios in a few weeks' time.

'We'd better try to get you a job on the production side for later on. You won't want to stay with me once filming starts.'

He has become quite fatherly. I rang Cotes-Preedy who is very excited. Naturally he believes the newspaper report that MM is going to stay in his house, and I did not disabuse him. Then I rang Garrett Moore,* who owns house No 2. A bit of panic when he said the whole thing was off, but I guessed the problem. '£100 a week is not enough,' he said severely. He is extremely astute and can somehow tell he has me over a barrel. I had told him, on pain of death to keep it a secret, that MM was going to be the tenant, and since he fancies himself as God's gift to women, I knew he was not going to refuse. I'll bet he secretly thinks that he will get to meet her and that she will be unable to resist his languid charm. Eventually we settled for £120 per week. Mr P had said 'Price no object', so I didn't bother to check back with him. But I did insist on going down to Parkside House over the weekend. I just can't resist meeting Garrett's wife, Joan.** She is incredibly beautiful. I hope the house is also as attractive as I remember it. Right now I'm going out to get sloshed at the Stork.*** To eat, drink and, as Al Burnett would say, 'Make Merry.'

---

* Lord Moore, later Earl of Drogheda, chairman of the *Financial Times*.
** Joan Carr, a concert pianist.
*** A nightclub run by a comedian called Al Burnett. The clientele was largely made up of rich young men of a type now known as 'Hooray Henrys'.

MONDAY, 18 JUNE

A great weekend. On Friday night I told all the girls about my job. They were very impressed and I succeeded in getting Yvonne into bed at last. She is tough as an alley cat on the surface but quite scared underneath – like an alley cat is, I suppose. She is really too moody for me, but she was just the company I needed to stop me getting big-headed. After all, I'm not exactly going to direct MM in a movie yet.

I had quite a hangover on Saturday, but I spent Sunday sleeping in the garden and today I felt really good.

This morning Mr P gave me quite a cheerful, for him, 'Hello Colin,' when he came in. Mind you, if you didn't know him, you'd have thought he was going to a funeral. He must have a wardrobe full of the same clothes as he never varies what he wears, day by day. Brown tweed suit, dark brown shoes, pale brown shirt, brown tie etc. Gilman said he'd never ever seen him in anything else. (There is a *Mrs* P. I wonder what she thinks?) After a bit, Mr P called me into the office.

'You might as well know everything we are doing if you are to be any use.'

He showed me a huge squared-off sheet of paper, covered in columns and names and shaded squares.

This is really Mr P's pride and joy, his *chef d'oeuvre*, his bible. It is called a cross-plot. It has been cunningly worked out so that Pinewood's studios A and B can be alternated, with different 'sets' being built on one stage while the other was being used for filming.

To get the most out of each set the film is not shot in chronological order. If there is a scene in a particular room at the beginning of the story and another scene at the end in the same room, then they will both be filmed together. This is especially hard for film actors who have to develop a character in fits and starts.

The major actors also have to be fitted into the cross-plot so that we get the most out of them in the shortest time. Dame Sybil

Thorndike,* for instance, is going to play Sir Laurence's mother-in-law (no more 'Larry' now that I'm officially working for him). But she is also booked for a West End stage play, so all her scenes have to be shot first if possible and most should be finished before the play begins. (Some of her scenes need special effects and these can be put in later.) SLO** and MM and Richard Wattis*** are in virtually all the scenes so they don't influence the cross-plot much.

MM has a terrible reputation for being late on the set, and not turning up at all on some days. Mr P has scheduled her to do all her scenes first with a long list of alternate shots, cutaways and reactions which can be put in at short notice if MM is not available.

'What happens if shooting gets a week behind? The whole plan will collapse.'

Mr P grinned a Machiavellian grin and pulled out a second sheet and a third.

'We just switch sheets. Warner Bros will never know.'

I gather that Warner Bros is lending LOP and MMP the money to make the film. Already I hear Mr P say: 'Charge it to MMP' pretty frequently. I wonder if MMP is MM herself, or a group of people backing her.

I don't dare ask anything about MM. It seems in bad taste, like asking about childbirth. Anyway my job is to be preparing for MM's arrival. Police, press, chauffeur, bodyguard, servants, redecorations, everything to delight her eye and soothe her nerves. She must be a very difficult lady. I can't believe anyone is so unreasonable and silly, that they have to be spoiled so much. What would Nanny have said?

---

* (1882–1976). *Grande dame* of British stage and screen. She was the first actress to play Shaw's *St Joan* (1923).
** i.e. Sir Laurence Olivier. When filming began the whole crew was to use this abbreviation.
*** (1912–75). He was playing Mr Northbrook of the Foreign Office in the film.

TUESDAY, 19 JUNE

Six weeks until filming starts and a lot to prepare. Mr P depends on me a lot now but of course he won't need me at all when it does. Today a David Orton came in, and Mr P warned me that on him my future in the production would depend. He is going to be 1st Assistant Director. This does not mean SLO's assistant (SLO being the director), but the man in charge of seeing that everyone in the studio does what they are told.

'He's a sort of sergeant major,' explained Mr P.

This didn't sound very attractive and I can't say I liked him at all. Blondish-mousy hair, a thin face and glasses which he is forever pushing up onto the bridge of his nose with his forefinger. He did not take to me either:

'Have you worked on a film before?'

'No.'

'Then forget it. If you haven't made a film already then you aren't in the union, and there is no way in which you can work on a film, in any capacity.'

Very funny! It seems the union is the ACT, the Association of Cinematograph Technicians, and they are a famous 'closed shop'. (No card, no film; no film, no card.)

So Mr Orton advised me to stay in Mr P's office. This is very disappointing. Mr P has already told me I can't stay in his office after production begins. And anyway I want to be a film *director*, not producer.

Mr P cheered me up by telling me to go down to see Diana Dors'* house tomorrow. It is somewhere near Ascot or maybe Henley. I've only got the phone number so far. Her agent has learned that MM is looking for something for the summer and thinks it might be good publicity if they could swap houses. Of course we already have two

---

* 1931–84, real name Diana Fluck. Popular British actress whose many films included *Good Time Girl*, *Lady Godiva Rides Again*, *Passport to Shame* etc.

houses, for MM and her manager, but I suppose some other creeps like APJ might arrive from America so I'll go and look.

Diana Dors always seems very sexy, even if extremely common. A bit of a tart.

WEDNESDAY, 20 JUNE

Diana Dors is divine. She's as vulgar and cheeky as I imagined from her films, but with a hilarious sense of humour. She never stops cracking jokes and telling stories. Her conversations peppered with F—s and C—s.

Her house is near the river, although I couldn't see it, as she has a huge indoor pool. She and a starlet friend were sitting by the pool in bikinis when I arrived. DD is smaller than you would think in real life. I suppose the camera exaggerates her on purpose. She is quite a pretty girl, and her friend was even prettier but not so vivacious. DD could not care less about the house swap but she did want to hear about MM. It was quite a let-down when I was forced to admit that I hadn't met MM yet. DD got bored very quickly, so to liven things up she and her friend both took off their bikini tops and jumped into the pool. That got my attention all right. There were two workmen hammering at something at the far end and their eyes stood out like organ stops. They just downed tools and stared.

Both girls have beautiful, quite small breasts but I must admit that they were so brazen that I was more embarrassed than rapacious. They must have been on the game together in the old days, is my guess.

The house is much too small for MM or her retinue, and has no class at all. With this film, MM is trying to go up in the world, not down. So I left silently and reported back to Mr P. He just chuckled. He hates film stars really.

THURSDAY, 21 JUNE

Thank goodness, I was completely wrong about David Orton.
Underneath that severe exterior he is a very nice man. He is just
awkward with people until he knows them.

He is married to a pretty, jolly make-up girl called Penny, who picked
him up this evening. His world is the film studio, where he is in charge
of course, and he is very experienced. He gave me a long explanation
about how film studios work. Like in every job, there is a hierarchy
which is very important. This is true in each department – the lighting
cameraman is head of one group, and pretty much above everyone
except the director, the designer has his crew – set-dressers, down to
chippies (carpenters); there is wardrobe, make-up, film editing etc.,
each with their own structure. The Director has an Associate Director,
but his right-hand man is the 1st Assistant Director – David in our case.

The lowest of the low is the *3rd* Assistant Director who is known
as a 'gofer'. Anyone can tell him to 'go for this, go for that'.

This is the job he'll try to get for me, but even a 3rd Ast Dir
needs a union card and that is the hardest thing in the world to get:
actually it is the same card as a director needs to work on a film,
but it is a different grade. David has promised to try and come up
with a scheme to get round the union 'closed shop' rule. I trust him.

Mr P has other worries and so has SLO. I'm not surprised. I
saw the play on which the film is going to be based: *The Sleeping
Prince*. Larry and Vivien did it together – at the Phoenix Theatre in
1953–4* – and it was a very slight piece indeed. Typical Rattigan** –
theatrical, charming and that's all. Vivien was enchanting as ever,
despite a funny accent. But I thought Larry was at his worst. He has
an old-fashioned notion that it is funny to play European royalty,

---

* Vivien Leigh had created the role of Elsie Dagenham, changed to Elsie Marina
when Marilyn played her in the film.
** Terence Rattigan (1911–77). Popular West End playwright (*The Winslow Boy*,
The Browning Version, *Separate Tables* etc.).

---

and he gets wooden and mannered. The whole play ended up like a sort of 1930s in-joke – hardly Hollywood. I can't see it being a good role for MM. I suppose she thinks it will enhance her new 'intellectual' image. She will certainly have been told what a fantastic opportunity it is to play opposite the greatest classical actor of the generation etc. But Rattigan is no Shakespeare. Unless MM is cleverer than she looks, she will find it jolly hard to mix her style with Olivier's. She is said to be reading Dostoevsky or *War and Peace* or something so maybe she will surprise us all. Diana Dors surprised me, but she's more a crafty cockney than an intellectual.

FRIDAY, 22 JUNE

SLO came in, in quite a state. Problems already. After a bit I was called in to Mr P's office to 'join the discussions' – providing I do not speak unless asked a direct question! It seems that MM is going to marry Arthur Miller* this weekend. What sort of an effect will that have on her? And on the production? Will Miller persuade her not to come, and whisk her off on a glamorous honeymoon? SLO says he is a self-satisfied, argumentative, pseudo-intellectual. Charming. Will he help MM or make her argumentative too? She has a dreadful reputation already among movie directors. She is always late on the set, often does not show up for days on end, and can never remember her lines. What on earth can be the matter?

Her producer, and the co-producer of the film, with SLO, is called Milton Greene.** It is for him that I have rented Tibbs Farm. He will be responsible for MM while she is here, making sure she does turn up and keeping an eye on the expenses. But it seems he does not like Arthur Miller. He got MM out of her 20th Century contract,

---

* 1915–2005. American playwright (*The Crucible, Death of a Salesman, A View from the Bridge* etc.).
** Milton Greene (1922–85) was a fashion and celebrity photographer who had formed Marilyn Monroe Productions with Marilyn Monroe a year previously.

together with a lawyer called Irving Stein.* Evidently Milton Greene has given SLO his assurance that he can make MM behave herself.

After all it is her own money that is involved this time. Marilyn Monroe Productions (MMP) has a big share in the profits, just like LOP. If MM doesn't turn up for work, then she (and her partners, Greene and Stein**) start losing money. That is the theory. I don't know if it has occurred to any of them that while the three men involved (MG, IS and AM) want money, MM may be more interested in her career, but I didn't dare say so. Poor SLO. He is already upset enough. He doesn't trust any of the Americans and is out of his depth.

'What have I got myself into, Colin?'

'I think it will be a fantastic success, Larry,' I replied (using Larry for the last time, I swear it).

Mr P beamed in the background. His prodigy had said the right thing. 'Success for her or success for me?' said SLO but he was comforted for the moment (so easily?!).

And on top of AM there is the problem of the Strasbergs.*** Lee Strasberg is the head of the Actors Studio in New York, where MM sometimes studies (like once??). He is her god. He doesn't want to come over to London and desert his other students so he is sending over his wife, Paula. Paula Strasberg is a famous menace. As MM's 'drama coach' she could undermine SLO.

Naturally SLO wants a professional actor's approach. MM learns the role and decides how to play it; SLO makes suggestions, they discuss them, MM alters her performance accordingly etc. What will Paula's approach be? How will she fit in between them?

Throughout all this, a new idea has occurred to me. A couple of years ago, Lee and Paula's daughter Susan completely stole my heart

---

* Stein, Chairman of the Elgin Watch Co., was killed in a car accident in 1966.

** Stein was not in fact a partner.

*** Lee Strasberg (1899–1982) founded the Actors Studio, famous for teaching 'the Method'. He went on to act, brilliantly, in films such as *The Godfather Part Two*. His wife Paula had been an actress.

in a film called *Picnic*. Susan played the kid sister of a blonde called Kim Novak. KN was meant to be the beautiful one and SS the ugly duckling – aged about 15, I suppose. Needless to say SS was 100 times more attractive than Novak in every way. I am a complete sucker for little skinny girls with big brown eyes. At the time I fell in love with Susan Strasberg, I had only just got over Pier Angeli marrying some dreadful Hollywood crooner.* I could hardly stop myself from asking whether Paula was bringing her daughter with her. I suppose not, but with luck, Susan might *visit* her Mum.

Anyway, I kept quiet.

Mr P and SLO had a long moan about Hollywood and Hollywood types and agents, lawyers, producers, stars. I don't think SLO is jealous. After all he and Vivien have both had huge Hollywood successes. He just can't stand the lack of professionalism. He sees 'the Method', which originates in New York, of course, but influences all the new Hollywood stars, as an excuse for self-indulgence.

Everyone is seduced by MM's particular form of glamour and SLO fears he has fallen into a trap. MM is not like any leading lady he's ever known and he can't fathom it. He can't figure out whether she has a brain in her head or not. He knows he's a very attractive man, but she doesn't seem to have really noticed him. She only sees his reputation. She'll be here in three weeks and then we'll find out.

It's true that I don't think of SLO as a movie star, despite *Henry V* and all the films he's made. I think of him as a great actor. How will a 'star' and an actor mix. They'll have to find somewhere to meet between the sky and the stage.

I know I want to be a professional, like SLO. If I get a job on the film, I must stick to him like glue!

---

* Pier Angeli: Italian actress, modestly successful in Hollywood in the fifties and sixties, who committed suicide in 1971, aged thirty-nine. She was married to the singer and actor Vic Damone.

MONDAY, 25 JUNE

The whole office is busy planning for MM's arrival. Frequent directions arrive from America about the colours she likes, the materials
she likes, the decorations she likes. The dressing-room suite at
Pinewood is to be all beige. In fact beige is the only colour everyone
agrees is safe. Red is out. Blue is out. Green is out. It is as if these
colours were enemies.

Garrett and Joan are having the master bedroom suite at Englefield
Green repainted white. They say they hate beige and won't change
it. I told them I was having their village renamed Englefield Beige.
For the money we (well, MMP to be accurate) are paying them,
they could repaint the whole house many times over, but Garrett
is too mean.

I made an appointment for Thursday with the police at Heathrow
Airport to plan MM's arrival on 14 July. The Inspector thought I was
kidding at first. But when I threatened 3000 fans he took me seriously.

Evidently when the crooner Johnny Ray came through, he – the
Inspector – had his little finger broken in the mêlée. Johnny Ray's
publicity people had gone down to the East End and filled up four
buses with slum teenagers. They gave each one 10 shillings to cause
as much pandemonium as possible when Ray appeared. This they
duly did, and Johnny Ray's arrival was instant front-page news.

The Inspector says if we plan something like this he will personally have me arrested. I assure him that SLO himself has entrusted
me with the job of getting MM into the country as discreetly as
possible. He is still doubtful but I can tell that even he cannot resist
the chance of meeting MM in the flesh. Her name has a magic effect.

People who are going to be associated with the production of the
film drift in.

Roger Furse* is going to be the designer. I have met him before

---

* Furse (d. 1972) had also designed the stage sets for the London production of *The
Sleeping Prince*.

with Vivien – I think at Notley. He always seems to have a hangover, never stops smoking. He ran out of Capstans and cadged three of my Woodbines. (I never get time to smoke anything larger.) Mr P won't allow me to smoke in his office, despite his continual pipe puffing. I find Roger very sympathetic but Mr P clearly does not.

'Never trust the dirty fingernail brigade, Colin,' he said after Roger had left. 'They pretend to be only doing it for their art, but they are always trying to wangle more money.'

I took a quick squint at my fingernails – not that clean. I need the job, not the money, but I suppose that I must admit I am prepared to wangle.

My worry is that Roger is rather too 'stagey'. The more SLO surrounds himself with stage people, the more 'stagey' the film will be. Perhaps that's the intention – to make the film a sort of period piece – rich, theatrical and far from MM's normal image.

Jolly hard to pull off though. SLO may like it and MM may like it, but will filmgoers pay to see it?

TUESDAY, 26 JUNE

Another 'old friend' today.

Tony Bushell* roared in at 12.30 to meet SLO and Rattigan for lunch. Tony looks like a bluff military man – bald, red faced and jovial. In fact he was in the Guards during the war and almost everyone forgets he is an actor.

David Niven told Mama that when Tony applied to join some grand regiment, the Adjutant asked him what he did for a living.

'Nothing at the moment,' said Tony, who, like all actors, was out of work.

'Thank goodness,' said the Adjutant, assuming Tony was idle rich,

---

* 1904–97. Actor in Hollywood and British films of the 1930s (*Disraeli, Journey's End, The Scarlet Pimpernel* etc.) who later became a producer. He had worked with Olivier on the films of *Hamlet* (1948) and *Richard III* (1956).

'I thought you might be an actor. The last actor chappie we had ran off with the Colonel's wife.'

So Tony got in, and sure enough, ran off with the wife of someone in the regiment.

Very adorable she is too. Anne Bushell is a great friend of Vivien's, as Tony is of SLO's. In fact Anne talks exactly like Vivien (though she is not an actress at all – she is an heiress), and when she answers the phone at Notley one can't tell the difference. She is not as beautiful as Vivien (no one is) but she is still very attractive – as well as a good deal easier to be with.

Tony boomed a great welcome to me. He is going to be the Associate Director. This means that while SLO is acting in *front* of the camera, Tony will take charge *behind* it, and 'direct' the film.

I don't think Tony could direct traffic in Cheltenham. Despite his imposing appearance he is really a pussy cat. But SLO needs a chum to guard his rear, as it were, and it is a great joy to have Tony around. He has a heart the size of a house which he loves to hide behind a glare. I've met Rattigan too, but he didn't remember me. He's queer of course, although I've nothing against that. He's charming to everyone but with a cautious look in his eye. I can't pretend I think he's much cop as a writer. Very 1920s period stuff. Of course, there's always an edge but if there wasn't even that his plays would just be blancmange.

SLO and Vivien probably know this but they love to have queer courtiers, and Rattigan's plays are quite good vehicles for actors.

They all went off to the Ivy in high good spirits. Like a lot of overgrown schoolboys, I thought.

'Hmph' said Mr P as we settled down to the cheese rolls and Guinnesses – which I buy and we now consume together in his office.

WEDNESDAY, 27 JUNE

Mr P has finally admitted that MM may need a bodyguard. The newspapers are making such a fuss of her and the upcoming visit. You would think that her fans are massing at strategic points to trample her to death in the rush for her autograph. 'Phooey' we say, but we can't take risks, and anyway the cost will come out of MMP's budget.

Mr P has no idea how to arrange a bodyguard so I rang Scotland Yard. When I finally got through to someone senior enough, they were incredulous and angry.

'Miss Marilyn Monroe will be adequately protected by the police while in this country like every other American visitor,' said some Commissioner sniffily. I patiently explained that if there was a retired Inspector around who would like to spend four months in Miss Monroe's company for a high salary I would like his name.

Once again the magical MM image made a strong man wilt. In fact I think the Commissioner sounded as if he might resign there and then to take the job. (Imagine what he could tell the wife – line of duty and all that.) He would have someone call me in the afternoon. And he did call – a real Inspector Plod. He was cautious and realistic – quiet sense of humour, not overawed. Sounds just what Mr P and I need. I invited him to come here to meet us in a week's time.

Tomorrow I'm going to Heathrow to see those police. (I may mention Plod's name.) It's to be a conference. I am afraid they are expecting someone older than me but it can't be helped. I'll just have to play the officer to the hilt. The RAF wasn't exactly the Life Guards, but I do know how. Most of those senior cops are just sergeant-majors at heart. As soon as they realise that I am serious, they'll settle down.

THURSDAY, 28 JUNE

The police at the airport were very suspicious. They assumed that I had come out there to arrange some sort of publicity stunt. Luckily I have experience of this sort of planning – defending Dalcross airport against infiltration* – and I managed to get their interest. Which corridor, which car park, which tunnel etc.

* While stationed there in the RAF in 1952.

SLO really does want a very low-key reception for MM. He and Vivien will come to meet her. The press can have a short question and answer session plus pictures in a room especially set up between Immigration and the cars. MM and AM have to go through Immigration and Customs, no matter what, but the police have promised to whisk them through alone.

So together we planned the whole thing like a military manoeuvre. I ended by telling them not to alter our plan in any way unless advised by me. (Milton Greene and Irving Stein and some publicity types are coming in ahead of MM and Mr P says that they are certain to try to change everything.)

In the end the cops became great chums. They all want to be the one who stands next to MM and protects her from the mob. She has that effect on all men, I guess. They certainly do not want a riot in their airport. Memories of Johnny Ray are all too recent. I was very Old Etonian Guards officer visiting the Sergeants' Mess, even though they are in black tunics covered in silver braid. But we understood one another.

David Orton came in again this afternoon. He gets nicer and nicer, and receives my plaintive enquiries about a job with twinkles and winks.

'Wait until next week. It's the middle of summer, you know.'

What can that mean? I know it is summer. It is extremely hot. But I trust him to help. I'm very lucky that he has become a friend.

FRIDAY, 29 JUNE

Garrett Moore is being very difficult about Parkside House again. What about the phone bill? What about the mess and the possible damage? I keep telling him that it will only be MM, AM and a Scotland Yard detective – although in reality I'm none too sure about this. There are always hangers-on, but they are meant to be at Tibbs Farm.

The Moores' servants will stay on at the house for MM, paid by Garrett who will be recompensed by MMP. This way, Garrett hopes not to lose them. Garrett is like a child, whining about someone playing with his toys.* Joan says nothing – just smiles and flutters those amazing eyelashes. She is the most seductive woman since Cleopatra. She and Vivien are in the same mould only she is passive where Vivien is active. Joan is older of course, but when she plays the piano for a concert, most of the men in the audience are close to fainting. I suppose Joan and Vivien know each other – it's not the sort of question to ask either of them – probably through Papa: lucky old man. I would be putty in Joan's hands, but I have to be tough with Garrett. I'm sure he can't resist £120 per week and I'm sure he can't resist the slightest chance to get his hand up MM's skirt. I know he is meant to be so brilliantly clever, but he is also extremely vain.

Mr P is pleased by the airport arrangements and by the bodyguard, although we haven't met him yet. None of the film production crew will be put on salary until 23 July, and he depends on me to negotiate with Garrett and Mrs C-P.

The costume designer came in to arrange her contract. Beatrice 'Bumble' Dawson** is a jolly, ginny neurotic old bird who SLO has used many times. She smokes continuously and grinds her teeth. In an effort to conquer this last habit, she is trying to replace it with twisting a lock of hair, a psychoanalyst trick which results in simultaneous grinding and twisting! She laughs a lot, between puffs, and is very sympathetic.

I can see why SLO has chosen so many chums. It is going to make life in the studio very easy. But I wonder if MM and Co will appreciate that sort of atmosphere.

---

* I later became fond of Garrett, and he was right about the house. AM and MM left a *very* large unpaid phone bill.
** 1908–76. Her many designs for Vivien Leigh's costumes included *Caesar and Cleopatra*.

MONDAY, 2 JULY

MM finally married Arthur Miller in New York over the weekend.
Nobody here knows if that is good or bad for the film. Rumour has
it that she panicked at the last minute and tried to get out of it.

Just before the wedding, a car full of reporters chasing the happy
couple crashed and the *Paris Match* woman was killed. MM was very
badly shaken and saw it as a bad omen – as if one was needed. The
poor girl seems to invite disaster. Perhaps she *needs* calamity, so that
she is permanently in that helpless condition from which everyone
wants to rescue her. But SLO, and Mr P for that matter, do not see
her in that light and have no desire to do so. SLO probably once
thought the whole thing would be a bit of a lark. He could have fun,
make money and add considerably to *his* glamour. SLO's charm can
be devastating – but will it work on MM? Of course, Vivien loves
SLO despite his charm, not because of it. She is very demanding of
his time and his attention – almost to the point of obsession. But
she always defers to him as the great actor and the great star – even
though she won an Oscar first* and is really more famous.

Vivien makes it quite clear that she regards SLO as more important than her, but I wonder if this will help him in his dealings with
MM. He must not be grandiose or condescending. MM is too big to
be treated like that.

Richard Addinsell** came in this evening to talk about music. He
is quiet and modest with a very good reputation for film music.
SLO wants a catchy romantic melody for the theme of the movie.
Evidently MM has agreed to sing it. She did sing in *Gentlemen
Prefer Blondes* and she has a low husky sort of voice, slight but not
unpleasant.

---

* For Scarlett O'Hara in *Gone with the Wind*, 1939. She was awarded a second
Oscar for Blanche DuBois in *A Streetcar Named Desire*, 1951. Olivier won a Special
Academy Award for *Henry V* (1944), and a second for Best Actor as *Hamlet* (1948).
** British composer (1904–77). His film scores included *Goodbye Mr Chips*, *Dangerous
Moonlight* (including the 'Warsaw Concerto'), *Blithe Spirit* etc.

The question of how much music there will be in the film has still not been solved. Rattigan wants very little but SLO disagrees and MM wants lots.

Meanwhile Vivien – who created the role MM will play – sides with Rattigan. I think the music might give the film another sort of appeal (i.e. to make up for the obvious deficiencies in Rattigan's script), but I couldn't say this, even to Mr P. The general line is that with SLO and MM in the same film, everyone will flock to see it since everyone is in love with one or the other. But the play seems to me a very doubtful vehicle for two great stars, and Rattigan is going to write the screenplay too. Perhaps enough people will go to see it out of curiosity. 'What on earth made him/her want to do a film with her/him?'

That's something I'm curious about too.

TUESDAY, 3 JULY

Dave Orton, first assistant director to be, has a plan to get me the job of third assistant director. He has a friend who works in the ACT union office. This friend is going to tell him when the number of unemployed 3rd Ast Dirs on the union books gets really low, which it does every summer. When there are only four or five left he will ring the union and ask for a 3rd Ast Dir right away. They will send him the list of names and he will say that none of them is suitable – which is probably true. Then he will tell them that he has a young man already working in the Production Office and ask them to issue a temporary card to him. This they will have to do, and then I can work on the film on a temporary card. Once the film is over, I will have done a film and can apply for a permanent card. This is the only way round the 'no film, no card; no card, no film' rule.

David is brilliant. He is a very nice man underneath that gruff exterior and rather like Mr P. Both of them expect their orders to be carried out to the letter.

Every morning when Mr P comes in he asks me: 'What's the first thing you do, Colin?'

'You check, Mr Perceval.'

'And what is the second thing you do?'

'You check again, Mr Perceval.'

'Grmph.'

I mentioned this to David who explained that the slightest mistake in the movie world, which causes filming to be delayed by even an hour, can cause chaos later and cost millions. Just imagine the problem if everyone made a little careless slip now and again – so no one must. Directors and producers only hire you if they can be absolutely sure you will get it right. This means that you must have a well prepared fall-back position just in case things do go wrong, even if it's not your fault. Eyes in the back of your head are a necessity not a luxury. Unlike in the Army, the blame will always fall on the lowliest person involved, and on this film that is going to be me. Never mind. I enjoy the challenge, and, for the first time, I think maybe I might have made the right decision not to do a fourth year at Oxford.

WEDNESDAY, 4 JULY

My policeman came for his interview today – first with me and then with Mr P. We have codenamed him PLOD to confuse the Yanks.

He is absolutely perfect. He looks like a favourite uncle. He has a great sense of humour but is very shrewd underneath. He only retired from the police force a few months ago, so he knows everyone in Scotland Yard. Thank goodness he is extremely unimpressed by the film world and even by MM's glamorous image. I made it clear that his principal duty was going to be to protect MM against photographers as well as lunatic fans. He gave a very wry grin and pointed out that it is not against the law to take a photograph of Miss Monroe, or anyone else.

'Yes, yes, protect her *person*,' I said, but of course he is right.

Since he is to live in MM's house at Englefield Green, all expenses paid on a huge salary, he isn't going to refuse. Mrs Plod will have to put up with this somehow, he said with a chuckle. 'I hope she's jealous.'

I wheeled him in to Mr P, who loved him of course, since they both hate showbiz. Mr P made it clear that he trusted me to make the appointment, he just wanted to discuss the sensitive nature of the job. My eyebrows went up but Plod's didn't. (I suspect they never do.) Mr P grumbled and rumbled round the subject for a while but what emerged was that Plod's second duty was to act as a spy for LOP, with me as his contact. He would be the only person in Englefield Green whom we could trust for a commonsense report on what was going on there. MM was notoriously unreliable and unpredictable. Plod would be her shadow and could keep us informed, not of her private life of course (of course!) but of any developments which might affect the progress of the film. This would be immensely helpful on the mornings when she clearly had no intention of leaving the house. Then we could arrange for other things to film. Mr P explained that it would take 2½ hours every morning to put on MM's make-up, wig and costume. She had to be at Pinewood Studios by 7 a.m. if filming was to start at 9.30 a.m. This meant that she had to leave Englefield by 6.30 a.m. 'Laurence will arrive at 6.45 a.m. promptly, Colin, and you will already be there to greet him,' Mr P said gravely.

On the days that MM had decided not to come at all, if we could be made aware of that by, say, 7.30, we could switch the schedule round to film shots without MM in them. Even these needed a couple of hours to set up and light, so every minute was vital.

Plod took all this in with a few gruff chuckles. I don't think Mrs Plod needs 2½ hours to do her hair and make-up in the morning. (I have known ladies take all day.) The other thing Plod had to do was sign a document swearing that he wouldn't sell information to the newspaper. I think quite a few people have to sign this as Mr P had the form typed and ready. I haven't had to sign anything. I'm sure (I hope) he knows by now that I am absolutely loyal to SLO and him.

Plod will start next Monday, 9 July – and I will take him round and show him all the relevant addresses then. Someone from the Legal Department at Pinewood has contracted Parkside and Tibbs from then on, so Plod can move in if necessary. He is a very honourable man, and I think he will be a great ally.

THURSDAY, 5 JULY

Mr P and I went down to Pinewood Studios in a hired car. We didn't tell the driver but he was on trial for the job as MM's chauffeur. I think he will be perfect. He is very stupid, and never shows any emotion at all. The car, an Austin Princess, has a glass division and normally Plod will ride up front with the driver, while MM rides in the back. I wonder if AM will come to watch his bride filming, or stay in his study and write plays.

Pinewood is guarded by a studio police force which is hell-bent on keeping out the press and other intruders. Every vehicle is checked at the gate just like in the RAF. Once inside there are three huge studios joined by a very long concrete corridor. The other side of this corridor are the star dressing rooms, crowd dressing rooms, make-up rooms, wardrobe rooms etc. Across a little private road is the club house, with bars and a restaurant. MM's and SLO's dressing rooms are going to be at the end of one of the side corridors, opposite the restaurant. It really is all very like an RAF base with its hangars, offices and officers' mess.

We are going to alternate between Studios A and B while other minor British films are being made in Studio C. There is a large 'lot' for filming outside scenes, but our film doesn't have many of these as far as I can see.

Mr P and I first inspected MM's dressing-room suite. Filming doesn't start for four weeks but she must have somewhere suitable to relax in when she comes for rehearsals in three weeks' time.

We were shown a series of what looked like old cowsheds which made me anxious.

'Don't worry Colin. The scene builders and set dressers only need 48 hours to convert this into the Dorchester. We are just here to check which ones have been allotted to us.'

We were shown round by Teddy Joseph, the production manager to be, who is still working on another film here at the moment. Small, bespectacled, a bit like a penguin, he will be Mr P's right arm when filming starts. Teddy showed me round the various departments. We will use Pinewood facilities for everything but the stars.

In the wardrobe department was one of the prettiest little girls I have ever seen in my life. This is very good news indeed since I am going to be working here myself for four months. Slim as a wand, curly brown hair, huge brown eyes and a wide cheeky grin. The head of the department is a large motherly lady. She definitely feels that it is her duty to protect her little lambs from prowling 3rd Ast Dirs. But the 'wand' was thrilled to bits. After all I was with Mr P – and Mr P is supreme boss, at least until SLO arrives. Teddy persuaded Mr P that all was well, Mr P caught me by the ear to prevent me bobbing up to Wardrobe for the sixth time and we returned to London. Pinewood strikes me as a bastion of professionalism and common sense. It is not at all like the Hollywood studios I have read about. With Teddy and David and Tony Bushell in charge, what can go wrong?

FRIDAY, 6 JULY

Last night I asked myself what could go wrong. Today the whole movie seemed in question, before the camera has even rolled. A rumour came from the USA at lunchtime that AM was going to have his passport refused after all.* This would mean that he couldn't come to London, and MM would certainly not come to London for four months without him. Since huge sums of money have been spent

---

* Miller had been under investigation by Senator McCarthy's House Un-American Activities Committee. His marriage to MM evidently convinced them that he was a regular guy.

already, this caused quite a panic. Everyone was on the phone, asking for reassurance which we could not give. Rattigan was especially put out. SLO was grim-faced and terse, firmly shutting me out of the office for his conference with Mr P and Tony B, and a series of calls to the USA.

No one could get through to MM and AM, but Milton Greene, on the transatlantic phone, was calm. It could be fixed, he was sure. But *he* couldn't find Irving Stein who had been with MM last night or speak to MM and Arthur at least. So the worrying went on all day.

Mr P has heard (from her last director) that MM often gets 'confused'. Surely he doesn't mean 'drunk'? Pills, more likely – as with Judy Garland. That may be the problem now, although I hope she isn't taking pills on the first week of her honeymoon. I suggested this to Mr P and got a very grumpy 'grmph'. But by 6 p.m. it was all solved. AM and MM had got up at last – 1 p.m. in the USA – and switched the phone on. Milton Greene was on the line to MM and SLO simultaneously and all was sweetness and light.

'Not a very good omen,' said Mr P, for the second time this week, as we finally left the office at 7 p.m. But he is always pessimistic. I'm really relieved that the film is on the rails again. Gilman whisked Tony and SLO off to Notley in the Bentley. Anne had been waiting for them in the car. My goodness, she is an attractive woman, and extremely nice too. She gave me a great welcome, as if I was an old friend. But she is not in the least seductive, unlike Vivien. I'm off for a weekend in the country too – but alone. I sure envy those two men their beautiful ladies. I wouldn't mind staying in bed till 1 p.m. like Arthur Miller if I was with either of them – or both!

MONDAY, 9 JULY

Back to earth. SLO started to distribute cigarettes when he came in this morning. He is delighted that they have named a new cigarette after him, and now he gets free packets of 'Oliviers' for life. I suppose I didn't look as thrilled as I might have at this news so he told me quite sharply that the same tobacco company had named a cigarette after the great actor du Maurier.* He could hardly refuse.

'Oh of course, yes, wonderful,' I cried, but to me the idea of someone as great as SLO advertising something is a shame. Du Maurier was of another era – and probably needed the money which SLO does not. I know nothing about du Maurier but I think of him as an old ham, although quite unfairly I'm sure. More importantly, du Maurier cigarettes are not a great success.

SLO went on to explain that his costume in the film has no pockets so he wants me to be on call holding the cigarettes at all times in case he wants to smoke. I am naturally to smoke 'Oliviers' also, and I can get as many as I want from Gilman, who has crates of them.

After one day's trial I don't like them that much – I prefer Woodbines – but that isn't the point. 'On call by SLO's side at all times' is what I wanted to hear, and have been planning to be anyway. As soon as the film starts, my pay goes up to union scale (£10.10s. pw), I get free cigarettes, and I have to be at the director's side at all times. Good news.

I told this, with glee, to David Orton who came in at 4.30.

'The hell with that idea!' he roared. 'You work for me and me alone and don't you forget it. You are my slave. I don't want my 3rd Ast Dir poncing around with the director, even if it is SLO.'

'Quite right, David. I was only kidding.'

I've managed situations like this before, and it's nice to be in demand. Just a matter of being very quick on the feet and polite at all times.

Irving Stein and Milton Greene arrive from NYC tomorrow on the overnight flight. I offered to go to meet them but Mr P said 'no'. He's sent the chauffeur.

'Let the buggers find their own way around,' he growled.

Do I sense hostility to our American cousins already?

---

* Sir Gerald du Maurier (1873–1934).

TUESDAY, 10 JULY

Milton Greene and Irving Stein are both very young. They came in like a couple of recent graduates from some Jewish university. Both were exhausted after the flight and looked wary, but very charming. Irving is more aloof; Milton more boyish, very slight, dark brown eyes always smiling. They must be extremely shrewd to have got control of the most famous film star in the world.

Milton masterminded the plot to break MM's contract with 20th Century and 'set her free'. I suppose these two are the up-and-coming Louis B. Mayers.

SLO was brimming over with bonhomie – always a bad sign. When he is irascible is when he is sincere. Milton treats me like an executive, which is nice! He asked me all the details of the houses, the servants, Plod and the airport reception.

SLO absolutely promised Milton that Vivien and he would be on hand 'to welcome Marilyn and Arthur' and join in the press conference.

'But let's keep it low key, old boy.'

SLO wants the minimum publicity of course, and Milton says he does too. I wonder if both men have the same definition of 'minimum'. I suspect SLO really means 'none' and Milton means 'front page of every paper in the world – but no scandal'. There is a new publicity man around who has been ringing newspapers all day – ostensibly to notify everyone about the press conference even though this has already been done by the Pinewood press office.

Whenever they have a chance, Milton and SLO go into very private conference, talking fast and low. 'MM worries' I suppose, that even Mr P and I are not allowed to know about.

WEDNESDAY, 11 JULY

Milton rang from Tibbs Farm – could we all go down there for lunch. He was tired after the flight. Mr P was delighted. He is more curious than he lets on! I drove down in the Bristol, behind Mr P and Tony in the Princess. That way Milton can meet the chauffeur MM will have. SLO met us there as it is nearer Notley. Everyone agreed that Tibbs is perfect – out of Milton's earshot that is. Nouveau-riche – bathrooms smelling of pot pourri and towels so thick and soft that they don't even dry your hands. SLO gazed round in genuine horror. He is used to Vivien's exquisite taste.

Gilman said, 'This is a bit of all right, Colin,' loudly enough to embarrass me and please Milton who thinks it is typically 'English'.

There was a huge bunch of roses in the Bentley from Vivien which Gilman took through to the kitchen to find a vase. A buffet lunch had been prepared by the Cotes-Preedy cook – mainly reheated delicacies from the Ascot shop which I recognised from my stay here. Milton had ordered salad and cold white wine, which made it seem American. SLO had also brought a lot of Olivier cigarettes.

'I get them free, dear boy,' he said with much pride, but I don't think Milton smokes. Perhaps he is a health and fitness addict.

After lunch Milton and SLO went into conference again, this time allowing Mr P and Tony in too. I hope Mr P has some gossip for me later.

At teatime we drove over to Englefield Green to see Parkside House. The Moores have left and only the servants are waiting for MM and her party. Plod will move in on Friday and the chauffeur will live out. Parkside really is too pretty for words. It is right on the edge of Windsor Great Park and has its own private entrance to the Royal Gardens – or so I'm told. It is in quite different taste to Tibbs – much more elegant and feminine thanks to Joan. The master bedroom has been repainted white. I never saw it when Joan was in it. (I wish I had though!) Everyone was delighted. Milton praised me very highly for both houses and Mr P beamed, for once.

SLO hadn't come, of course. He'd been to the house as a guest of Garrett and Joan's. I don't think SLO likes Garrett any more than I do. Garrett is famous for sneering at people less clever or less titled than himself – which means pretty well everyone. I must admit that I am pleased with the arrangements so far, but everyone warns me that the day MM arrives, the rules will all change. She is the most famous woman in the world, though, so I would expect her to be pretty wilful. The worst thing is to have all that clout and not know your own mind. If she says her favourite colour is beige, that has to be a definite possibility. Then she will be as dangerous as a Chinese Empress. We'll see in three days' time.

THURSDAY, 12 JULY

The press are really getting worked up about MM's impending arrival. They phone me up hourly, demanding interviews with MM and SLO. I tell them that there will be a press conference at the airport and another at the Savoy Hotel on Sunday but of course they already know this and they want more. Any request for MM has to go through the loathsome Arthur P. Jacobs who is coming back to the Savoy tomorrow. It isn't that MM wants to avoid publicity – publicity more than anything else has got her where she is. But you have to control how much money you print. Even publicity has to be rationed out to get the maximum effect. APJ is meant to be the expert on this.

But there is a new publicity/personal relations man who is very nice. He is an Englishman, who nevertheless works from Hollywood, called Rupert Allan* and he is the opposite to APJ, quiet, dignified, polite. Perhaps he acts as the antidote to APJ's type of poison.

MM's personal make-up man has also flown in. He came in to the office this morning, unannounced, 'just to say "Hi"'. His name is Allan Snyder but 'Call me Whitey' is his opening remark to everyone. Impassive, and courteous, he is a great contrast to the Hollywood types we were expecting. Evidently he used to be a great influence on MM and is still a great friend. She insists on his presence on each of her films. I wonder if he was ever her lover, too. In our case, he only has a limited work visa so he is doing her original make-up and

---

* Allan (1913–91) was actually an American educated in England. He was the grandest personal publicist in Hollywood: his clients included Marlene Dietrich, Grace Kelly and Bette Davis.

then someone English will take over. Frankly I wish he was staying for the whole movie. He has a wonderfully calming presence which could be a great help. But he clearly doesn't want to stay more than a few weeks anyway.

'I love Marilyn,' he said with a nice open grin, 'but I do not want to find myself responsible for her behaviour.'

Now he has wandered off to explore London. He gives no address and simply says he will see us at Pinewood next Tuesday. Even Mr P, who deeply distrusts all Americans, seemed to like him. I hope he doesn't come to any harm in Soho! He is probably not as naive as he seems.

FRIDAY, 13 JULY

Mr P's distrust of Americans was justified. Arthur Jacobs went to London Airport and changed all our careful plans for MM's arrival tomorrow. Once again the police there assumed the worst, jumping to the conclusion that all we all want is maximum disruption and publicity. In the end, one of them thought to telephone me. I didn't even know APJ was out there so I got very cross. I pointed out that they had promised to listen to no one but me; that APJ was a publicity man whose job was to get publicity whether his client wanted it or not; that SLO and MM's producers had both instructed me to arrange MM's arrival with minimum fuss etc. But the papers are nerving everyone up and the police are edgy.

Luckily APJ is so loud-mouthed and overbearing that they would much rather disobey him. I have promised to get there really early tomorrow morning and go over the details again. I do remember from the days of Gaby Pascal and Jean Simmons* that once show business

---

* Gabriel Pascal (1894–1954) was a Hungarian film producer who owned the screen rights to Bernard Shaw's works. He first had the idea of making *Pygmalion* into a musical (*My Fair Lady*, as it became). Jean Simmons (b.1929) appeared in his film versions of Shaw's *Caesar and Cleopatra* (1945) and *Androcles and the Lion* (1953). My sister and I spent the summer of 1948 with them in Venice.

retinues get on the move, it is very hard to influence them or deflect them. They are like rivers. They jolly well go where they want to, so you have to make the banks good and high. London Airport is very big and if we lose control there will be chaos. The police are efficient and charming, but like all men in uniform they will take orders from anyone in authority. It's going to be a close-run thing.

APJ did have one success out there, I must admit. So oogle-eyed are the junior cops about MM that four motorcycle riders have volunteered to escort her car from the airport to Englefield Green. Evidently that is an honour never granted to anyone before except visiting royalty. I hope MM is impressed. It is not the sort of thing SLO and Mr P meant by minimum fuss, but I must agree it sounds exciting.

SATURDAY, 14 JULY

The first problem was that it rained.

After all the fine weather we've had, a light rain was falling when I woke up and it got heavier. I got to the airport early and went straight to the police office to make everything as clear as possible. But within an hour APJ and his minions were there trying to make everything as confused as possible.

Milton Greene arrived, very nervous, and was all too ready to listen to APJ's panicky lies. Quite soon he too was trying to change the plans around. Rupert Allan also had ideas of his own, even if they were expressed a bit more calmly.

Luckily I had Plod on my side, and he could speak to the police in their own language. But he is so unflappable and monosyllabic that we often did not get heard.

As the time of arrival grew near, everyone began to get very crazy. MM is like Desdemona: 'It is the very error of the moon; She comes more nearer earth than she was wont and makes men mad.'*

---

* *Othello*, Act V, Scene ii.

By the time the plane from New York actually landed there were reporters everywhere. The first I saw of them was a bunch of yelling waving men in raincoats in Immigration. The Customs officers had lost their heads and been swept away. I suppose the very thought of searching MM's person had been too much for them.

In the middle of this rabble stood Arthur Miller, teeth clenched on an unlit pipe, grinning like an amiable crocodile. The girl he had his arm around was unmistakably Marilyn Monroe. She looked so exactly like her publicity photographs – blonde hair, white face, scarlet lips in a pout – that it was hard to see the person. Added to this she had on huge very dark dark-glasses.

Poor woman. She must have been very tired after the flight. I suppose her life is permanent chaos. As for Jacobs, on whom she depends for help and guidance, he clearly had only one aim – namely to create the maximum confusion and even physical danger. Then he could step in and appear to save her from the very problems he himself had generated. In the blur of faces and cameras, he would be the only one she would recognise, and turn to with gratitude.

AM had clearly decided to grin whatever happened and be steered by the crowd. He recognised no one, not even APJ.

Milton Greene was too small to have any effect. Plod and I are total unknowns. We flung ourselves into the crowd and only added to the confusion.

Somehow the police managed to steer this whole mad rabble into the hall set up for the press conference where SLO and Vivien were waiting. I left the main group and went to defend Vivien, with Gilman, as the riot spread all over the room. MM and AM were lifted bodily onto the podium, and I was glad to see one of the cops giving APJ a good jab in the solar plexus. (He later threatened to have all the police at Heathrow fired!) Everyone was shouting at once and MM just looked confused and frightened. Finally Rupert Allan got onto the stage and quietened them all down. He announced that MM would make a short statement and then leave for a private destination to rest, until the main press conference at the Savoy tomorrow. Then

MM took off her dark glasses and gave that famous smile and every flash bulb in the room popped at once creating such a blinding flash that she put the glasses back on immediately.

In a breathy little girl's voice, MM said that she was very glad to be in England at last, with her husband (looking fondly at Arthur), and how excited she was to be making a film with SLO. SLO got up to reply but no one took any notice and they all started yelling questions at MM. So he gave up and we literally strong-armed it to the exit.

MM and AM got into the Princess with Milton and APJ and they swished off with the four motorbike policemen in dangerously close formation. SLO and Vivien got into the Bentley with Gilman and followed right behind. I had to go to get the Bristol with Plod so the press cars got in between us.

When we arrived at Parkside House the press were lined up outside the gate with the four cops preventing them from going in. Plod persuaded them to let us through and we found AM and MM and SLO outside the front door on the gravel. MM had meant to thank the police outriders but who had got in and was trying to interview her but that little creep Donald Zec of the *Daily Mirror*. How *did* he get past the others? Plod and I moved across to chuck him out, but he suddenly put his hand round MM's waist. His photographer jumped out of the shrubbery and 'flash', before they both raced off. I suppose MM is used to this sort of behaviour from total strangers, but it drove the pressmen at the gate crazy.

AM whispered in MM's ear, MM whispered to Milton and he nodded. Then he sent me over to the reporters to tell them they could all come up the drive for one last photo. MM and AM stood in the doorway and smiled, arm in arm, before disappearing inside. Plod and I followed and Milton introduced Plod (but not me) to MM and AM. I don't think MM took in a word, but as Plod is going to live in her house she will soon get used to him.

'Well, we are going to bed,' said AM with a huge leer.

I thought this pretty vulgar. I saw MM notice it without much pleasure, but she pretended not to catch on so perhaps she is smarter than she looks. AM certainly doesn't behave like America's most eminent intellectual. More like an overgrown schoolboy. But MM has a very appealing aura, even if physically she is not my type. A bit too exaggerated.

Before SLO left he had said: 'I hope things are better organised tomorrow.'

I'll do my best but I think that even he has underestimated the press hunger for MM.

SUNDAY, 15 JULY

Except for the large crowd outside – and who organised that I wonder – the press conference was orderly. In fact it was predictable and dull. SLO arrived without Vivien. He was already in a bad temper – nose out of joint, perhaps? Mr P came sniffing around to have a look at how things were going on and a squint at MM. Irving Stein and APJ were already there – what a pair. APJ had clearly lost centre stage to Milton, who arrived with MM and AM.

The Savoy Hotel had organised itself much better than the airport police. MM's party was 45 minutes late which allowed the flower of the nation's press corps time to make many ribald jokes. D. Zec was telling everyone who would listen that MM was a personal friend of his.

MM still had on her dark glasses and barely spoke above a whisper. AM mainly grunted past his pipe. I would say that they both had hangovers of several different kinds.

SLO made a speech of welcome, which I thought was a little bit patronising – although I'm sure not intentionally. Cecil Tennant,* SLO's agent, was also on the stage. He is a bit of a bully and

---

* Cecil Tennant was to be killed in a motor accident in 1967, on his way home from Vivien Leigh's funeral.

interrupted most forcefully if he didn't like a question. Rupert Allan was much more diplomatic and more friendly. Tennant would not dream of acknowledging my presence, even though I am clearly attached to SLO's party. It is true that I'm pretty inferior but I don't like people who act as if they were 'superior'.

Plod seems to be happily installed at MM's right elbow. He is like a lovely gruff uncle and when MM finally wakes up, she will be jolly glad to have him. I notice that she gives her coat to AM and AM gives it to Plod, so AM has already seen the benefit.

It's a bit like starting a new school. Everyone has to settle down and find out who the other boys are.

MONDAY, 16 JULY

Very quiet day after the hectic weekend. Only Mr P, myself and Vanessa. We will leave the Tibbs group and the Parkside group to themselves, although I am sure there will be a lot of traffic between the two (about six miles). Everyone asks me: 'What's she like? Is she beautiful?'

Well, she certainly looks like Marilyn Monroe, and not all film stars do look like their image. She has got a cute smile, but so far she only turns it on for the cameras. Her figure – and especially her bust – is fantastic but a little on the plump side. Problems – too much fakery: peroxide hair, dead white make-up, heavy lipstick, but that is her image. She looks confused too, lost, troubled. That's the MM image too, I know, but even when she's shut the door on the reporters, she still looks in distress, not just acting it.

She doesn't seem to be able to shrug off the image in private, to throw off her coat, slump down on the sofa and say: 'Phew, let's have a drink.'

She gazes at AM as if he is a superhero, but I don't think he is that nice. He's clearly very handsome and very attractive, but good hearted, no. And she hasn't really got anyone else to depend on. A girl like that really needs her mum, like Margot,* but I'm told her mum is in a bin.** Milton is clearly dependent on her, rushing round like all the others trying not to upset her, frightened of her even.

SLO is much too remote. He's going to be her director and that should be a close relationship, but he is quite clearly not in any way concerned with her personally. He is the supreme professional, expecting and assuming that everyone else will be professional too. (You can see why he and Vivien get on so well.)

MM does have the dreaded Strasbergs, one or both of whom are going to turn up any day now. (Their darling daughter Susan will not be coming for a month, I'm told. But Rupert Allan, who knows everything, says she is expected one day. Hooray – hope springs eternal.)

I wish SLO could be cosy with MM. He's strong and romantic with most women but he only gets 'cosy' with men.

Speaking of which, Tony B is now permanently installed. He is delightful company, and he is going to be behind the camera most of the time. But I doubt if MM goes for that English charm stuff. She clearly adores the strong silent intellectual type, and Tony certainly isn't that. He is SLO's AdC at all times, and keeps his eye on him only.

I must admit it is exciting to be working on this production. The most famous film star and the most famous actor. But they should change the name. *The Sleeping Prince* always confuses people. They think I mean 'The Sleeping Princess', as in 'Sleeping Beauty', and they miss the slight Rattigan pun. If the film was called 'The Naughty Chorus Girl' it would be more dramatic and easier to explain, but I suppose that would be like the old MM image, the one she wants to shed.

* The ballerina Margot Fonteyn (1919–91), an old family friend, whose mother was omnipresent.
** MM's mother had been certified insane in 1934, and spent the rest of her life in various hospitals. She died in 1984.

TUESDAY, 17 JULY

Milton phoned in a nervous state. He has heard that MM's dressing room at Pinewood is not ready yet (true) and he wants to show it to MM tomorrow when she will be there for the make-up test. (This is what is called the screen test, which I always thought was an audition. MM hardly needs an audition since MMP own half the film.)

Mr P is grim because he was specifically told by Milton that MM would not need a full dressing-room suite until filming begins in three weeks' time; and the main dressing room isn't even hired yet. She would normally just go into a make-up room with Whitey and then go home. Teddy Joseph was reassuring however. The dressing-room suite will be 'made' today, and if necessary it can be used by someone else for three weeks and then done again.

I pointed out to Mr P that MM might not like the decor, and then it would have to be redone anyway.

'Hmph.'

It is true that Milton is a fusspot and a perfectionist, but then so is Mr P so he can't complain. At lunchtime I phoned Plod at Parkside.

'What are they up to?'

'Playing trains,' said Plod, with a chuckle.

I hope they are going to get to Pinewood Studios by 9.30 tomorrow morning. Whitey has created a new make-up to match her new hair (a wig, of course)* and her new image.

'We will be ready to leave here by 8.30,' said Plod. 'I heard her mention it to Mr Miller.'

So not only does she remember her appointments but also Plod overhears her doing so, which is very good news.

'You'll have to leave the house at 6.30 when filming starts,' I said. Another chuckle.

I will get to the studio by 8 a.m. to meet David. He is responsible

---

* MM's hairstyle was created by the famous Hollywood stylist Sidney Guilaroff. He flew in for a few days but did not mix with the British crew, except to instruct the film's hairdresser Gordon Bond.

for getting everyone to the right place at the right time, and it is time
I did some work for him.

WEDNESDAY, 18 JULY

It goes without saying that she was late – but not very late, only half
an hour. She seems to have a tendency to leave the house about the
time when she is due to arrive at her next appointment.

Milton arrived early and was quite cheerful. He was very relieved
to see Whitey. 'She'll be on time for *you*,' he grinned.

The dressing-room suite is beige of course, but very very pretty,
like a film set in the 1930s. There is an anteroom and sitting room
and bathroom, all covered with deep Wilton carpet. The curtains
are permanently drawn shut, and low table lights give a soft glow.
There are flowers everywhere – a big bouquet from SLO and Vivien
in the front.

Of course the studios themselves are very forbidding and I wish
the sun had come out. It didn't look at all like California – more
like RAF Dishforth.*

When MM did arrive we all got a shock – except Whitey, I suppose.
She looked absolutely frightful. No make-up, just a skirt, a tight
blouse, head scarf and dark glasses. Nasty complexion, a lot of facial
hair, shapeless figure and, when the glasses came off, a very vague
look in her eye. No wonder she is so insecure.

She bolted into her dressing room with Milton and Whitey and
stayed there for 20 minutes. Eventually they coaxed her out, looking
very tense indeed, and walked her to the small studio.

The whole idea is to film her first without make-up on, so she sat
on a stool, under the bright lights, like a prisoner of war.

Milton spoke to her and SLO spoke to her but she did not listen.
Then Jack Cardiff** stepped forward. Jack is going to be the lighting

* Where I was stationed as a Pilot Officer in 1952.
** 1914–2009. He won an Academy Award for his work on *Black Narcissus* (1946),
and later turned to directing.

cameraman. He is very well known in the business, and has some excellent films to his credit – *The Red Shoes* etc. He is also very charming in a completely natural way. MM is smart enough to know that the lighting cameraman is the one who makes her look beautiful, but she clearly liked Jack as a person. He is kind and tolerant and doesn't put on that awful old public schoolboy charm that Englishmen so often think is the best thing.

I hope I can be natural too. At least I was in the RAF not the Guards. Of course MM never noticed me, but then why should she?

David Orton was in charge of the studio, and he's the Sergeant Major all right. He has a very loud bark when he wants quiet. After half an hour of filming from every angle, MM dived back into her dressing room and Whitey got to work. We had taken a whole reel of MM sitting there like a naked sausage and it was time for the transformation to take place.

'Three hours,' said Whitey cheerfully, so we went to lunch. SLO, Tony and Jack went to the restaurant, David and I to the canteen. Pinewood eating facilities are set up to look democratic – everyone eats in the same place. In fact the wood-panelled restaurant with waitress service is set so deep in the canteen that the stars are very much apart from the hoi polloi. The prices alone keep everyone in their allotted place. David explained that he has already started his efforts to get me the temporary union card so that I can be 3rd Ast Dir. I can tell from his twinkle that he is going to be successful so I don't push it. David looks mild but he doesn't suffer fools gladly – like Mr P.

After lunch there was a long wait until MM emerged, now fully made up with her blonde wig and chiffon top. At first sight she had just changed from a slum kid to a huge gift-wrapped dolly, but that's Jack's problem. He started playing with the lights again, changing their filters and shutters until he was satisfied, and the camera whirred away. For some reason SLO put Tony in charge of the afternoon shoot. There isn't much to do I suppose but stand around and look as if you are in charge, and Tony is very good at that.

Plod and the Princess reappeared. MM had sent them and the driver back to Parkside, I suspect to look after AM. Then MM left at high speed, as if she was afraid of being kidnapped. She reminded me of General Franco when I saw him in Vigo last year.* Milton and Whitey went after her in Milton's car. I notice that Plod now carries MM's handbag!

We are all going to see today's film in the viewing theatre here tomorrow morning, before more tests of make-up, wardrobe and wigs. David says 8 a.m. again tomorrow.

This is fun.

THURSDAY, 19 JULY

MM late again but this time no one cared. Everyone was only thinking about the 'rushes' – the film that was shot yesterday. At 9.30 Milton and SLO led the way into the viewing theatre, and we all held our breath. Jack and Whitey had already seen it together, early on. They were looking pretty smug but said nothing. They were going to MM's dressing room to start her make-up again and discuss technicalities.

The film was magical, and there's no other way to describe it. The stuff we shot in the morning, although it resembled a police line-up mug shot, was quite heartbreaking. MM looked like a young delinquent girl, helpless and vulnerable under the harsh lights. The afternoon footage was even more extraordinary. What an incredible transformation. Now MM looked like an angel – smooth, glowing, eyes shining with joy (Jack's lights), perfect lips slightly parted, irresistible. Quite a few people had wandered in to look and they were stunned. We all fell in love there and then. Milton was triumphant. He and SLO rushed to MM's dressing room to tell her the news, although I suppose they could not exactly explain how very relieved they were.

---

* I had spent the previous summer in Portugal and Spain, and saw Franco arrive in the port of Vigo, where he was very unpopular.

The rest of us joined Bumble Dawson for the wardrobe test. Now it was her turn to be nervous. We had only seen MM wrapped in chiffon so far. She need not have worried. MM finally appeared in a long white dress that suited her perfectly. It made her walk with an amazing wiggle, but a wiggle which is somehow naive not brazen. It also showed just enough of the famous Monroe bosom.

Bumble made various tiny alterations and then announced that two more fittings would be needed to get it right. (These will be at Parkside.)

MM did some twirls for the camera, but this time no one held their breath and Jack hardly bothered to adjust the lights. We all know what it will look like – ravishing.

At the end of the day, I was the last to leave. SLO had gone back to Notley with Tony, in high good spirits, after calling everyone to tell them the news. I went over to the bar for a drink. It is out of bounds during the day but empty after 6 p.m. Sitting alone I saw Whitey Snyder quietly sipping Scotch so I joined him.

'What an amazing transformation,' I said.

'Nothing to it,' said Whitey in his calm Yankee accent. 'The camera just loves some people,' he explained, 'and it sure loves Marilyn. Look at Bogart. Funny little man you wouldn't notice in a crowd, but on camera . . . ! Look at Gary Cooper. Wonderfully tall and good looking, yes, but can't act for toffee and never even tries. Doesn't ever change his expression by a hair's breadth, and yet when you see him on camera, everyone with him seems to be overacting. Just born with the magic. And so is Marilyn. However confused or difficult she is in real life, for the camera she can do no wrong. I tell her that all the time but she doesn't believe me. And sometimes I feel like telling her directors – don't fuss her, don't tell her what to do, just let her rip.'

I can see that he is genuinely fond of MM. The only person I've met so far who is. I wish I could sit him down for a quiet chat with SLO, but that's out of the question.

FRIDAY, 20 JULY

Last day of the tests. This time the hairdressers had lots of wigs to try, but we ended up with the first choice which has been so successful. MM arrived in the car with Milton. Clearly he is trying to reassert his control, which may have temporarily been taken over by AM. He never stops whispering into MM's ear. Is this the fashionable way of communicating with film stars in Hollywood?* We also ran a test to choose MM's stand-in. Jack chose a skinny little blonde who doesn't look a bit like MM to me – no more a real blonde than MM either, I would guess. But it is Jack who will have to light her every day to get the set ready for MM, and he mumbled something about 'perfect skin tones'. Hmm. Who is perfect is the little Wardrobe girl. She could not be cuter or more flirtatious, and I made many more visits to the Wardrobe Department than were strictly necessary.

I hope David hasn't noticed. I didn't have the nerve to ask her out this weekend, but I stressed that I would be back on Monday and come to see her again then. I definitely have to get my hands on her!

I have had to learn my way around the studios in a hurry. David is always telling me to check something at one end or fetch someone from the other, and I spend a lot of time dashing along that long concrete corridor. Before the camera rolls, or 'turns over', a bell rings, red lights flash and the soundproof studio doors are locked automatically. It seems like an age if you are the wrong side of the doors, but actually the camera never runs for more than a minute or so. It is stopped between 'takes' to save film and it is returned to its starting position if it has been moved.

David told me that for the filming, there will be two 2nd Ast Dirs on call, one in the office and one in the studio. However that will not alter my role as his slave: I do not work for *anyone* else (except for SLO, Tony, Milton, Mr P and Vivien, think I).

Tomorrow I'm going down to the country for the weekend, to boast about MM.

* Yes it was, and still is.

MONDAY, 23 JULY

We were all at Pinewood again today, this time to listen to the music, which has been specially written by Richard Addinsell. SLO, Milton, Tony B, Terry Rattigan, David and I were all crammed in a rehearsal room. RA hummed and sang the main song he had written, accompanying himself on the piano. He is a very gentle, sympathetic man and we were all on his side. I'm not musical and I find it extremely hard to catch a tune the first time I hear it played. I remember M and D playing us the record of *My Fair Lady* when they came back from New York after attending the first night. The songs that had brought the house down in a live performance left us unmoved until we had played the record several times. It was the same now. Out of nerves, RA had put in so many decorations and variations with his left hand that it was too hard for us. Nothing could obscure the melody from him, but we were baffled. There was a polite, embarrassed silence.

'Can you play the tune alone,' asked SLO, 'to make it easier for us dullards, dear boy.'

RA was clearly very anxious. But he played it slowly and lyrically and gradually a very charming little waltz began to appear – the Sleeping Prince waltz.

'Bravo!' shouted Tony, and everyone began to applaud.

Then RA sang the song MM will be singing in the film, to another round of applause.

There is no doubt such a pretty tune could help the film immensely. David tells me there will be a grand ballroom scene with 500 people ('extras') waltzing to it in full evening dress. That is where the movie will differ from the play and hopefully be more of a spectacle.

After lunch I sneaked up to see my little Wdg* again – pretty as ever. She is no Einstein, but who cares about that. I just want to get my arms around her tiny waist and squeeze. She doesn't have a boyfriend, so I intend to make my move next weekend.

* i.e. Wardrobe girl.

TUESDAY, 24 JULY

More arrivals from the USA. Most important is Paula Strasberg. SLO and Tony B have worked themselves into a lather about her already. She is MM's drama coach and current Svengali. SLO has been warned by Josh Logan (MM's last director on *Bus Stop*) that she is a total menace. She contradicted everything and she muddled MM up. I thought Lee Strasberg was the drama coach. I don't know what qualifications his wife has, except by association, although I hear she used to be an actress herself.

SLO has determined to ban Paula from the set while we are filming. Several times he has given me a diatribe about her and drama coaches in general. Finally, he told me to throw her out if I see her!

'She can stay in Marilyn's dressing room.'

'What about MM's dressing room in the studio?' (MM is to have her own sort of pre-fab, or 'portable' dressing room built for her right by the set. It too will be all decorated up in beige and soft lights.)

'Oh, the devil take her!' shouted SLO, seeing that he wasn't going to win.

Other arrivals from the USA are Amy and Joshua Greene, Milton's wife and baby son. Milton almost looks too young to be a father. He is evidently a famous photographer, although I hadn't heard of him. He does look a little like Bert Stern,* but that is hardly enough of a qualification. I will find an excuse to visit Tibbs tomorrow and meet everyone.

There is also a lady called Rosten who used to work as AM's secretary and now is going to be MM's secretary.** She is said to be a chum of MM's but I suspect she is still loyal to AM. She will live with them both at Parkside.

---

* A well-known New York photographer, married to Balanchine ballerina Allegra Kent.
** Hedda Rosten was the wife of Norman Rosten, a well-known New York novelist and poet. They both remained friends of MM all her life, and after her death Norman Rosten wrote a book about her entitled *Marilyn: A Very Personal Story*. He died in 1995.

WEDNESDAY, 25 JULY

I drove down to Tibbs in the morning – with Mr P's blessing. He loves a bit of spying, and I'm afraid he already sees the American and British camps as 'Them' and 'Us'. As I know Tibbs so well, and I was the one who arranged it, I went in through the back door as if I was the boss. This has a calming effect on the servants who are already in semi-revolt. It seems that Milton and his friends never give them a thought and are very untidy. The Cotes-Preedys are definitely going to lose their staff if we are not careful. I persuaded everybody that the arrival of *Mrs* Milton Greene would change all the bad habits. They countered that by saying they had never been told there would be children.

'Just one,' I said, 'very small, and I have been told he is very well behaved.' (Absolute lie.)

But they may still walk out with no notice despite their huge wages. 'As good cooks go . . .'

Milton, to his credit, does not seem in the least surprised or upset when I wander into his living room unannounced.

'Hi Colin. Want a beer?'

I explained that I was just checking if he was comfortable and well looked after.

'Sure am. Stick around and meet Amy. She'll be down soon.'

Amy looks even younger than Milton. She is also extremely attractive – small, pale, dark hair, intense – very much a contrast to my little Wdg with her empty eyes.

The little boy is about 2½ and known as Josh. He toddles all over the place, pretty much unhindered and with very little sense as yet. Milton seems very involved with both of them. Perhaps he is not as much of a rascal as Mr P implies. I absolutely can't help liking him.

In the afternoon I drove over to Parkside. Plod opened the front door cautiously (I don't know the staff here so I can't go round the back). It seems that MM and AM spend all their time upstairs, having meals and newspapers sent up. I met Hedda Rosten, MM's 'personal secretary'. She is very New York, middle-aged, but sympathetic and clever. She had a drink in her hand and seemed to me a little tipsy. I suppose she is still exhausted from the overnight flight.

Plod seems happy enough. It is a great relief to have him there.

As I was leaving AM appeared in a white towelling bathrobe and gazed round slowly over his hornrimmed specs. Plod explained who I was – the house etc. – but AM just grunted and went back upstairs.

And to think that this is the man the whole world envies – on honeymoon with Marilyn Monroe.

THURSDAY, 26 JULY

Mr P and I and Vanessa went to Pinewood again to check everything once more. (Vanessa is going to be Mr P's production secretary.) We already have Studio A and the major set – or scenery – is being put up there. It is going to be the purple drawing room in the Carpathian Embassy in Belgrave Square, and it is built so that each of the four walls, with their windows, fireplace, doors etc. can be swung away, and the camera can film the other three. There will be various bedrooms and dressing rooms leading off it which will be built later. It is meant to be on the first floor of the Embassy, and a huge columned hall and grand double staircase will eventually be put up in Studio B when we have finished in A.

There is a lighting grid or gantry all over the ceiling of each studio, with literally hundreds of lights hanging from it. They are on telescopic, rotating metal rods so that they can be altered by the electrician working up above. The lighting cameraman, Jack Cardiff, will work out which of these lights he wants lit, how high they should hang and where they should point. He will make a plan beforehand and give it to the lighting foreman, or 'gaffer', to set up. Then Jack will fine-tune all the lights using the stand-ins – one for MM, one for SLO, one for Dame Sybil Thorndike etc. until all is ready for the stars to walk in and perform.

The stars will be made up in their dressing rooms and walk in costume to the set. MM will do most of it in her main dressing room and then walk to her 'portable' dressing room for her costume. The idea is to have her ready to go in front of the camera at the same time as the set has been lit and prepared, and all the technicians are ready.

I get the strong impression that the technicians are the bosses here. If MM has to be kept waiting, so be it. Woe betide the actor or actress who keeps the technicians waiting!

That seems to be the attitude to British stars, anyway, but I doubt if MM will see it that way. Nor do I. There is no doubt that the technicians are admirable men – calm, professional, efficient. But basically they are replaceable and MM is not. Skills are common. Talent is rare. One day someone will have the courage to sack every technician in the industry and only rehire them if they promise to do what they are told.

However if I said that, even to David, I'd get lynched, so I better keep my mouth shut.

To go back to the filming – you never shoot a scene in one go. You shoot all the bits with the camera pointing in one direction and then swirl round and shoot the others later. And each shot is done many times to get it just right. The boy with the clapperboard marks each one so that the editor can put the whole thing together in the right order later. The film goes off to a laboratory to be processed overnight. The sound is transferred from thin magnetic tape to wider tape in the Sound Department, and the editor uses the 'Clap' of the board to 'sync' the two up on his machine. The board also tells the production name, the shot number and the take number. The lab only prints the takes that look successful to the director – sometimes only one – in order to save money, but even so the editor ends up with hundreds of strips of film in his office, each one with a parallel piece of sound tape. I had asked David to explain all this and he took me round the studios showing me the various bits of equipment we would use. Cranes, dollies, B-P screens, arc lights, booms, concealed microphones etc!

I've got a lot to learn but David and Mr P have been very patient teachers. I really need to know as much as I possibly can before filming starts, so I don't get caught out.

The editor of the film will be Jack Harris. He is an old pro. Thin, grey hair, stoop and perpetual cigarette. At the moment he is finishing up another (British) film here, and normally he wouldn't join our production team until the actual filming was nearly over. An assistant would log all our footage, and sync it up for us to see in 'rushes' each evening.

But SLO (and Milton, I suspect) wants all the insurance he can get, so Jack H will start to work a week after filming starts in 10 days' time. Then he can double-check that every single thing has been covered by the camera.

David explained that with an 'inexperienced' (his word!) actress like MM,* there might be a little 'um' or 'er' or breath that the director didn't notice at the time. The editor will catch it on his machine – which he stops and starts while he examines every frame. Then they can either look for another 'take' or the director can shoot something to cover it.

This seems a good idea, especially as SLO will be acting in most shots as well as directing them. Tony B, bless him, could easily miss something. He's really not a professional director.

Jack Harris is as dour and thorough as Mr P – what politicians used to call 'a safe pair of hands'.

FRIDAY, 27 JULY

Pinewood again. Mr P was occupied with the accounts and legal departments of Rank Films who run Pinewood. They will rent us the necessary facilities. Very dull!

I spent the entire morning flirting with the little Wdg. Very exciting!

I finally bucked up courage to ask her for a date.

---

* *The Prince and the Showgirl* was in fact her twenty-fifth film.

'Not tonight,' she said sternly.

'Why not?'

'I've got to wash my hair, of course.'

I didn't quite understand the 'of course', but pretty girls must be allowed their little ways.

'What about Saturday night then?'

'Oh, all right,' smile, giggle and wiggle.

She really has the smallest waist and the most enchanting laughing eyes I've ever seen. And all those beautiful natural (I suppose) brown ringlets hanging down to her shoulders. I'm hooked. I wish I could decide where to take her.

David and I checked the MM dressing room which had needed some alterations – not, I hasten to say, at MM's behest. I don't think she has even noticed where she is yet, but Milton feels he can interpret her wishes best. MM will use the suite to rest in from Monday, when rehearsals start.

We also checked the security arrangements. The idea is that no one can get in to our area unless they are on a casting call-sheet. For some of our scenes – the Coronation route, the Abbey, the ballroom – we will have as many as 500 'extras' and it would be very easy to smuggle a journalist in, so everyone will have to be especially careful. The 'extras' belong to a union – the FAA, or Film Artists' Association. It, too, is a completely closed shop – the film business seems full of them – and their members are the only ones who can do walk on parts in British films: passers-by, crowds, people in shops etc. It is a small union so '500 extras' means using virtually all of them.

David says most of them, women as well as men, are total rogues. They all try to skive off rather than work, even though 'work' only means standing around in a costume. It will be our job to get them all in front of the camera, and keep them sober. We can be tough, but if we are not scrupulously fair they can all walk out on strike and stop the filming completely.

I met the chief security man at the gate. As I will be first to arrive each morning, I won't need a pass – but they will issue one anyway.

I would imagine any reporter who did want to get in would be smarter than the Pinewood security men, and would have prepared a convincing story to fool them. But it would be tough to get past David.

I'm going to pick up my little Wdg at seven tomorrow night. She was very impressed that I have a car. Heavens, how adorable. I haven't decided where to take her yet and I am a bit nervous. I have no idea what she expects.

SUNDAY, 29 JULY

What a super weekend. Not much to do with my film career, but all part of my film life, so I can't resist writing it down. The little Wdg is as sweet and tasty as a sugar mouse. I am head over heels with infatuation. I picked her up last night in the faithful Bristol. (I fear it has rather a musty leathery smell to it but she didn't seem to notice.) We went to Soho for dinner and I ordered champagne(!). She had one tiny glass and I nearly finished the rest. Lots of smarmy Italian service had a good effect. I didn't dare take her to a night-club. She might have been frightened by their dark, red, velvet corners. So we simply drove round the West End for an hour. She is very naive and all the sights were greeted with oohs and aahs. We chatted and held hands, where traffic allowed, across the handbrake. Finally we came back here.* It is hard to invite anyone in for purely social reasons since I only have a kitchen and a bedroom, but we were both flushed with passion and fell onto the bed immediately. Her figure is picture perfect, she kisses like an angel (so I'm not the first) and she happily allowed me to stroke her all over.

Neither of us wanted to go the whole way. It is much too soon, and she is a good girl and not a tart. But it was impossible for her not to see how excited I was. She was curious, I explained, and finally

* The servants' quarters of my parents' flat in the Albany, Piccadilly, which they had loaned to me.

out of kindness she put her little hand where the tension was and I was soon in heaven. Actually I think she enjoyed herself too, if not in quite the same explosive manner. When I took her home we were still delirious and spent ages kissing goodbye in the car. Finally a light came on in the house and she fled. Now I can't wait to see her again.

MONDAY, 30 JULY

Rehearsals at Pinewood all day. The principal cast members arrived at 9 a.m. David and I were outside to greet them and show them to an upstairs studio. It is just a large gloomy room with a few chairs scattered about, but David explained that to have rehearsals at all for a film is a great luxury. They are the essential preliminary of plays in the theatre, but evidently films very rarely have them.

MM will certainly never have had this sort of rehearsal before and I expect she was nervous. The normal procedure is to rehearse a scene 10 minutes before it is filmed. This is simply because an act of a play runs 45 minutes and a film shot lasts 45 seconds, more or less. I expect SLO has arranged for rehearsals on this occasion to ensure smooth, level performances right through the movie (a smooth level performance from Marilyn Monroe, to be precise). MM was only 45 minutes late, and was accompanied by Paula Strasberg.

Mrs Strasberg is not, at first glance, a very formidable figure. She is short and plump, with brown hair pulled back from a plain, round, expressive face. She has big brown eyes which are usually hidden by big dark glasses – like her protégée. Her clothes are also brown and beige – bohemian but expensive. Her influence over MM seems to be total. MM gazes at her continuously and defers to her at all times, as if she was a little Jewish Buddha. SLO was clearly put out by this, but remained theatrically gracious. He introduced MM to the assembled cast. First Dame Sybil, who radiates love and good fellowship so genuinely that even MM could not resist her. Then came Jeremy Spenser, who'll play Dame Sybil's grandson, very polite and bright-eyed, and Richard Wattis, who looks exactly like the Foreign Office dignitary which he will play. These three, together with MM and SLO, really *are* the movie.

Richard Wattis is in virtually every scene except the love scenes, and he even has to barge into two of those. Luckily he has a wonderful sense of humour behind his austere appearance.

Then SLO introduced Tony B, who had directed MM at the screen test, but whom MM had clearly forgotten, and then David and then me (two more blanks for MM).

Well, it has been 10 days since she saw any of us but frankly I don't think she'd recognise Milton Greene in a crowd – especially if she was nervous. In this case she definitely was not at ease. The whole thing was rather theatrical and I sense that she doesn't understand the language.

All these people (except for David and me) are old cronies of SLO's. Paula understands them OK – she was once an actress herself – so she becomes MM's interpreter, and MM relies on her alone. SLO, whom I love and worship, can be a bit condescending. He treated MM like a doll from a faraway land. It is almost as if he is already in the character of the film, and she is just 'a little bit of fluff'. When SLO isn't completely at ease, he tends to retreat into a role, and in this case that is a little unfortunate. If MM is working with 'the greatest classical actor in the world' to acquire a serious dramatic image, then she won't be liking his attitude at all. Paula didn't say a word but she radiated disapproval, which definitely means that MM is upset.

Then SLO introduced the film. He told the whole story, most magically, and in a dozen accents, from start to finish. We really should have filmed his performance and then gone home. MM listened, eyes and mouth wide open like a child, completely carried away by the little fairy story. At the end everyone clapped and MM joined in enthusiastically. Then David and I handed round marked scripts and SLO chose certain key scenes to read aloud. I must say that MM was enchantingly unspoilt. Compared to those 'old stagers' she sounded most refreshing and delightful. But her voice does seem to be coming from another world, floating out of the sky like a little moth. I hope it all mixes together in the end. It *is* a fairy story, I suppose.

TUESDAY, 31 JULY

MM and Paula were 45 minutes late again today and it was enough to irritate SLO. He sees it as a great professional discourtesy, especially to Dame Sybil. This is a pity because Dame Sybil really doesn't care, or hardly notices. I think MM actually enjoyed yesterday's readings and SLO should have taken advantage of this.

MM just doesn't seem to know late from early, so when she is scolded she often can't understand why – or is it that she doesn't want to understand why?

I took MM and Paula up to the rehearsal room where everyone was waiting. Dame S is so divine; she was warm and welcoming to MM – as if really glad to see her, as a human being. SLO tempered his greeting with a hint of menace which I could see MM pick up. Paula was icy to me but I am incredibly polite and charming to her at all times. As she does not know that I am in love with her daughter (sorry, little Wdg!) she was rather taken aback, but obviously flattered. MM, of course, totally ignores me, and quite right too. In the film industry I am right at the bottom and she is right at the top.

Actually she seems a strange mixture of self-centred and sensitive, like a child, I suppose. I have heard adults like that described as 'mimophants' – as fragile as mimosa about their own feelings, as tough as elephants about other people's.

I always thought being a big, big star would give you an armour-plated ego, but MM certainly has not got that. In fact I don't think SLO realises, or perhaps even cares, how fragile she is. He takes the line that all actors and actresses are nervous, but they should have learnt to suppress their nerves by the time they work with him. I hope he remembers that MM is his *partner* in this production – his equal business partner. Milton Greene is just his partner's stooge. Charming him won't help much!

I didn't stay for the rehearsals in the morning but went on the set with David. I've been on sets before and one thing hasn't changed. There is nowhere to sit! That's why directors and stars have their names on their chairs. The only place I know is the wheel of a sound boom, which is not popular with the sound boom operator. David thinks a 3rd Ast Dir should never sit, night or day, by definition. 'A 3rd Ast Dir is "he who never sits",' he barked.

I also had to pop up and see my little Wdg (sorry Susan!). Very sweet and soft and I stole a kiss behind the racks of costumes. The wardrobe mistress, her boss, has obviously been told the news of our night out together, and gives me looks which are both fierce and benevolent. 'Don't hurt my baby,' she implies.

I took a spare copy of the shooting script home, from rehearsals, and I'm going to study it very carefully tonight. Work before pleasure – but Saturday night seems far away.

WEDNESDAY, 1 AUGUST

MM was very late this morning. I phoned Plod to find out what was the matter but he knew nothing. Neither MM nor AM had come downstairs yet, and no one had had the courage to go up and knock.

'Could they have committed joint suicide?' I asked.

'No.' There had been bumps.

'What sort of bumps?' I heard Plod grin down the phone.

'Oh no. Surely not.'

I can't repeat *that* to SLO. He is extremely grim. It doesn't bode well for the 6.45 a.m. filming days. Tony B is fuming. Dear Tony, he always mirrors SLO so closely it is touching. He genuinely feels SLO's emotions as soon as SLO does. And his wife Anne is so like Vivien – in manner, of course, not in looks. Did he choose her like that, or did she become like that to please him?

The rest of the cast seem quite relieved. Esmond Knight paid us a visit – even though he is half-blind.* No one seems to know how much he can or can't see, but he's very kind and nice.

Rehearsals went on, punctuated by hilarious theatrical jokes, mainly from Dicky Wattis. What a pity MM can't join in this sort of 'actors' band'. I'm sure it is much more relaxing than the method group in New York. But perhaps you have to be a professional, as these actors are, to be able to join in and relax.

At noon MM did turn up with Paula and Milton. I wonder if they are fighting over her. She seemed confused and frightened. The script might as well have been *Alice in Wonderland*.

She had trouble in following the other parts and so failed to come in when her cue came. No one could be cross; they were just embarrassed. Paula had gone off to 'confer' with Milton, so Dame S went and sat by MM and coaxed her through. I wish Dame S was going to be in every scene but she is only in about 15%. Something definitely seemed the matter with poor MM so perhaps it will pass. It could be her monthly period, I suppose, but she was clearly very upset. By the look in her eyes she has been taking tranquillisers. She went to lie down in her dressing room at lunchtime and Paula came tiptoeing out after a few minutes so she must have gone straight to sleep.

At 2.30, when she didn't appear, SLO told David and David told me to go to get her. Milton opened her dressing-room door, grinning, and said she'd be up in 10 minutes. I could see, and smell, a champagne bottle open on the table. My heart sank. I didn't mention what I'd seen to SLO. Not booze as well as pills?

Actually MM was much better in the afternoon. I suppose the tranqs had worn off and the champagne had cheered her up. SLO left her alone to do what she could and Paula sat silently in a corner glowering.

Milton must have won a round there, I guess!

---

* Esmond Knight (1906–87) had been partially blinded in the Navy during the war. He acted in many films, including Olivier's *Henry V*, *Hamlet* and *Richard III*, and *The Red Shoes*. In *The Prince and the Showgirl* he played the Regent's security officer.

THURSDAY, 2 AUGUST

MM arrived early, *for her*, at 10.30 a.m. Paula and Hedda Rosten and AM were with her in the car. (No room for Plod!) Tension seemed high to me but MM was quite jolly.

AM and Hedda just looked round the studios a bit and went back to Parkside. Paula took a firm grip of MM on one side and Milton, who had been waiting outside, took a firm grip of the other. They hardly bother to conceal their battle for control. And not just them – AM wants control too.

There is no doubt MM is a huge star. Everyone is simply hypnotised when she appears, including me. Everything revolves around her, whether she likes it or not, and yet she seems weak and vulnerable. If it is deliberate, it is incredibly skilful, but I think it is a completely natural gift. All the people round her want to control her, but they do so by trying to give her what they think she wants. What a paradox. Only Dame Sybil, with a heart as big as a house, can bypass all this nonsense. She can get away with being natural with MM because she is so naturally nice. Which none of the rest of us are, of course.

We are all really thinking of what we want underneath. 'Oh what a nice pot of gold you are. Can I help you, pot of gold?' etc. Dame S simply is not interested in gold.

Meanwhile life goes on. Filming starts on Monday and everything needs to be ready. Studio A is now bursting with technicians, preparing the equipment. The first shots on Monday will be unimportant – just there to make sure everything works, camera, lights, sound etc.

Jack Cardiff has to have the right lights hanging from the grid. It looks a total muddle but it has a pattern which only the gaffer and he understand. The lights get very hot – I dread to think what the temperature is up on the gantry. Whenever possible the lights are all switched off. 'Save the lights' is the cry, and there is a great clunk and what seems like darkness for a moment. But actually there are work lights which always stay on. They make everything look tawdry and pathetic. Carpenters are hammering, scene painters are finishing back-drops, curtains (drapes) are being hung and ornaments are being selected to decorate the set (props).

Roger Furse is meant to be in charge of the scenery but his assistants hardly seem to have time to listen to him.

Bumble Dawson is clearly close to a breakdown. She has all the costumes to worry about and some aren't to her liking.* My little Wdg, who works for Bumble of course, is too busy to give me anything but a smile, but we do have another date for Saturday night.

FRIDAY, 3 AUGUST

Tony B is incredibly nice. It seems he and Anne have rented a large house near Ascot, at Runnymede, where King John signed the Magna Carta. They want me to come to live with them there while filming is going on. It is much nearer the studios than London, of course, and not far from Tibbs and Englefield Green. Since I have to be at Pinewood by 6.40 a.m. every morning from now on, that is very good news.

But the real joy is to be invited to be part of 'the family'. Tony B and Anne are very much part of SLO and Vivien's 'family' and now I will be too. I always have a tendency to feel lonely unless I am with people. It is an absolutely lovely idea and I accepted with much gratitude.

Rehearsals ended at lunchtime and all the cast dashed off for the weekend.

'Not you,' said David sternly, and we stayed to see the last person leave. I don't mind. My mind is firmly fixed on tomorrow night.

I will go out to Tony and Anne at Runnymede on Sunday afternoon.

* Some of the costumes had been designed by Cecil Beaton, but he had asked for too much money to do the whole production.

SUNDAY, 5 AUGUST

This is a glorious Edwardian mansion, with leaded windows, mahogany furniture and large Turkey rugs. The garden is very green and lush as we are near the river. The house is dark and cool. Anne is enchanting – slim, pretty, vivacious. She has filled the rooms with flowers and put the excess bric-a-brac in the attic. Tony is gruff and jovial. He brings generous drinks before dinner. I feel I have landed in Paradise! Anne cooked a delicious meal and the conversation sparkled.

My poor little Wdg is rather heavy going. Not a brain in that pretty little head. Anything that wouldn't go in a woman's magazine goes straight over it.

Lack of sophistication can be so attractive, and yet it's also rather tiring. Last night was delightful but I'm not sure that I can keep it going. What she likes is Romance. Well, I'm a great romantic, but she sees it only in terms of clichés. One step away from these simple terms and she is startled; one original remark and she gets suspicious. Alas, one cannot just kiss all evening. It might be different if we were sleeping together – then there is always something to do – but of *course* we are not.

Tomorrow we start to make a film.

The strain on SLO is going to be terrific. He has to direct as well as act. His confidence in his co-star and partner is minimal. Already late, already prone to be detached from reality, MM is the sort of star he just does not understand. It's no good treating her like 'a pretty little thing' who must do what she is told. When he does talk to her directly, she just gazes at him with those huge eyes, and it is impossible to tell whether she is even listening or not. I've never heard her reply. So SLO is forced to go through Milton, and he is sometimes forced to go through Paula. We must all be very careful not to take sides, or we will make things worse.

I feel as if this film has really become my life.

MONDAY, 6 AUGUST

I am officially 3rd Ast Dir at last.

'Your most important duty right now,' said David, at 9 a.m. in a crowded Studio A, 'is to get me a mug of tea and a piece of bread and dripping.'

We had all been there for over two hours by then, and we were very hungry indeed. A sort of NAAFI wagon appears in the concrete corridor at nine and my task is to queue for David's breakfast (and my own).

The studio is usually pretty dark except for the 'work lights', not to save electricity (money is no object in this film!) but to stop the set getting too hot. There is a real danger of the actors breaking out into a sweat – which is especially embarrassing if the action is set on a cold day.

Jack stands in the middle of each set, gazing at the stand-ins and giving orders to his 'gaffer'. Different lights are raised and lowered, switched on and off. Strange filters are added – 'barn doors' and 'gauzes' – and fingers are burned.

Except for the areas the cast acts in, the floor is completely covered with cables, camera rails and other hazards, so 'Have a nice trip?' becomes a much too frequent joke.

There are also a lot of people – electricians, camera assistants, boom operators, property men, make-up 'artists', wig-dressers, carpenters, drapery men, painters, plasterers, set decorators, etc., some of whom are busy, and a lot of whom are just milling around in case they are needed.

A journey from one side of the studio to the other with two mugs of scalding tea and two pieces of floppy 'Bread and Drip' is a truly hazardous experience. There must be at least 40 people in the way now, and I'm sure it will get worse when MM appears tomorrow.

The crew are all very English, very professional and clearly not easy to impress. They, of course, can see me for what I am – the lowest of the low.

There is Elaine, the continuity girl, whose job it is to make sure that every scene blends perfectly with its neighbours. Without her, cigarettes would suddenly lengthen or shorten, or jump from hand to hand, doors would suddenly open, and dresses rearrange themselves. Elaine is cool and competent and I get the impression that nothing will frustrate her.

There is Denys [Coop], the camera operator, and his crew. I didn't realise but Jack never even touches the camera. Very occasionally he is allowed to peek through it while everyone gives him odd looks. The camera is usually at the end of a long crane, or on rail tracks or both. Denys sits behind it, on a little chair with his legs either side, and twirls wheels to move the camera around. He also has two young men to push and steer, despite the use of electric motors. The sound recordist is Mitch, a very quiet, very patient man, who is often ignored by everyone. He has a metal console, linked to a microphone on a boom and to another recordist in a soundproof room somewhere.

Actually Mitch and this crew are more dangerous than they look, as they demonstrated while we were waiting this morning. Mitch saw Roger Furse and his assistant hobnobbing in a corner. A nod to his boom operator and the 'mike' was extended across all the obstacles until it was over Roger's head. Then a quick whisper to his recordist and the secret conversation was being played over the Tannoy system. Incredibly, even though their conversation was booming out from every loudspeaker, they didn't realise what was going on for over a minute. It could have been very embarrassing.

When we are ready to start filming David shouts 'QUIET, STUDIO. Going for a take. LOCK THE DOORS.'

A claxon goes PARP, PARP, PARP. Red lights flash. Denys says 'Camera rolling.' There are two little beeps from Mitch's console and Mitch says 'Speed.'

David says 'Mark it.' The clapper boy steps in front of the camera, names the film and the shot and the take number: '*The Prince and the Showgirl* (which is the new title) shot 3 take 1,' then he goes 'SNAP' with his clapper, on which the same information is written. Then the director – SLO or Tony – quietly says 'Action,' and filming starts.

This is essential for the editor. It gives him all the information on the sound tape *and* the film, so he can join the two up very easily. But it must be awfully off-putting for a nervous actor or actress. I suppose they have to learn to ignore it. It's all very well for the director to say 'Action' in soft and persuasive tones, but four other total strangers have just barked out their contributions, heedless of acting nerves.

As almost all scenes are very short, often just a few seconds, the director will be saying 'Cut' almost immediately and, nine times out of ten: 'Let's do it again.'

The happiest words you can hear are 'Print it' – you only print the very best takes – but even that is often followed by: 'Let's do it just once more, shall we, to be sure.'

Then Denys says 'Check the gate,' and his assistant opens the front of the camera and looks inside with a torch, to see that no fluff or 'film debris' has got caught on the shutter mechanism, and scratched the film.

All this is part of an inflexible routine. It happens every time a scene is filmed, no matter how often that scene is repeated. I can't understand how actors put up with it. Do they do the same in Hollywood? David says they do, but David's 'bark' alone is enough to frighten the lines right out of an actor's head. I suppose I will get used to it all, like any ritual.

Many of the people in the studio today were finishing up the set for tomorrow. The first set to be filmed – but not the first scene in the story of course – is the private drawing room of the Carpathian Embassy. SLO plays the Grand Duke, the Regent of Carpathia, and in this drawing room he will try to seduce the showgirl, Elsie Marina, MM. Also built is the Queen Dowager's sitting room, so that Dame Sybil's scenes can be shot as soon as possible.

The art director is a small intense lady with short grey hair, cut like a man's. She is Carmen Dillon, who has done many similar films. She works with a set dresser called Dario Simoni. Together with Roger Furse, they are responsible for the 'look' of the whole film. They are all completely professional, and only think about the scenery, and the props, and the costumes. They didn't even glance at MM when she walked in to look at the set for a moment last week, even though MM was quite excited by the whole thing.

This professionalism pervades the entire crew. In fact I am sure that they are all extremely proud of it. But I don't find it exactly 'welcoming' and I'm sure MM won't either. A top actor like Dicky Wattis will take it for granted. A director like SLO will insist on it, but a stranger, a foreigner, a 'new girl' like MM may be put off by it. I know I am. I admire and envy all their skills but it is possible to be human too, isn't it?

Anyway we did a couple of early shots which gave SLO and David a chance to get to know the crew before MM makes her very considerable presence felt. I had to stay until last so I only just got back here in time for Anne's dinner.

Tony B is buoyant for a change. This certainly means that SLO is optimistic, despite the omens. I expect he is happy to be working in a studio again, on a 'closed' set (no visitors) where Vivien's social demands have to take second place.

TUESDAY, 7 AUGUST

I left Runnymede at 6 a.m. sharp. Quite cool – no traffic on the road, so I was at Pinewood before 6.25. One sleepy guard who couldn't care less. After 20 minutes of pacing up and down outside the star dressing rooms, a black hire car arrived bearing . . . Dame Sybil.

'Oh Colin. How kind of you to meet me. Dear me, you look cold.' (I was.) And she is over 70. I called make-up and hair and settled her in a warm dressing room. Five minutes later came Gilman in the Bentley, carrying SLO.

'Hello boy. Marilyn arrived yet?'

'Not yet, Sir Laurence.'

'Well wait here until she does and let me know directly.'

He is an optimist. At 7.05 Dicky Wattis arrived in a London taxi. With him was Paul Hardwick who will play the Embassy Major Domo. At 7.15, Milton Greene.

'Hi Colin. Is she here yet?' Who is he kidding? Then a long wait. I remain poised outside on the pavement. David emerged from the studios.

'What's going on? I thought you had a contact in her house. Have you phoned yet?'

'Not yet.'

'Phone.'

Plod answered. 'We are due to leave right now. We've been on standby for 10 minutes. Paula is here. She and Hedda are waiting too.'

Report to David. 'ETA, 8.15.'

Report to SLO (being made up) and Milton. 'ETA, 8.15.'

Scowl.

At 8.30 MM arrives with Paula. Plod, carrying her bag, winks. MM wears dark glasses, beige nylon scarf, slacks.

'Good morning, Miss Monroe.'

'Oh, hi.'

Whitey is already in her dressing room. He has been there for nearly two hours. Everyone but Paula is firmly shut out. I report to SLO again.

Now I must make a note: 8.30 a.m. arrival at the studio means 11 a.m. on the set. It just isn't possible to hurry the Make-up – Hair – Costume sequence. Even if one could it might upset MM and then where would we be? Well, where? I expect we'll find out, sooner or later.

SLO had expected MM to be late and had planned 'cut-away' shots to use up the time.

The main scene of the day was Dame S – the Grand Duke's mother-in-law – greeting MM – the showgirl – in that purple drawing room. Jack had lit the stand-ins by 9 a.m. and by 9.30 Dame S and Dicky W were waiting on the set in full costume.

SLO offered profuse apologies but they didn't seem to mind.

'Poor dear. I expect she's nervous,' said Dame S.

'I expect so,' said Dicky dryly, but SLO did not get the point.

We shot a 'reaction' on Dicky, eyebrows up in mock surprise, and then I went to check on MM. As I was waiting outside her dressing-room door, she suddenly burst out, with Paula, Milton and Whitey surrounding her, like warders with a violent prisoner. They all swooped off in the wrong direction down the corridor, until I could run and catch up. When I got them into Studio A, they all bolted straight into the 'portable' dressing room on the set and slammed the door. This left Bumble, grinding her teeth and curling her lock of hair, MM's dresser (skinny, rather sexy), a hairdresser and a make-up assistant all marooned on the outside rather wondering what to do.

When they were eventually admitted it must have been like the 'And two hard-boiled eggs' scene from the Marx Bros.* The answer was to expel Paula and Milton but that is not so easy.

Finally at 11.30 a.m., MM did emerge, fully dressed and looking, I am bound to say, ravishing. What a beautiful creature she is, to be sure. Paula whispered in her ear, and she walked straight on to the set.

No apologies to Dame S for a two-hour wait. But Dame S could see that it was quite an act of courage to be there at all and gave her a warm welcome.

'QUIET STUDIO. Going for a take. Hit the lights.'

The whole sequence began without SLO giving MM any direction, let alone MM asking for it. I suppose he just thought he would see what happened. He was sitting quietly behind the camera, in full costume as he was in the next shot.

'Action.'

Dame Sybil's performance is rock steady and flawless. All MM had to do was remember her lines.

When, by take 8, she had done this, we had a 'print' and MM's first shot was 'in the can'.

* In *Monkey Business* (1931).

What a relief for us all, not least her.

Between takes MM cannot lie down, or even sit. Bumble's gorgeous dress does not allow for that. So MM has a strange white resting board with armrests on which she can relax. She dashes to this on every possible occasion, flicking her fingers up and down in the air. She has been taught this trick as a 'tension reliever' by one of the Strasbergs. It does not look very effective to me, and it gives her the appearance of being in a flap.

Paula's lips are never more than two inches from her ear, muttering and whispering continuously. Not unnaturally, SLO has a hard time coming to terms with this. He wants to talk to MM about the next shot, but it is hard for him to interrupt. I'm sure he had originally expected her to rush to him, and lap up his words of wisdom etc. Not a chance.

I hover equidistant from him and David while Jack re-lights as quickly as he can. During re-lighting, MM retreats to her mobile dressing room and once again the door is slammed. This time SLO knocked and walked in. Through the gap I could see a determined Paula trying to shield him from MM but he took no notice and shut the door behind him. David called 'the half' – union-esc for delaying lunch for half an hour – and we did another shot.

After lunch we did two more set-ups, and then David called 'That's a wrap, gentlemen,' signalling enough for the day.

We were all exhausted. MM got straight into her car with Whitey and Paula. Whitey will remove her make-up at Parkside and, I hope, calm her down. SLO and Milton retired to SLO's dressing room for 'a conference', and I could hear angry voices. I think SLO wants to nip 'this idiotic behaviour' in the bud. The trouble is that Milton does too, but he doesn't know how.

I went to the bar for a drink.

Thank goodness for Tony and Anne. I don't think I could have driven all the way back to London. I'm completely whacked. But I've sworn I will write this diary every night and that's going to be a good discipline.

WEDNESDAY, 8 AUGUST

Has anyone told MM that she's meant to be at the studios at
6.45 a.m.? Perhaps no one has dared? Perhaps it wouldn't make a
scrap of difference?

I wonder what the usual time is in the USA. She turned up at
8.30 again this morning, quite jolly, and I even got a smile. But 8.30,
early though it is in normal circumstances, is 1¾ hours late for us.
Once again, we couldn't start filming with MM until 11.30. All the
other actors have to be called for 9.00 on the set, just in case MM
does turn up on time, and there are only so many shots we can shoot
without her.

Lunch is almost due by 11.30 so David had to 'call the half' again.
For some reason this annoys the crew. I know they are hungry but
it's more than that. It is as if management was taking advantage of
them in some way. 'Calling the half' is meant to be the exception,
not the rule.

At least we all have time to explore the set and get to know each
other. As usual I popped up to see my little Wdg. She is so pretty
that I can't resist her, but she is also so silly that I jolly nearly can.
I asked her for a date on Saturday.

'Of course,' she giggled. Of course. Already? Hmm.

Then I nearly brought the studio out on strike.

Dame Sybil was on the set in full costume and I asked her whether
she would like to sit down.

'Why yes,' she said, 'let us all sit down,' so I went for her chair.
Everyone froze.

'Are you a member of NATKE?' or some such bunch of union
initials, asked some nameless man in overalls.

'No.'

'Chairs is Props. Props is NATKE. If ACT members (and I'm
not even that yet) is going to do NATKE jobs, we're off.' They all
grumbled and rumbled in agreement.

David stepped in to calm them down. 'Colin is a new boy,' etc., and put in a humble, official request for the chair for Dame Sybil, which took 10 minutes to fetch from the 'Prop' department (and should have been there from the beginning).

Now I know why it is so hard to sit down in a film studio! And they went on about what I had done all day. But Dame S is as bright as a lark, no matter what happens, and gossips away with Dicky W. They are a real theatrical pair.

The set is the drawing room on the first floor of the Embassy. Even allowing for the difference between Carpathian taste and mine, I find it completely hideous. Dreadful purples and mauves everywhere. But it is an effective background for the long white evening dress which MM will wear in every scene. I suppose Roger F was thinking of this when he designed it.

When MM is all made up by Whitey, in that sparkling outfit with her blonde wig, she really does shine like a star.

After we had done another four shots today (of the five that were planned – not so bad) we all went to see the film that had been printed from yesterday's material (the 'rushes').

It was only the best takes – two of each shot for comparison – but we were enraptured, all over again. The fluffs and the lapses of memory were forgotten. MM looked sublime and even acted old Dame S off the screen. She looks far more natural and less 'stagey'. SLO looked wooden and uncomfortable by comparison, although this is partly his role as Grand Duke. One can't tell anything about the film from one day's shooting, but one thing is for sure. You just can't take your eyes off MM.

SLO was still grim. I think he senses loss of control on many fronts. Well, he is nearly 50, poor man.

THURSDAY, 9 AUGUST

Now I know the secret of Paula's control over MM . . . total, abject sycophancy, continual flattery, blatant pandering to every nerve-end.

'Drama Coach' – phooey! It's Lee Strasberg who is the coach. But Paula certainly is an actress.

This morning Plod had reported serious insurrection among the staff at Parkside. I decided to go to talk to them, and to offer them a little more of MM's money, so at the end of the day I went back there in the front of MM's car. Plod had gone back at lunchtime. Of course I could have gone in my own car, but, to be honest, like everyone else in the world it seems, I couldn't resist getting more of MM's company. Anyway I don't think Paula minded. Nor did she notice that the glass division in the car was down.

As soon as we drove out of the studio gates she started: 'Marilyn, you were wonderful. You are the most wonderful actress I have ever known in my life, Marilyn. You are superb, Marilyn, you are divine.'

At this even MM demurred a little, and in truth she was not good today, having great trouble to remember even the simplest line. We had only completed two scenes.

Paula went straight on: 'Yes, Marilyn, you are a great, great actress. All my life, Marilyn, I have prayed for a great actress who I could help and guide. All my life, Marilyn, I have prayed on my knees.'

There was a bump and I sneaked a look. Paula was now on her knees on the carpet of the car.

'. . . prayed on my knees for God to give me a great actress. And now He has given me you, and you are that great actress, Marilyn. You are . . .' all the way back to Parkside.

I was curled up with embarrassment, trying by sign language to get the chauffeur to put up the glass division, but he was much too stupid to notice – or to listen to what was going on. Paula was like a hypnotist on stage – you can't believe it will work, but it does. Gradually I could see MM relax, and regain the self-confidence which SLO and his gang had drained from her.

When we arrived I jumped out and opened the door. 'You really are great, Miss Monroe,' I said, and I meant it.

'Why thank you, Colin,' she said with a dazzling smile.

I didn't know that she'd noticed me, let alone remembered my name. I floated into the house and agreed to all the servants' demands – more money as I thought. I'll square Milton later.

The car took me on to Runnymede, still under MM's spell. But Tony and Anne brought me back to earth. After all, we have a long, complicated, expensive colour film to make somehow.

Tony will take me in to the studio tomorrow morning. If I am late, as he sometimes is, David can shout at him. No chance of MM beating me to it anyway.

FRIDAY, 10 AUGUST

Dame Sybil really is an angel. On time as usual this morning – she is now the only person who is – she handed me a bright red woolly scarf as she got out of the car.

'I thought you looked cold, so early in the morning, so I bought you this.'

I was overwhelmed. I'll wear it every morning from now on. Typical Dame S thoughtfulness. It is exactly what I need.

MM arrived at what is now her usual time. It seems there is nothing Plod, or Hedda Rosten, can do to get her out of the house before 8 a.m. I must say I sympathise. If I was the most famous film star in the world I wouldn't get up before nine. I know films don't work like that, and that if she is late it is phenomenally expensive, but couldn't she have asked SLO to schedule all her shots for after lunch? It would prevent a lot of friction.

As it is, he seems most upset by what he sees as MM's discourtesy to Dame S. This morning, through clenched teeth, he actually told MM to apologise to her. He strode onto the set when she arrived, took her by the hand as if he was dealing with a naughty schoolgirl, and led her over to Dame S. We didn't hear what he said but he had been rehearsing it for an hour. We all held our breath. SLO was doing what we were all dying to do, at last.

But MM wasn't at all upset – just surprised. I really don't think she realised that her lateness affected anyone. Plod says she gets called, goes back to sleep, gets called again, rushes round the house, changes clothes quite a few times, goes up and down stairs etc., without ever thinking of what the time is. Finally she bucks up her courage and dives into the car. Paula, Hedda, AM and Plod can all be flapping around her but it has no effect. Most of the time, and it is unpredictable, MM takes as much notice of other people as a cow does of rabbits in the same field.

However, Dame Sybil did get through: 'My dear you mustn't concern yourself,' she said. 'A great actress like you has other things on her mind, doesn't she?'

MM beamed, and behaved well all day.

We were only filming scenes with MM and Dame S, so SLO could stay behind the camera, and that makes things a lot easier. Then AM turned up to watch the 'rushes'. MM was thrilled, and giggled and wiggled like a teenager. When we got into the viewing theatre, to everyone's embarrassment they went into the back row and started snogging as if they were on a date!

'Love birds,' said Whitey with a grin, and we watched MM on the screen, endlessly repeating her lines, while the real-life MM heaved and panted a few rows behind us. Very un-British, but I suppose they are on their honeymoon. (MM's third, I guess.)

SUNDAY, 12 AUGUST

Saturday night was a bit of a failure. Oh, how quickly a beautiful bloom can fade. Already the little Wdg doesn't seem quite as charming as I thought, and not even as pretty. It is as if she belongs to the fringe – not really relevant, something I must leave behind.

Terry Rattigan is giving a party next Saturday night and I can *not* take the Wdg to it. Of course this is difficult to explain to her and in fact I can't even begin, so she has decided that I am going to take some other girl. The more I protested, the more she became convinced. Finally I told her, quite sharply, not to be silly. That caused a coolness which I fear may turn to ice. One problem is that she can never understand how I feel about my work. It really is so much more than just a job. It's my whole life, and I'm afraid that she is right to feel excluded. But there is nothing I can do to change that. Today Tony and Anne took me over to Notley for tea. Vivien was radiant. Without any doubt she is still the most beautiful woman in the world and she knows it. Terry Rattigan was there. He did not ask me to the famous party; but Vivien did, twice, in front of him, and anyway SLO had already done so on Friday. Also there were Roger Furse, Bumble and Bobby Helpmann.*

No one was there to represent the MM point of view so there were a lot of unflattering jokes about the Americans. Vivien was very funny and very catty and so was Bobby (well, he always is – even about Vivien).

Vivien, who knows I worship her, asked me confidentially how MM was working out. I dare not say anything or she might quote me, so I just rolled my eyes to heaven. Naturally she was delighted.

In the end we stayed much too late. Vivien hates to let good guests leave. It is already 11 p.m. and I have to be up at 5.45 as usual. Groan.

MONDAY, 13 AUGUST

We have now settled into a routine in that damn purple set. MM is late every morning and every morning it is treated with the same shock/horror/gloom by SLO and the entire crew.

SLO gets fully made up and costumed and the stand-ins are lit for the main scene. The equipment is checked and rechecked. We all eat bread and dripping and drink mugs of tea. Then we cast around for something to shoot – SLO speaks MM's lines to Dame S who has to pretend that MM is sitting opposite her. Finally MM appears, breathless and beautiful, and hope rises, only to be dashed as she disappears into her dressing room Mk II.

* Robert Helpmann. Australian-born dancer, choreographer and actor (1909–86), knighted in 1968, who often partnered Margot Fonteyn. His film appearances included *Henry V* and *The Red Shoes*.

Fifteen minutes later – after goodness knows what little ritual – MM appears again and we all stand by. MM shakes her hands vigorously, one ear bent down to Paula (who is 10 inches shorter than her) for final encouragement.

If she gets panicky now it can mean another half hour in that portable Nissen hut, so Paula really is essential. MM might easily ruffle 'her' hair with one hand, and that means a 20-minute delay, or rub her eyes, half an hour. And SLO has yet to give her direction. Only he, after all, really knows what all the scenes are about, and he feels he must pass this on. Whether in fact he can say anything which has any effect whatsoever, I very much doubt. But he tries.

Then there is another hazard. Completely innocently, he may contradict something that Paula has just said. If she notices this, MM will summon Paula and Milton. Together they will go back through the corridor to the main dressing room and put through a long-distance call to Lee Strasberg in New York, usually waking him up. Advice from the great oracle.

Quite apart from the tremendous cost, in phone bills and Strasberg bills, this is hardly a vote of confidence for SLO. He is the director of the damn film, for heaven's sake, as he often points out angrily – to me and to Milton, but not to MM. And it doesn't help the action much, since Lee Strasberg is normally sleepy, and has absolutely no idea of what is going on over here (I don't think he even has a script).

When we do re-start, if SLO lets so much as a glimmer of his rage appear, a bright red flush suffuses MM's famous chest and neck which even Whitey cannot make disappear. Then filming has to stop for an hour while MM calms down and prepares to try again.

It's true that MM doesn't notice much of what is going on around her, but the knowledge that 60 actors and technicians are waiting for you, and at enormous cost to you personally, is hardly one to induce calm in anyone, let alone someone with such a fragile grip on stability as MM. So there is a lot of handshaking and conferring, and finally she goes back to the main dressing room again to lie down. This in turn means that the dress must come off, and the wig must come off, so at least one and a half hours' delay is inevitable.

When we finally do get the shot, it is hardly as fresh as a daisy. SLO gets so tense that he can hardly act at all. Dame S stays as sweet as ever, but she loses that imperious edge that Martita Hunt* gave to the original role. Dame S is just too nice to be really royal. She has become like MM's dear old granny and this spills over into the part.

And yet, after all that grief, when we see the 'rushes' it is *MM* who lights up the screen.

It is very bad luck on SLO. After 'rushes,' he goes into his dressing room with Tony and Milton for yet more 'urgent discussions'. I see MM into her car and then go to the bar for a well-earned snort (brandy and water).

But this evening I had a hunch, and after half an hour I went back and started walking up and down outside the dressing rooms, while trying to look busy. Suddenly SLO stuck his head out, just as I guessed he might.

'Ah, Colin dear boy, could you pop over to the bar and get me some more cigarettes and a bottle of whisky?'

Well 'Colin' is determined to be the best damned 'gofer' in the movie world, so I opened the door of the empty dressing room next door, picked up the 100 Oliviers and the bottle of whisky I had left there, and marched straight in.

'Ah, thank you, dear boy,' said SLO, not bothering to question how I had got to the bar and back in 15 seconds. But Milton jolly well noticed and he gave me a very quizzical look.

From now on I must stay within range, and prepared, until SLO has left the studio altogether.

I can't even gossip with Gilman outside in the car. One quick drink and then back on duty. I want SLO to think of me as *indispensable*, and take me on to his next production, as he does so many of his loyal crew.

* (1900–69). British stage and screen actress, often cast in imperious roles (e.g. as Miss Havisham in David Lean's film of *Great Expectations*).

I'm afraid this all made me late for Anne's delicious supper, but Tony understands without me telling him and he is big-hearted enough to be happy about it.

From now on dinner will be at eight and not 7.30.

TUESDAY, 14 AUGUST

To forget one's lines in midstream is evidently something no professional actor ever does. In a long play in the theatre it might just be forgiven once or twice. But in a film . . . ?!

Speeches in a film are usually very short. Four or five sentences must be the longest scene MM has to remember in the whole movie. Anyone watching a well-edited film won't notice the cuts and will think they have just seen one continuously acted scene.

MM doesn't really forget her lines. It is more as if she had never quite learnt them – as if they are pinned to her mental noticeboard so loosely that the slightest puff of wind will send them floating to the floor.

This is very disconcerting to the other actors. Like going down a familiar staircase and missing a step, MM is suddenly not there. She can be in mid-speech, and then she gives a little frown, her lips part, her eyes look puzzled, and she stops. She doesn't say 'Oh drat, what is the next line?' or anything. She just stops.

Sickening pauses are not permissible on film. SLO says 'Cut' quietly (and grimly), or sometimes 'Keep rolling' to camera and 'Would you like to try again?' to Marilyn. This has not yet been a success. Even if MM does have another try before the camera stops running, she is too flustered and her eyes are glazed.

Most actresses would take a quick peek at the script – which Elaine has, ready to hold out – say 'Oh yes. I'm so sorry. I know it now,' and have another try. They would only need a brief reminder to get it right. Not our MM. She walks off the set, leans on her recliner and waits to be powdered by Make-up and pandered to by Paula.

She's almost like an athlete taking a little rest before having another try at the high jump. And it may be that she feels that that *is* exactly what she is doing.

Dame S had a long line about Eleanora Duse being a much greater actress than Sarah Bernhardt. MM simply could not remember when to reply. Dame S is babbling on and ends with a rhetorical question: 'You agree. No?'

All MM had to say was 'No' at the right moment, but today even this proved too complicated. In the end we broke the shot down. We filmed the whole Dame S sequence, with MM missing out the 'No' altogether, and then filmed MM in close-up saying 'No?' which the editor will cut in later.

Halfway through, SLO tried a controlled explosion. MM was stunned, as usual, but SLO had reckoned without Dame S who promptly gave him a good ticking off.

'Don't you realise what a strain this poor girl is under? She hasn't had your years of experience. She is far from home in a strange country, trying to act in a strange part. Are you helping or bullying?' Poor SLO, who naturally thinks he is the injured party, was stunned.

MM was radiant.

'Oh thank you so much, Dame Sybil. But I mustn't forget my lines. I promise I'll try to remember them from now on.'

And she was good as gold for the rest of the afternoon.

Tony B thought this vastly amusing – 'Laurence got a scolding from Grandma,' he told Anne at dinner.

But SLO did not. 'It's high time someone gave that silly girl a real telling off,' he said to me, after Milton had left.

I worship SLO but I am afraid he is wrong.

WEDNESDAY, 15 AUGUST

I suppose you could say that today was a red-letter day. This morning I definitely saw more of MM than I ever expected to, and she went up in my estimation in more ways than one. She arrived really early, for her, and nearly caught us on the hop at 7.30 a.m. She was still in a jolly mood – I expect she and AM had had a good laugh over SLO's discomfiture.

As lunchtime drew near David caught me in the corridor, and told me to look for MM's marked script which was missing. I assumed this meant MM was on the set so I just barged into her dressing room and straight into the inner sanctum. What David had not told me was that filming had already ended.

There stood MM, completely nude, with only a white towel round her head.

I stopped dead. All I could see were beautiful white and pink curves. I must have gone as red as a beetroot. I couldn't even turn and rush out, so I just stood there and stared and stammered.

MM gave me her most innocent smile.

'Oh Colin,' she said. 'And you an old Etonian!'

How did she stay so cool? And how did she know which school I had gone to and what it meant?

When I managed to get out of the room and pull myself together, I realised that behind the fog MM could be a bit brighter than we all think. How much of the MM image is contrived? Acting dumb is a good way to make other people make fools of themselves. What fun it might have been to make a movie with MM when she felt everyone around was her friend.

Dream on, Colin

In the afternoon we filmed Dame S putting her jewellery onto MM in preparation for her going to the Coronation, as Dame S's lady-in-waiting.

I don't know what happened at lunchtime – I hardly think it was my bursting in on her that did it – but MM had become really confused.

As Dame S and her original lady-in-waiting fuss round her, Elsie Marina has to ask 'What's happening? Is it a game?'

All light-hearted stuff, but by now MM was so frightened of missing her cue that she got frantic.

'What's happening?' she screamed in genuine distress. 'Is it a game?' like someone who is afraid they are being kidnapped.

No one could calm her down, so that's how it will go into the film. I hope it works.

We saw the 'rushes' of yesterday's footage, when her previous long scene with Dame S was broken down into three shots, and frankly I don't think that does work. When Jack lights a wide group shot he lights it quite differently from a close-up, especially MM. For the close-up he darkens the background and uses all sorts of filters to make MM look her best. That's fine, and MM does indeed look extremely beautiful, but it doesn't seem to match up with the wide shot which it will have to fit into. The wide shots look like a stage play, the close-ups are as intense as Garbo.

Yesterday MM had to look a little confused and say 'No?' It isn't hard for MM to look confused, so that worked fine. But today, when she looked very confused, it was almost too real for a light drawing-room comedy.

That is what this film is meant to be, and indeed that is what MM can often play so well.

SLO might have been able to handle this if he was left alone. But everything has to bounce off Paula, and Paula always sees things in dramatic terms.

No wonder Jack Harris, the editor, haunts the studio like a gloomy vulture. He is going to have a tough job.

THURSDAY, 16 AUGUST

Nearly finished with Dame S – only three more shooting days. She starts in a stage play next week and is very tired. She is already in rehearsal, but she is still the only one to arrive on time (6.45) and we always have a little chat (she knows M and D of course). SLO's arrival is nearer to 7.15 these days and is always grim. Dicky Wattis and Paul Hardwick come tumbling in at the same time, but all the others use a different entrance.

Dicky and Paul have become my special chums. Paul plays the Major Domo, and has hardly any lines. This is a pity because he has a wonderful rich, dark baritone voice. I suppose this is his main asset as an actor. On this occasion it is wasted, but it certainly means that David has to 'sssh' him more than most when we are gossiping on the set. Dicky is always impeccably dressed in his Foreign Office uniform, with its gold braid and white stockings. He has a very 'camp' sense of humour, with lots of 'double entendres'. He is always ready with his lines, and never flustered by whatever MM does, or doesn't do. But he is so quintessentially British that she usually gazes at him as if he was from another planet. Dicky and SLO and Dame S can go through a scene like a knife through butter, and if MM is in the scene too, but doesn't have a line to remember, she quite enjoys herself, like a schoolgirl on a train. It is extraordinary that an actress can get so far without ever really being taught. MM just relies on her native savvy. Imagine what she would be like if she'd spent a year in rep. Or would the magic disappear?

Talking of magic, I now have a real problem with my little Wdg. She is convinced that I am going to take someone else out this Saturday, and won't even let me explain. The atmosphere in the Wd department is so tense I can't even go in there. Wdg hides behind the racks of costumes, crying, while the wardrobe boss growls like a tigress. No sympathy from David when I explained the problem.

'The first lesson on any film production is not to shit on your own doorstep. Now you're stuck with this for another three months. I'm not having you unable to go up to Wardrobe for the rest of the film, so SORT IT OUT!'

What a nightmare. The trouble is that you can't discuss things logically with a little Wdg. I'll have to find the right cliché.

FRIDAY, 17 AUGUST

Dame S has left now and will be much missed. She had a calming, reassuring effect on MM, while SLO definitely puts the poor girl on edge. This morning MM had to eat a late supper, on screen. She had herself chosen caviar and chicken salad, but there were problems. It requires many 'takes' under hot lights to get a scene right, so fresh caviar and a new chicken salad were produced for each take. However there is a limit to the number of times that even the greatest actress can tuck into caviar and chicken salad at 11 in the morning.

I thought she did jolly well.

SLO kept telling her not to eat, 'just mime', but MM is now a '*method*' actress. She has to know what her motivation is for each action and each word, and miming does not come naturally to her. Nor did she appreciate the substitution of apple juice for champagne. Real champagne was produced, but it quickly got warm under the lights. By this time MM was supposed to have drunk lots of vodka (which was water of course) and she began to slurp on the real champagne a bit too greedily. SLO as the Grand Duke was on the telephone in the back of the set and couldn't see what was happening. Tony began to get nervous about continuity. How drunk was she meant to be? Soon Elaine, the continuity girl, was beginning to direct the movie. MM liked this but the rest of the crew did not.

SLO sensed impending chaos and got frantic, huffing and puffing away from the far corner.

MM was enjoying herself. She also had a chance to be patriotic about America and raised her glass to toast 'the President' (Taft), which was an action she found profoundly sympathetic to her mood. I'm sure she feels that the British treat Americans as if they were idiots every bit as much as the Carpathians did in 1911. As MM got more confident, SLO began to fade, very rare for him. It is hard to believe that even a Carpathian Grand Duke would be quite so wooden to a young lady he is hoping to go to bed with in half an hour.

In the afternoon, Jeremy Spenser* appeared for his first entrance. He looks 16 but I suppose he is about 22. I recognise him from

* Former child star, b.1937. He was playing the part of Nicky, the young King.

somewhere. Did he play Sabu, the elephant boy?* It's the sort of question that is hard to ask.

In this part his carefully contrived royal charm, flicked on and off as if by a switch, is more convincing than SLO's, and he is equally smooth off-screen. MM seems to like him but perhaps it is also because his character in the script is so sympathetic to hers.

It is clear that she does sometimes have difficulty separating fact from fiction, as many actresses do. Vivien, after all, has never quite escaped from Scarlett O'Hara. In the *Sleeping Prince* story, SLO plays an insensitive seducer, and MM must have come across a great many of those in her early career. In real life, he plays an insensitive director, and she has come across those before too. It is not a happy combination.

And we still have to get through the love scenes!

SUNDAY, 19 AUGUST

Terry Rattigan's party last night was as formal and artificial as his plays.

He has a typical expensive show-business house on Wentworth golf course – 1920s classical, and very nouveau riche; thick carpets, chandeliers, flowers.

I got there early, and alone, and the first person I saw was Mr P. I got a shock as it was the only time I'd ever seen him not in his brown suit. He was wearing an old-fashioned dinner jacket, and a wing collar, but at least he still had his pipe and hornrim specs. With him was Mrs P. She is just as conventional as he is, and clearly very proud of her old stick of a husband. Perfect casting!

Terry R was in a white dinner jacket beaming urbanely at everyone (though not me).

Milton was there with Amy – small and attractive, both of them.

---

* In fact the title role in *Elephant Boy* (1937) was played by the *actor* Sabu (Sabu Dastagir, 1924–63).

Finally AM and MM. AM looked very dashing, also in a white dinner jacket – strong jaw, intense gaze, the perfect he-man intellectual. I fancy he is very vain indeed.

MM looked a bit straggly. She had done her hair herself and she had not been made up by Whitey. She even seemed a bit scared, not of us, but of AM. He really is unpleasant. He struts around as if MM were his property. He seems to think his superior intelligence puts him on a higher plane, and treats her as if she is just an accessory. Poor MM. Another insensitive male in her life is the last thing she needs. I can't see the romance lasting long. She is the one who could be forgiven a little vanity but, strangely enough, that's not in her make-up at all.

I hung around SLO in case I could be of help, but he was soon surrounded by people of greater assumed self-importance, mainly agents.

Cecil Tennant treats me like an office boy, which I am I suppose. He is married to a Russian ballerina* and even she is not very friendly, which is a surprise. All the ballerinas I've ever met are adorable. Karsavina,** who we once met in Hampstead, was as lovely as Margot, although very old.

The party just never gelled. I bet it would have been another matter if we were all queer. (Gaiety, everyone!) I left early and went up to London. I went to the Stork Club and in the end I was unfaithful to the Wdg – so she was right!

MONDAY, 20 AUGUST

A bad start to the week. MM did not show up until 11 a.m. Frantic phone calls to Plod at Parkside were to no avail, although he did hint darkly that AM and MM were not on such friendly terms as usual. I thought so on Saturday at the party.

---

* Irina Baronova, star of the de Basil Ballet in the 1930s.
** Original Prima Ballerina of the Diaghileff company, partner of Nijinsky.

I reported this to SLO. He said that AM is short of funds, and has finally figured out that when MM is late at the studio, she loses money. And when MM loses money, he does not exactly get richer. Like many American intellectuals he is extremely mean – or maybe meanness goes with vanity, like Garrett Moore. In any case he has been trying to get MM out of the house earlier in the mornings.

I suspect he also wants peace and quiet. I certainly wouldn't want a frantic MM in my bedroom all morning, unless of course we were 'playing trains' in Plod's immortal words. Now, it seems, AM has lost some of his powers of persuasion. Nobody knows, or will say, what the trouble really is.

We did all the shots of SLO and Jeremy which MM isn't in, but we couldn't work with her until after lunch. When we did it was a long scene and not all that easy. She comes in through the door of the purple room with Dicky W and says, 'Oh, we are the first to arrive, aren't we?'

Then there is a change of thought, which is always tough for MM unless very carefully explained by one (and only one) person. She looks round the opulent room and is supposed to say: 'Gee, this is all right too, isn't it.'

Alas, it was not carefully explained (and never by one person) until after tempers had already begun to fray (about take 5). In she came each time:

'Oh, we are the first to arrive, aren't we?' Fine so far.

'Gee, this is all right, isn't it?'

'CUT.'

'Wonderful, Marilyn darling, but the line is "Gee, this is all right TOO, isn't it?"'

Much conferring. Much 'Oh yeah, gee, I guess so,' much leaning, flicking of fingers, whispers from Paula, powder reapplied, wig patted, dress straightened and off we go again.

David shouts: 'Going for a take. Absolute QUIET please.'

The lights come on with a crash. Bells ring, doors lock with a clunk, red lights flash.

'Camera running.'

'Sound.' Beep, beep.

'Speed.'

'Mark it.'

'*Prince and the Showgirl* shot 48 take 6.' SNAP.

'Action.'

MM and Dicky come through the doors.

'Oh, we are the first to arrive, aren't we?'

We hold our breath. MM looks round.

'Gee, this is all right, isn't it.'

'CUT!' etc. etc.

In the end it was Dicky who explained to her that in an earlier scene, not yet filmed, she had come in to the hall of the Embassy and said 'Gee, this is all right.' That is why it was now so important to say 'Gee, this is all right too!'

Finally she got it right and carried on to the end of the scene without a hitch, but what a painful hour it took.

Like a Greek tragedy, it really isn't anyone's fault. SLO would normally take his leading lady quietly to one side and explain it after the first mistake. But MM is all revved up by Paula, before each scene, to go it alone. And after she makes a mistake, which in this case Paula probably didn't even notice, it is Paula and not her director to whom she runs. When the wretched director does intervene, simply to get his film back on the rails, MM is already upset, and it is hard to talk to her on any level.

What is so frustrating is that we all know that in the end only the good take will be printed, and tomorrow evening MM will fly out of the 'rushes' like an angel.

At this rate the film will take forever. I don't know why we are all so fed up with that purple room set but we are. It is cut in half, and sometimes in quarters, so that the camera can shoot in different directions, across the table, above the sofa, looking at the fireplace, or the windows or the door. But it always feels claustrophobic. I expect it is the colour. The whole crew feels the same. Only Dicky's camp, unprintable comments break the tension.

Whenever something goes wrong in the studio during filming, the blame either falls on MM or on some technical mystery. But today I think the blame fell on the doors – those doors into the purple room through which everyone has to enter. Mind you I'm not sure if SLO or Tony or David would agree.

In the opening shot of the day, MM was due to burst in through these doors and surprise Dicky and SLO. She had been 'below stairs' with Nicky, the young King, and the Grand Duke has only just been told that she is still in the Embassy. He is expecting an old flame, Lady Sunningdale, to come to supper. Lady Sunningdale is late and he says he wishes she had grown out of that habit. His line is: 'She has had, after all, time,' and that was MM's cue. Her line is: 'Hello. Oh – supper! How thoughtful of you, darling. I'll just run down and say goodnight to Nicky. See you in a minute.' Then exit. Not too hard for her – all one 'thought'.

David shouts: 'Let's go for a take. QUIET studio.' MM is tucked into a little bit of corridor outside the doors, where she can hear SLO's cue. We go through the ritual as usual. Lights, Camera, Sound etc. 'Action.'

SLO: 'She has had, after all, time.'

Nothing. The doors do not move an inch. No sound. No clues. Nothing.

'CUT.' Controlled passion now from Tony.

'Marilyn? Is anything the matter behind there?' Muffled grunts.

'COLIN!' Would you go behind those doors and see if you can help Miss Monroe!' I dash round the corners of the set (quite a long way, as it happens) to find MM smiling mildly in her little alcove. She seems as mystified as everyone else.

'Any problems, Miss Monroe?' She shakes her head with wide eyes.

I am not empowered to say 'Well, what the hell is going on then?'
so I squeeze into the little alcove with her and wait.

'Going for a take, studio?' I hear distantly.

'Lights.'

'Camera.'

'Sound.'

'Action.'

SLO: 'She has had, after all, time.'

I am holding the handle of the door, and I pull it firmly towards
me, so that MM can burst in with her line. Nothing. The door doesn't
budge. Then and only then do I remember that the doors open inward
and not out into the corridor. Too late. There is a bellow of rage
simultaneously from Tony, David and SLO. 'COLIN!'

I caught MM's eye and we both dissolved into total, helpless
giggles. The more they cursed from the other side of those nice
strong doors, the more we laughed. The tears literally ran down
our cheeks and we were both incapable of speech. David marched
across the set and flung open the doors to expose us to the whole
studio, helpless as naughty school children. MM buried her face in
her hands and rushed off to Make-up for half an hour – plenty of
time for me to get an old-fashioned roasting from David and Tony.
I couldn't really explain, and nobody in the whole studio thought it
was funny – except for Marilyn and me. She really can be adorable
when she is human like that.

Tony was very gruff at dinner tonight, but Anne thought it hilarious. How like a married couple.

WEDNESDAY, 22 AUGUST

'Vivien is coming to pay us a visit today,' said SLO when he arrived
this morning. 'Call me when Marilyn gets here. I'd better butter her
up a bit first.'

Gilman gave me a wicked grin. Vivien is famous for being unbelievably catty while at the same time being unbelievably charming. I

did not think Vivien's visit was a good idea, under the circumstances, but of course no one can stop Vivien doing something if she has a mind to it. It was Vivien who created MM's role on stage, and MM knows this well. I suppose Vivien would have liked to do the movie herself too. 'But Larry went and fell in love with Marilyn, silly boy,' she said to me at Notley: 'And a fat lot of good that did him.' (Vivien is *always* right.)

I suggested caution to SLO, but he had a mischievous look in his eye. Perhaps he thought Vivien might inspire MM to greater efforts.

Vivien arrived at lunchtime, after we had endured another painful session in the purple room. SLO, in full costume, escorted her on to the set as if she were royalty.

'Hello, Colin darling' – that got the crew's attention – 'Are you looking after Larry for me like you promised?'

Me: 'Gulp.'

Tony: 'We are all trying our best, Vivien.'

Vivien advanced and, to MM's intense surprise, kissed her lightly on both cheeks.

'Marilyn,' she sighed, 'Larry tells me you are quite, quite superb. He never stops singing your praises. I'm getting a little jealous.'

Very sweet, very sincere, what an actress! MM smiled and fluttered her eyelids, easily flattered although not quite convinced. Since Vivien was looking stunning in a little Jacques Fath suit and MM was looking like a plump frump in a towelling robe, the crew could hardly imagine Vivien being jealous. But still, it was a true meeting of the stars. Everyone was impressed, even Paula. Vivien quickly made her excuses.

'I know how frantically hard Larry makes you all work etc.,' and she vanished in a cloud of very expensive perfume. Even David, who has bellowed at every film star in Britain, was in a bit of a dream.

MM took a long time to emerge in the afternoon, but she did definitely seem more committed and we got a surprising amount done. Tomorrow we do the love stuff on the armchair. Fingers crossed.

THURSDAY, 23 AUGUST

I have been watching MM very closely. She is really like a lovely child. Whatever possessed her to become an actress? I suppose it was some sort of clichéd idea about Hollywood. In America pretty blondes with buxom figures often think that they are meant to be film stars. Or perhaps it was some man who found that the quickest way into her pants was to promise that he could get her into movies. MM is certainly very ambitious. Once she got to LA,* I'm sure she found a whole string of men who told her that they could get her into the movies, and she must have been very single-minded to get where she has. Many pretty girls are convinced that they are 'someone special', and she was proved right!

A natural on camera MM certainly is, but a great actress she is not. When SLO, or Dicky or Dame Sybil act, they stop being who they are and become the character who they are acting. They enjoy changing into someone else completely. It feels natural to them, often better than real life. They can become heroes, villains, lunatics, poets etc. depending on the script they are given.

With the minor actors on the set it may be different. Take the footmen, for example. One or two may be burning with ambition. They will be acting footmen with all their might – dreaming of the day when they will be acting the Grand Duke. The other two may be earning their living the easiest way they can, and just walking where they are told to, without a thought in their heads.

MM is different again. She desperately wants to be an 'actress'. She has been told many times, by the people who see her magic in front of the camera, and also by unscrupulous people who just want her money, that she is a wonderful '*actress*'. She is not. MM is always MM. Can one imagine her playing a ruthless spy? Most of the time she is desperately trying to remember her lines and the 'motivation' of the character who speaks them. This automatically

---

* In fact she was brought up in Los Angeles.

precludes 'being' the character. The *character* doesn't have to think of lines and motivation. So the process of acting is very frightening for her. She needs Paula a few feet away and Lee at the end of a phone to reassure her. But there is no easy formula, no short cut. I suspect that there have been quite a few 'Paulas' in the past, and all of them will ultimately fail because they are substitutes for a training which is just not there.

FRIDAY, 24 AUGUST

MM's scenes are made even harder by the idiotic Rattigan script. In the middle of her first love scene, after the Grand Duke has finally kissed her on the sofa, she is supposed to run her fingers through his hair. Well this is very difficult and unpleasant because SLO's hair is greased absolutely flat, but would she really ask him what he used on it? She's not a beautician. But this is what the script would have her do.

'Oh, a little pomade,' the Grand Duke replies abstractedly, and she is meant to reply 'You should use Pinaud's "Lilac".'

What on earth is this interchange doing in the love scene between Marilyn Monroe and Laurence Olivier? It's hardly the place for a witty quip, or a laugh for that matter.

It was far too much for MM to remember – no 'motivation' at all. She plunged in bravely, forgot, desperately tried to remember after all, and finally blurted out: 'You should use' – loud squeak – 'I know, er, er, er, PINAUD'S "LILAC"' giggle giggle. SLO, his face two inches from hers and due to kiss her passionately in the next shot, was trying frantically to cover the gaps and keep a straight face.

'Think of love, my darling,' he gabbled. 'Don't forget our *love*.'

After many attempts, he decided to print everything and choose the best one. Everyone hopes it will work, but it may look a little odd, to say the least. Perhaps it will be a triumph of nature over art.

It has been a tough week. SLO and Milton are shattered. So is AM. He came over to collect MM but ended up sending her on ahead with Paula and Whitey and Plod. I went into SLO's dressing room with fresh whisky and cigarettes.

'I've had it,' said SLO. 'I think I'll go off to China for a month.'

'I'll come with you,' said Milton, laughing.

'So will I,' said AM grimly.

'Come now, dear boy,' said SLO. 'Your new bride.'

'She's devouring me,' I heard AM say as I left.

Three strong, famous men all in awe of that young lady. Luckily they take no notice of me whatsoever, which I *think* is a compliment.

Before I left the studio, Plod rang from Parkside. MM had announced that she wants to go shopping tomorrow – incognito. Plod is nervous and wants me there too. Parkside at 10 a.m. But no one is to tell Milton. I went and told Milton right away and then came back here for supper.

SATURDAY, 25 AUGUST

I arrived at Parkside at 9.45 a.m. Milton was already there.

'Colin. What's the smartest shopping street in London?'

'Bond Street.'

'OK. We'll go there.'

Plod went off to make a discreet phone call (to Gerald Row Police Station I expect) and Milton and I sat and waited . . . for one and a half hours. Milton is a great charmer, very easygoing and direct. He told me he used to be a top photographer which is how he got to meet MM.* He genuinely feels that MM was being exploited by 20th Century Fox – nothing new about that – and he wanted to help her escape from her contract. And that I can understand too. Everyone who meets MM wants to help her, even me. It is another part of her magic. Milton teamed up with a lawyer called Irving Stein who Milton said is as brilliant as he is unsympathetic. (The 'unsympathetic' bit is right. I 'met' him when MM first arrived.) Together they succeeded

---

* They had had a brief affair in 1949.

in getting MM free and Milton set up Marilyn Monroe Productions. But he underestimated the power that MM generates, and the number of people who are determined to get a piece of that power. Trying to control MM is like riding a tiger. With the best will in the world, you can't really control, or even forecast, which way it is going to go. So Milton is forever trying to *manipulate* MM with promises, threats, even drugs* – and he has to compete with Paula, AM, Hedda Rosten, various psychiatrists and doctors and, ultimately, SLO and me. I feel sorry for Milton. He wants to get the film made as much as we do, and he has a very difficult job, as pig in the middle.

When MM did come down at 11.30 she was in a sulky mood. She was all in beige as usual – tight blouse, slacks, head scarf – and dark glasses, with very little make-up. She looked like she had when she first turned up at the studio. She was not in the least surprised to see Milton, or me. AM and MM and Milton and Plod got into the Princess and I followed in the Bristol. When we got to Bond Street, I could immediately see a problem. We were late, as usual, and all the shops were going to shut at 12.30 (Saturday early closing). Nobody else in the party seemed to mind, however, so we all got out and trooped along behind AM and MM. As AM is pretty tall and MM is pretty wiggly, we expected quite a reaction, but no one seemed to notice. The most famous couple in the world (bar two, I suppose**) were strolling along a busy street with no protection, and nothing happened.

All of a sudden Milton realised that MM was *not* happy about this. She wanted to be incognito, but she didn't want to be *that* incognito. Not mobbed, perhaps, but a round of applause might have been nice! But the shops were now shutting and the crowds were thinning out.

'Where are the big shops, Colin? Where is everybody?'

I wheeled the party into Regent Street. I could see a few policemen

---

* Though never hard drugs.

** The other two couples I had in mind were Jacqueline and John F. Kennedy, and Prince Rainier and Princess Grace (Grace Kelly).

around, winking at Plod, so I felt reassured. Then suddenly we were surrounded. I don't know who spread the word, the police or Milton, or perhaps some reporter Milton had called earlier. The crowds picked up the scent of a 'star' and it took all Plod's chums to help us fight our way back to the cars. For the first time I saw how dangerous a leaderless mob can be, although in this case they were driven only by curiosity. Poor MM was quite upset and shaking, despite AM's arm round her. But perhaps she is used to this sort of horror, and even welcomes it, to confirm her view of the awfulness of her life. AM had also had quite a fright, though nothing really shakes his air of smug complacency. He is much more pleased with himself than MM is with herself, that's for sure. Plod worships MM, and can't stand AM, and nor can I. (And to be honest, we are probably a little bit jealous too!)

MONDAY, 27 AUGUST

No MM today. Calls to Plod yielded no clues, and at lunchtime we gave up hope. Finally AM called to say that MM wasn't well. A fever. Hmm. We had some shots we could do with SLO, Paul and Dicky. We also have prepared the corridor outside the purple room for shots of the valet and the other staff playing music in case MM doesn't come tomorrow.

When MM isn't on the set, SLO is a different man – tough, direct, clear-minded. Filming goes like clockwork, of course, because the other actors know him so well. But we all seem to feel that the centre of the film is missing, that what we are doing is peripheral. It's almost too easy. MM is so difficult to work with that even hardened technicians are driven crazy. But when she doesn't show up, we miss her! What a paradox. All of a sudden, filming is so routine that there is nothing to write about.

TUESDAY, 28 AUGUST

Despite our fears, MM did show up this morning, and at 8.30, but she didn't look well. I reported as much to SLO in his dressing room. A lot of people see each of them as soon as they arrive, but I'm the only one who sees them both.

'What shall we do, Colin?' he said wearily. 'What can we do?'

'Can we switch to something simple? It's that or nothing, I fear.'

'OK, send Jack (Cardiff) along. And Elaine (Continuity). We've got time to change things around.'

I explained the situation to Jack, and to David. Jack went to see MM for himself, but came out after a few minutes.

'I think she's drugged,' he said to SLO. They looked at the shot list to find something easy which we could use in the only set which was already built and lit. Luckily there were two shots of MM in close-up, lying on the floor. Jack went off and spent an hour with MM's stand-in and the lighting crew. At this stage in the film, MM is supposed to have drunk too much vodka and passed out just as the Grand Duke is about to seduce her. So all she had to do this morning was to lie back and giggle 'Oh, look at those lovely cherubs on the ceiling,' and 'Good night, my darling. See you in the morning.'

Even in her woozy state, MM managed to do this quite quickly, so after lunch we filmed her and SLO on the sofa. By now she was so relaxed that she was actually very funny. Dicky W has to burst in and interrupt SLO and MM in a clinch. He has an alibi that MM no longer needs.

'Your aunt has been in a serious motor accident, Miss Marina.'

'Oh, go away you silly man,' giggled MM. 'Serve her right. She shouldn't be out at this time of night. She's 93!' More giggles. Suddenly she really was *acting*. And for a moment we forgave her everything.

WEDNESDAY, 29 AUGUST

MM was very late this morning. Paula was tense and Milton was even tenser. Plod told me that MM and AM had a row in the night, and AM could not control MM at all. She was wandering around the house in a very distressed state. There had been a lot of phone calls, many of them transatlantic. Finally Milton had gone over with extra pills. MM had called for Whitey Snyder, but of course he is long gone. In the end one of the doctors in New York talked to her until she was calm enough to go to sleep. (Imagine what *that* cost!) AM had completely washed his hands of her, and Paula, usually her best friend and sort of surrogate mum, couldn't help on this occasion. Although Paula does want to control MM as an actress, she genuinely does not want to get between MM and AM.

We managed one long-shot of MM warning the Grand Duke that he'd better watch out because she is falling in love with him – just before she passes out.

SLO had to murmur 'Oh my darling, my beloved' or some such nonsense just to keep her going, and this did seem to test *his* acting skills to the limit. MM was in another world – quite cheerful but ga-ga. Booze *and* drugs I suspect. Nothing seemed to get through to her. But she is meant to be drunk in that scene, so I expect it will look wonderful, as usual. At least the scene is 'in the can'. When MM went back to her dressing room, it was clear she wouldn't be back on the set again, even though she didn't leave the studio.

We did reaction shots on SLO but our troubles weren't over. A piece of painted ceiling to go over SLO's head – referred to by MM yesterday – 'Oh what pretty cherubs . . .' – was not ready and there was a great row. Teddy, Roger and even Carmen were all in a flap. I think it was partly the aftermath of the tension with MM. When she is so removed from the everyday world we live in, it is very hard to keep patience. The whole studio gets 'on edge'. One thing is certain, however. If you scream at her or even frown, she retreats further into her unreal world, and gets even harder to reach. SLO calls it the Ophelia Complex. We don't expect her in tomorrow.

THURSDAY, 30 AUGUST

AM went off to Paris today, which may explain why MM was in such bad shape yesterday. Rumour has it that he is going back to NYC after Paris and will be away for over 10 days. AM seems big-headed, insensitive and super-selfish. I never saw him look tenderly at MM, only with what looks like a sort of boasting self-satisfaction. What bad luck on MM. Why couldn't she have found what she really needs – someone sympathetic to support her? She doesn't move around with those sort of people I suppose.

We've finished all the 'cut-away' shots we can in the purple room. We will do the Grand Duke's dressing room next, and then we will move on to the hall and staircase.

In the meantime, we have scheduled a day on the lot for tomorrow. We have ordered all the 'extras' available – about 500 – from the FAA. The costumes are already prepared, which means a lot of visits to the wardrobe department. The atmosphere up there is arctic, but, alas, there is nothing I can do. It is over. Poor little Wdg. She'll probably be married in a couple of years. Two kids and a family car. Wdg heaven!

Milton spent a long time with SLO and they decided to give MM a day off tomorrow. Then she can have a long weekend to rest in. She doesn't claim to be ill, but there is definitely more than one problem on her mind. Perhaps with AM gone, she'll get a chance to work quietly on the script with Paula. A lot of film stars first look at the day's lines while they are being made up – as MM does – but no other actor on this film does that. SLO expects them to know the whole script by heart before they arrive, like in a play.

FRIDAY, 31 AUGUST

500 extras are a hell of a handful. Just as David warned, they go to amazing lengths to avoid working. They also make desperate efforts to get paid double and the combination of both these pressures is bizarre. If they are in a medium shot with a principal actor, what they call 'cameo', they get more. If they have any special responsibility – whistling, juggling, grinning, they get more. If they wear any item of their own clothing, they get more etc. They are each issued with a pay slip and it is up to the assistant directors to add on bonus items. We also have to sign each slip before they can get paid at all. Our ultimate threat is to sign them off early, or refuse to sign. This is very often threatened, all day long, but almost never done. Poor things, they are the absolute bottom of the acting profession, but some of them have a pathetic desire to be appreciated. Quite a few get steady work, especially if they are chosen to be a stand-in. Most of them have other professions to keep them going. The oldest are in their 70s – wise, benevolent, seen it all, and looked up to by the young ones. They are successful career extras! But a lot of the ladies look like ageing nightclub hostesses, and the men like street buskers. Quite depressing.

Today we had to get them all done up like a 1911 Coronation crowd. Then they had to be individually vetted to make sure they weren't wearing modern spectacles, watches and so on. Finally they were arranged in a long stand lining the roadside. The 'roadside' was actually a track for the camera to run on with a wide column at either end. The camera rode down this on a 'dolly', panning past the waving, cheering crowd, from column to column. Then we 'cut', re-arranged the crowd, pulled the camera back to its original position, and did it again. By splicing the film, or mixing from shot to shot, as the camera went past a column, the crowd could appear to be as large and long as was needed. It will be projected behind the coach with SLO and MM in it on its way to the Abbey.

Needless to say, when we filled the stand, it was only half full.

David roared and stamped and we all went off like hounds, in search of the rest. The men's lavatories yielded 14, playing cards, with a bottle of whisky between them. Many threats and pleadings later they were on parade. The ladies' lavatories were the same. There was even a card game going on under the stand itself. The canteen, which was off limits as they will be given lunch boxes, had almost 30! At last we got about enough and we stopped counting. (They are very adept at confusing a count to protect their 'mates'.)

David and I and another two second assistant directors yelled and applauded and waved and cheered to encourage them to do the same. Then we mixed them up and did it again. It was a lovely sunny day, which helped us a lot, but apparently that is a very *bad* thing for the film. It seems we have some real Coronation footage (Elizabeth II) which will be cut in with our footage to make it more impressive, and of course on QE's Coronation it never stopped raining, so the two footages might not match. How perverse.

We did the whole operation about 10 times, until everyone was fed up, not to say rebellious. We then took the opportunity to audition some of them for the ballroom scene, in a rehearsal room with a piano. We will need a mass of dancers for the Grand Ball, and we can get them from ballroom dancing clubs, but NOT until every member of the FAA who can put one foot in front of another to music has been given a chance. Otherwise we will have a strike. They all want to work, so many of them claimed to be experts, but in the end we took only eight couples, and they are not much cop. It was a sop to the union to take any at all, but hopefully they won't be noticed in a crowd of professionals.

SUNDAY, 2 SEPTEMBER

Last night, after an excellent dinner, Tony told me of a rumour that MM was pregnant!! He is very alarmed. Will we soon have to cope with morning sickness, depression etc. as well as everything else? He wanted me to try to check it out with the household before he told SLO and started a panic. So this morning I rang Plod and went over to Parkside for a quiet chat, on the pretext of talking to the staff. (They are restless, as usual.) Plod was very jolly. He would confirm nothing but just put a finger beside his nose with his lips sealed. I'm not quite sure if this means 'yes' or 'no', but I assume 'yes'. Plod is the only one who never seems to be affected by the lunacy going on all round him. As he is now more loyal to MM than to me, and quite rightly so, I couldn't ask for details. Plod and I are close, but MM is his employer. She never speaks to him. He's like a stout walking-stick for her to lean on and he's very happy just to be that.

Paula appeared, looking as if she was trying to keep calm in a whirlwind. I sympathise with her. She has definitely bitten off more than she can chew. In the beginning, it was Milton who undertook to deliver MM's person, and Paula who undertook to deliver her performance. Now they are both facing failure. The whole film – and a lot of money – depends on their success but they both seem to have run out of ideas.

AM has left the country, and Hedda Rosten is no help at all. Plod says she encourages MM to drink champagne with her at all hours of the day. Naturally this makes MM feel ghastly and so she starts hitting the pills. There is no discipline whatsoever, and when Paula and Milton try to impose some, they become very unpopular and have to back off to survive. Hopeless.

I came back and told Tony there was no truth in the rumour about the pregnancy. Why give SLO another worry when there is nothing we can do about it? If the rumour does turn out to be true, we will all simply have to adapt as best we can, or the film will grind to a halt.

MONDAY, 3 SEPTEMBER

Once again, MM surprised us. Today she was inspired to make an enormous effort by the music. She has two music scenes in the film and they are being shot 'back to back'. The first was her dance to the music of a barrel organ, which was coming in through the open windows of the purple room. Richard Addinsell has written two pretty tunes for her, and this one is light and happy. MM is, as always, in that gorgeous white figure-hugging creation of Bumble's, and it is perfect for dancing.

The dances in this film are all 'choreographed' by Billy Chappell.* He is as camp as coffee but he is very sweet and cosy and gets on well with MM. All in all it was a delightful scene and MM did it exquisitely. The dance is interrupted by the young King, Jeremy Spenser, and it was easy to see that he was genuinely impressed by MM's performance. He is now almost the only person whom MM still likes, so it ended up a successful day.

One has to remember that even though MM is making a film with SLO, it is up to MM to make it something special – a super-star creation. SLO has made many films – some great and some mouldy. Only on stage, to a very limited audience, can he be seen as the great actor he is. And MM is carrying quite a lot of other burdens as well – a husband who is unsupportive, and away; a manager who could be seen as exploiting her, and 'best friends' who are sycophantic and weak. 'Ruth amid the alien corn' really. MM rose to where she is now by being stronger, more talented and more ambitious than the competition. I dread to think how many blonde bombshells there are in Hollywood right now, trying to get where MM got by any means, fair or foul.

Whenever I meet anyone who has got right to the top, I always notice that they have something extra that ordinary people – including me alas – do not have. And that 'little extra', whatever it is, does not mean that they have a happy or an easy life – quite the contrary. We have no right to demand that they share that little extra with us and then criticise them for being different or difficult or 'dangerous to know'. MM has more than a little extra, and yet the technicians expect her to behave like a twopenny Rank starlet. If I was SLO I

---

* Chappell (1908–94) started out as a dancer with the Rambert company. He went on to design ballets, light reviews and plays.

would tell them off, and lay out the red carpet for MM every day. But that would mean telling himself off too, and admitting that while he is great in many ways, it is MM who is the MOVIE STAR.

TUESDAY, 4 SEPTEMBER

Inspired by the success of the dance scene, MM was in a more confident mood than I have seen her for some time. The set was declared 'closed' (i.e. no spectators) — as if it had ever been open. This was because MM had to sing the whole of the Sleeping Prince Waltz to SLO, in a close two-shot.

It did at least mean a minimum of hangers-on, with no Drapes, Chippies, Plasterers and Props, who are usually hanging around, 'just in case'. Those who were essential but not absolutely essential — i.e. most people — were kept firmly out of sight. MM was kneeling over SLO on the purple sofa, in the purple room. She had quite a long, difficult speech, leading into the song. SLO was prepared to break it down into two extra shots. Instead of one shot for the whole scene it could have been made up of a close-up of SLO, a close-up of MM, and then the two-shot favouring MM for the song, but this wasn't necessary. Earlier, when the Grand Duke wanted to seduce Elsie Marina, he had arranged for his valet to play the violin in the corridor. Now it was Elsie's turn to seduce the Grand Duke, and she arranged for a veritable orchestra of valets and footmen in the corridor, all waiting to play on her cue.

Close-up Grand Duke (genuinely puzzled): 'Where's that music coming from?' (He knew he hadn't laid it on this time.)

Two-shot favouring MM. MM giggles: 'Oh never mind. It's just that Hungarian, I expect.' (She knows now that the 'Hungarian' had really been the valet.) 'You told me he plays every night.' She paused and sang the waltz:

'I found a dream, I laid in your arms,
The whole night through,

I'm yours, no matter what others may say or
do . . .

'My sweet . . .' she said and gave SLO a passionate kiss.

It was very good – singing *and* acting, and indeed the scene went
on for another couple of speeches. For the first time MM behaved
like a trouper. She is really happiest when she sings. Perhaps it is
because it is a nice uncomplicated thing to do, something she often
does when she is alone, or frightened.

In the previous films she's always seemed a rather reluctant
chanteuse, but not this time. I should add that she didn't have to
sing the final version. Today's voice will not be in the film – that
will be 'post-synched' in the sound studio much later. But her lip
movements today will be vital so she had to sing properly, nonetheless. And she did, in fact, give a performance which impressed
everyone. What a pity SLO can't build on this, but it is really too
late. After lunch, things weren't quite so easy. MM had to declare
her passion – 'Oh gosh, your Grand Ducal Highness, how I love
you' – and throw herself into his arms. Then they were interrupted
by the hapless Dicky W, once again with a phoney excuse, this
time on the Duke's behalf.

I don't know if MM had had a drink in the break, or a pill, or
both. (MM loves champers but she does not ever drink too much
on its own.) Anyway she seemed to be on another plane. She was
jolly enough, but communication got more and more difficult. By
the end of the day, when she had only one close-up left to do, she
had become wistfully sad – and completely lost. Her only line was
'I didn't quite catch that' – referring to the Duke's declaration of
love in Carpathian – but even that was almost impossible for her
to say. The hair got tousled, the red rashes came and went. Then,
suddenly, she got it right, like catching a butterfly in mid-flight. I
do see why directors dread working with her, poor lady. You never
know *which* MM you will get next – or how long it might take to
get anything at all.

WEDNESDAY, 5 SEPTEMBER

They have finished building the Grand Duke's dressing room, which leads into the purple room. This means there are a lot more scenes we can now shoot without MM. She did not turn up until lunch, and again she wasn't in very good shape. If she hasn't arrived by 9 a.m., and I haven't been able to learn from Plod when she is due to leave Parkside, I have to go to help David in the studio. I don't know until lunchtime whether she is there or not. It is academic really because she needs to be in Make-up before 9.30 for any work to be done with her before the lunchbreak.

This morning we did the follow-up to the Grand Duke's attempted seduction. Elsie has passed out and four footmen have been summoned to carry her into a bedroom. The sleepy valet, who has been dragged out of bed to play his violin, wanders into the drawing room, still fiddling away, gawping with curiosity. The part is played by a little old Greek actor called Andrea Melandrinos. It was hard to tell whether he was acting or really in a dream. When SLO yelled at him to shut up, he jumped out of his skin exactly like a real servant would have done and the crew dissolved into laughter. Neither he nor SLO could decide whether to be pleased or not by this comic success. The shot had to be done several times, and was never quite so funny again.

In the afternoon we did MM's long silent walk around SLO. He is being shaved by the same valet and is totally preoccupied. Elsie comes out of the bedroom in the background, walks through the purple room, into the dressing room, takes a cup of coffee, walks right round the Grand Duke and returns to the bedroom. She was draped in a pink bedspread, totally dishevelled with her blonde hair (a different wig) hanging loose down her back. The Grand Duke only does a double-take as the bedroom door shuts. For some reason, this scene bothered MM a lot. Perhaps it was a situation with which she could identify all too closely? She had no lines to remember but, in her confused state, even little details like when to collect the cup of coffee gave her maximum trouble. And, wrapped up as she was, it wasn't easy to carry anything. Although the camera could hardly see her face, her general appearance was frightful. Her walk, however, was unmistakable, especially from behind. If that wiggle of the rear end comes out on camera, the film will be saved!

Finally we did the shot of her collapsed on the bed, under the pink coverlet, where Dicky discovers her and, presumably, wakes her, before that walk. There was nothing anyone could do to make this shot presentable. The truth was that she just looked like a tart, the morning after. It is a very hard thing to define, but I've seen it (to my shame), and SLO could certainly recognise it too. No amount of fussing by drapes and set dressers could alter it. Something in the way MM sprawled on the bed, I guess. We'll see in 'rushes' tomorrow.

I just can't see how MM can keep this up all week. She looks shattered, washed out, in a dream. LOP and MMP have a huge insurance policy in case SLO or MM are ill. Filming must be stopped for five days before they pay and an independent doctor has to examine the 'ill' person. Mental illness does not count. Of course this does not apply to MM yet, but SLO had Mr P check the policy because he can see the writing on the wall. The most difficult question is – what will make MM recover her composure? What will help her to start working properly again? AM is not due back for a week. Plod says MM phones him in NYC for hours and hours, but that does not seem to make her any better – sometimes worse! And what if she is pregnant? Suddenly it looks possible that the film will never be finished . . . and we are only four weeks in.

THURSDAY, 6 SEPTEMBER

Sure enough, at 10 a.m. we had an official message from Parkside to say MM was not well, and a doctor had been called. I reported this to SLO. He wanted to know which doctor. A local GP? A specialist in nervous diseases? There was quite a difference. I rang Plod and spoke to Hedda. AM had found the name of a London physician from a friend and had recommended him over the phone. Hedda had arranged for him to call that afternoon. But whatever he says, Hedda thinks that MM will not return to the studio before next Wednesday (Sept 12th). As AM returns from NYC next Tuesday (Sept 11th) this seems a likely guess.

Milton arrived late. He had been to Parkside, and even he had been kept waiting for an hour. He and SLO immediately went into conference, frantically calculating whether a claim could be made on the insurance, and how to get the insurance company to examine MM for a second opinion (some hope!). I do not know if it would be necessary to shut the film down for five days in order for a claim to succeed. Presumably we would all still be paid – by the insurance company. But such an interruption is a horrendous thought. In the meantime, there are cut-away shots to be done with SLO, and scenes in the dressing room with SLO, Dicky, and Jeremy Spenser. Most of these are done very quickly and efficiently, with the only delays being for moving the camera and relighting. But they filled today and will fill tomorrow too. Mr P and Teddy Joseph have arranged for a day on location at the Foreign Office (the real one) for Monday which means a lot of work for the Ast Dirs. The road outside the FO in St James's Park has to be closed from very early in the morning, and filled with horses and carriages and extras dressed as passers-by. Everyone concerned is being very helpful. Even though MM is not going to be there herself, her name alone always works magic.

The dressing-room set is much more sympathetic than the purple room, although it may not be so dramatic on camera. It is a bedroom/dressing room which must have been quite rare in 1911 in such a large mansion as the Carpathian Embassy in Belgrave Square. Since this script is taken from a play in which all the action took place in one room, and it has been stretched to take place in one house, the rooms must interconnect. SLO has many changes of extremely handsome military-style uniforms – but somehow they do not suit him. He has chosen an ultra-teutonic bearing for the Grand Duke, his short hair slicked down, his collar buttoned up to his chin and a monocle in his eye. This worked well with Vivien on stage. She knew exactly how to play against it, and she could melt your heart with her combination of bright intelligence and vulnerability. (She certainly melted mine.) But with MM – as naive and well-intentioned as a puppy – the Grand Duke seems stiff to the point of absurdity. He never seems to relax. I don't know if that is in the script or because SLO feels so unhappy. It certainly takes away the romantic appeal and makes Elsie falling in love with the Duke stretch credulity to the limits. We can already see this in the 'rushes'. Of course Tony B is full of 'how wonderful Laurence is' but I feel there isn't enough for SLO to get his teeth into. Rather, the role has got its teeth into him. He gives the impression of a director who has walked onto the set and into the leading role. And that isn't make-believe – which is what the film is meant to be about – it is exactly what has happened.

FRIDAY, 7 SEPTEMBER

Another long scene of the Grand Duke being shaved, in his bedroom/dressing room, by Andrea Melandrinos, the valet who played the violin. Since he still behaves exactly like a valet, one must now assume he is a brilliant actor. There is another valet, played by Dennis Edwards, who is tall and thin, and quiet to the point of seeming in another world. When Elsie Marina, wrapped only in a bedspread, did her long walk round the Duke, Dennis was directed to stare in amazement. The trouble is that in the meantime, no one has told Dennis to stop staring in amazement. So all through today's scene, when nothing untoward is happening so far as he is concerned, there he is, still staring in amazement. SLO couldn't see him, of course, because he is acting in the scene, and Tony B did not notice. I must admit that I was not brave enough to point out the problem, so it will be in the movie. It is not the job of the assistant directors to assist the director to direct. Years ago I was

invited, by Vivien I suppose, onto the set of *Caesar and Cleopatra*.*
Gaby Pascal was directing a crowd scene. Caesar's troops had just
landed in Alexandria or something, and the people were in a panic.
After a couple of takes, I pointed out to Pascal that quite a few of
them were just wandering around, looking blank. I now know that
this was because he hadn't told them what to do. Extras who are not
told what to do wander around and look blank. But my observations
were not well received – (I was 12 at the time) – so I didn't risk
repeating my mistake. When I am a director . . .

SATURDAY, 8 SEPTEMBER

Plod called me over to Parkside for a chat. He could say nothing
directly, but he hinted that MM had been pregnant but had now
miscarried. The baby must have been no more than a month. This
seems very young to be called 'a baby' but I know nothing about
pregnancy, I must admit. Plod is very concerned. He adores MM
now, even though she doesn't seem to notice that he exists. (You
never know with MM, she has very good peripheral vision.)

'Does anyone else know?' I asked.

'Milton Greene, I suppose.'

'Does Arthur?'

'I don't think so, no.'

So much for marriage!

I went over to Tibbs Farm to check it out. When I arrived, Milton
and Amy were in a dreadful state. Josh, their son, had fallen out of
their car as they were going down the driveway. A doctor was with
him, but, amazingly, he wasn't hurt, just very shocked. Poor little
guy. For once Milton wasn't remotely concerned with MM. They
assumed that I had heard the news about Josh, and come over to

---

* Vivien Leigh played Cleopatra in the 1945 screen adaptation of Shaw's play, at the
time the most expensive British film ever made.

sympathise about that. So I said nothing about Plod's news and I never will. I just hope MM recovers. She must have had a pretty bad shock too, if Plod is right.

MONDAY, 17 SEPTEMBER

I haven't written for a whole week and I feel bad about it. We've had a very difficult five days in the studio. It is dark outside when I arrive at 6.45 a.m. – dark, cold and depressing. The addition of the Grand Duke's dressing room to the purple room did not give us the boost I hoped for.

Jack Harris, the editor, has started to visit every day which makes SLO nervous. There is nothing so bad as finding you have a gap in the film which can't be covered by another shot. If actors hesitate, or click with their teeth or let their eyes flick off-camera it can look very embarrassing when blown up on the screen. When you watch 'rushes' you see so many mistakes and overlaps that it is easy to miss the ones that you can't cover. Only the editor can tell this, as he starts to build up the 'rough cut'. Retakes are very expensive, because you can't afford to keep all the big sets built, 'just in case'. So Jack has to be absolutely sure that all is well before the purple set is destroyed. We will certainly store a small corner of it and then we will have something in reserve.

Poor MM has been very depressed. She missed Monday and Tuesday altogether as forecast. She seemed pretty drugged on Wednesday despite AM's return. We soldier on, getting a good take here, and an adequate take there. The 'rushes' have become much less reassuring. We can only see the agony it took to get the shot, and the confusion in MM's eyes. Even so, MM looks just as beautiful. When she is on the screen you can't take your eyes off her. Tomorrow we will start in the big new hall and staircase set in Studio B. Let us hope we all get a new lease of life. If it wasn't for Anne and Tony, I don't think I would have survived.

TUESDAY, 18 SEPTEMBER

The Embassy hall and staircase set is almost as hideous as the purple drawing room, but not as claustrophobic. Neither set *should* be claustrophobic at all. They are opened up to allow the camera in, dissected one way or another, and set down in this vast, aircraft hangar of a studio. However when three sides of a set are built and the camera, sound, lighting and production crews all squeeze into the fourth side, it feels very cramped. The ceiling is 40 feet up but it is impossible to see past the bright lights hanging down, and they get very hot, so the effect is like working in an underground power station.

The design of the hall is quite impressive. It is a bit like a set for a 19th-century operetta, and I suppose that is intentional. In the script, when Dicky enters with Elsie Marina for the first time, he says 'Personally I find the decorations a little vulgar,' which must have given Roger Furse a good clue.

The walls in the bottom half are pale blue, and above the stairs they are lilac. In these walls are round alcoves, painted black, with white plaster busts, like some travesty of Wedgwood. All the columns are marbled to death, and so are the steps and the door surrounds. But the wide double staircase has a good sweep to it, and the gallery running round the top has a pleasing dimension. The whole thing could have been designed for dramatic entrances and exits (*à la* Evelyn Laye*), although there aren't any of these in our film. Four footmen are usually stationed in this hall, in costumes as exaggerated as the decor. It is they who will be summoned to carry Miss Marina to the spare bedroom when she passes out. The Embassy exterior, which we will shoot on the 'lot', is a copy of the Portuguese Embassy in Belgrave Square. (I wonder what that building looked like inside in 1911 – or looks like now for that matter. I must ask Roger if he's seen it.)

When I am not running David's errands, or standing beside SLO

---

* 1900–96. British musical comedy star, chiefly on stage.

in case he wants a cigarette – (I am official cigarette bearer) – I spend most of the time gossiping with Paul H (the Major Domo) and Dicky W. Dicky has his own chair – what luxury – as his is really the third most important part in the film. Paul is very good at commandeering one too as his costume is tight. He is in a great many scenes and his face is wonderfully expressive even though he hardly ever speaks. They have a few hilarious scenes between them. When Dicky arrives the morning after Elsie has passed out, Paul rushes to tell him the news – that the chorus girl is still in the Embassy. Then Paul adds a *sotto voce* – and obviously vulgar – joke and Dicky freezes him with his sternest look. It was done so economically and understatedly that it was a delight to watch. Exactly what Rattigan had in mind, I am sure.

Dicky and Paul can swap jokes all day – theatrical jokes, camp jokes, drinking jokes. They are very enjoyable company and they prefer me as an audience to the crew. (I am much more likely to know the people involved.) Tony B joins in sometimes, but when the jokes get risqué – which is very often – he gives them the same look Dicky gave Paul in the film, and marches off. Dicky and Paul also drink a great deal together in the evenings. I was in the men's lavatories this morning, and all the time I was standing there, the most appalling noise, of retching and defecating, came out of one of the stalls. Then, as I was washing my hands, out came Paul.

'Morning, my boy' he said cheerily, as he marched off into the studio. I was expecting someone to call for an ambulance. What a constitution these actors have.

WEDNESDAY, 19 SEPTEMBER

AM returned yesterday, and by midday today he had been universally cast as villain of the piece. SLO is cross because he had hoped that AM would help MM to turn over a new leaf, and this clearly has not happened. She arrived at the studio late and demanding. In fact she is clearly fed up with AM and also disenchanted with Milton whom she cuts dead. She complained about her dress, and her hair, and her make-up, which is very unusual for her.

It is also pointless, since Elaine, the continuity girl, has absolute control over how she looks now. Elaine has to keep track of exactly how everyone looked in the preceding shot even though it may have been filmed at a totally different time. If MM even ruffles her hair a tiny bit, there could be a mismatch in the final film, and Elaine is determined that such a thing will never happen.* Like all the crew, she has to be a perfectionist or she might as well not bother to turn up at all. Film discipline is that strict.

Milton blames AM for the change in MM's attitude, both to her work and to him. Milton is in a very difficult position. He wants to control MM and her career, but he has to get this film finished on time and on budget if MMP, and he, is to make money (not to mention LOP and Warner Bros). And this means he has to co-operate with SLO and all of us, even at the risk of upsetting MM. So it is easy for someone (AM) to poison MM's mind against him.

Paula is treated by AM with extreme disdain. I have heard him describe Paula as a charlatan to Milton in SLO's dressing room and I'm sure he does it in front of MM. This is hard luck on MM since she totally depends on Paula when AM is away. She has no one else except the tipsy Hedda. Finally AM is not above snide remarks about Milton to Paula, which quickly get repeated, so Milton gets upset even though he has nothing concrete to go on. What a crew.

This evening MM told Milton that she was not satisfied with her car. She wants it replaced with a new Jaguar (a Mk VII saloon I suppose). This seemed pretty reasonable to me. A star like MM ought to be able to travel in any car she wants. Think of Gary Cooper's Duesenberg. SLO just shrugged, but to Milton, and to Tony B, it is an affront. They can see the dark hand of AM at work. Who will pay for it, MMP or LOP? As part of the British production obligations, it should be LOP. But it is for MM's special use, so it should

---

* It never did.

be MMP. 'He is trying to pull a fast one. He wants us to buy it and then he will ship it over (Right-hand drive??) to the USA for his own private use.'* And they were livid. I think it is funnier that a left-wing intellectual should want to drive round in a Jaguar with Marilyn Monroe. (Although didn't Lenin have a Rolls-Royce?) That is not the point, said Milton and Tony B, together, when I teased them. 'AM is going to ruin the movie.'

Actually the problem with the Jaguar will be that it has no glass division between the passenger compartment and the driver. I think Plod likes the peacefulness of the front of the Princess.

MM left the studios in a huff. She does not like being crossed when she has made her wishes clear; no more than any other film star before her. Quite right too, I say, but Plod looked gloomy.

THURSDAY, 20 SEPTEMBER

Today SLO took MM as far as he possibly could and then even further. He was directing only, not being in the scenes himself, so he was more in control than usual. We were in the hall and staircase set and he had planned a long-shot on the stairs, a continuation of MM's arrival at the Embassy with Dicky, her Foreign Office escort.

In the end it took 29 takes before we got it right. 29 takes is an historic amount, even for MM. I really think SLO wanted to break all records as proof, actual visible proof, of how difficult it is to work with her. It was a complicated shot, with the camera on a big crane following MM and Dicky up the stairs and walking round the gallery into the door of the purple room. (The actual purple room was in Studio A, of course, and is now destroyed.)

David: 'Going for a take. QUIET studio please.'

'Lights.' Clunk.

'Camera running.'

---

* They did get the Jaguar, but it was unreliable and I don't know if they took it back to the USA or not.

'Sound.' Beep beep.

'Speed.'

'Mark it.'

'*Prince and the Showgirl*. Shot 137 take 1.' Clap.

'Action.'

Dicky W: 'This way, Miss Marina.' (His voice combines disapproval with resignation.) They climb the stairs. MM looks around, asks about dinner, asks about the Grand Duke's wife ('Passed over' says Dicky). They reach the gallery. Dicky starts to explain which Royal Personage she might meet and how to address each one.

MM: 'Wow, I'm shaking. This is worse than a first night.' Exeunt. CUT.

Repeat 29 times!

Everyone was frantic. MM's rash came and went. Each time the camera was difficult to reposition correctly and the cameraman, Denys, was grey with fatigue. It is a big set and needs a lot of lights, so the lighting crew up on the gantry was nearly cooked. We could have broken the shot down into two or three shorter bits by shooting close-ups of reactions on MM and Dicky, to be cut in later. But SLO had the bit between his teeth, so on and on we went. Dicky is incredibly professional and he never wavers, or misses a word. But he was sweating so much in that hot braided uniform that he must have lost several pounds of weight.

MM simply could not remember all her lines, and when she did remember, she did not say them correctly. The lines were often silly and inconsequential and there were many changes of thought and direction. It is true that they were the sort of things one might say, going up the stairs to supper in a strange house, with strange people, but it was quite a risky challenge to put them all in one long continuous take.

As they went up the stairs, MM had to say 'Think of the trouble of bringing the food all the way up from the kitchen.'

Dicky replied: 'I fancy it will be a cold supper, Miss Marina.'

MM: 'They still have to bring it, don't they?' Then a change of thought: 'Is his wife still alive?' etc.

This sort of dialogue is written to illustrate Elsie's charming naiveté and it could have worked. When MM blurted it out, having just (only just) remembered it in time, it did not sound 'off the cuff', even to her. So then she started to forget the other lines, one by one, almost as if she wanted to wipe them out. Back she would go to Paula, hands flapping as if she was hoping to fly. There was much whispering, much looking at the script as if they were trying to translate it from a foreign language, and then back to the set for another try.

Amazingly enough we did get the shot on take 29, but at what cost we will not know until later. In his dressing room, SLO admitted to Milton that he should have broken the scene down. But by this time MM and Paula were speeding home in what mental state one could only guess at. For the record, and perhaps this influenced SLO, we had filmed virtually the same shot in the morning only with Dicky and Paul going up the stairs and meeting Jeremy Spenser in the gallery. We had done that in four takes, the first three having had minor camera problems.

FRIDAY, 21 SEPTEMBER

Today the hall and stairs set was readjusted so that we could shoot MM and Dicky going *down* the stairs.

It went much better, mainly because MM only had one thought in the scene – namely to escape the clutches of the Grand Duke. The exercise of authority by SLO yesterday seemed to have a good effect, to Milton's surprise. After all, we did get the shot. MM respects authority as much as she fights against it. Her relationship with SLO seemed a little more professional at last, and as a result the filming was easier and quicker. Of course there were problems. In her hasty exit from the purple drawing room, Elsie Marina had tried frantically to get her coat on, and failed. We shot this scene a couple of weeks ago and Elaine had noted it and had the film to prove it. MM's 'coat' is a frilly, lilac, silk taffeta affair which looks most elegant and becoming when it is on. But it is almost impossible to slip into in a hurry. So when MM emerges into the corridor at high speed, she still has to have it twisted round one arm. There was no real problem with this but it is the sort of thing that can easily put MM off. In the event it all went smoothly, and MM did manage to get the coat on over the next few shots, without letting it interrupt her thought processes. Dicky is an absolute rock, but alas MM treats him like a non-person. (This is how she treats most of us now.) She is in so many scenes with Dicky that it would have been a great help if she could have got cosy with him. Perhaps it is because he is queer, and doesn't look at her the way most men do. I don't mean that he is in the least effeminate, but I'm sure she can tell, and that makes him a 'non-man'. Of course he is also quintessentially British, and that is not her favourite nationality right now.

After lunch we filmed Dicky trying to persuade Elsie Marina to stay for her supper engagement. MM is convinced the Regent is only out to seduce her: 'He's a Carpathian Grand Duke, for heaven's sake.'

Dicky: 'Educated in England.'

MM: 'That's just what I mean.'

All this went on as they dodged around the marble columns in the hall, Dicky desperately pulling MM back onto her camera marks as she blundered about. But it worked again, and when we saw the four printed takes from yesterday's historic labours, MM looked lovely, acted well, and stole the scene. Let that be added to the story of 'the 29 takes'.

SUNDAY, 23 SEPTEMBER

Phew, what a weekend. I certainly celebrated my 24th birthday (in two weeks, actually) with a bang. On Friday night I had made a date to go out on a 'pub-crawl' with Dicky and Paul. We spend hours and hours gossiping on the set every day, and we all enjoy each other's company, but the outside world changes things. After a few drinks it became obvious that all Dicky wanted to do was pick up some gorgeous hunk of a man, and all Paul wanted to do was to get drunk out of his mind. I don't disapprove of either of these activities but I wanted dinner too, so we went to a 'bistro' Dicky knew in Soho. It was a queer's bar really. The food was delicious and I ate it, but Dicky just flirted and Paul just drank. (I don't know if Paul is queer or not. There's no Mrs Paul as far as I know, so maybe.) Just as we were wondering where to go next, in came Gordon Alexander, the dresser, camp as coffee as usual. He knew a very special and very exciting place, he said – giving me the eye, I noticed – so we all piled into a taxi and set off. Going along Piccadilly, Dicky got completely hysterical. He lay on the floor and said he was going to die. He and Paul were completely drunk by now, so we stopped the cab and tumbled them both out onto the pavement.

'Drive on!' screamed Gordon at the cabbie, who was only too relieved to do so. 'Thank goodness we've got rid of those two old queens,' said Gordon, putting his hand on my knee. 'Let's go home and you can fuck me.'

Peter P-M* used to talk like this so I'm used to it, although I wish he had closed the taxi-driver window first!

'I'm not sure I want to do that,' I said. (I was sure I didn't.)

'We'll go back and have a nightcap anyway,' said Gordon, giving the driver new instructions. Gordon's flat was really very nicely done up – watercolours, comfy sofas, pretty lamps etc. Gordon brought some gin ('Gordon's' he said, giggling) but he had no cigarettes and I had run out hours ago which made me nervous.

'Never mind,' said Gordon, grabbing me by the crotch. 'I'll give you a nice blow job.' I had heard this phrase before, but I didn't know exactly what it meant. It sounded sexy, so I said OK. It felt great to

---

* Peter Pitt-Millward owned a castle called Paco da Gloria in northern Portugal. I had spent the previous summer there. In 1978 Peter died, and I acquired the castle and lived there, off and on, until 1987.

start with but in the end I got restless and found it unsatisfactory. Gordon seemed to be having more fun than I was. I don't really like sex unless I can take an active part. However it all worked out in the end, and Gordon seemed grateful.

'We must do that again,' he said. I'm not so sure.

I slept really late yesterday and then went to the Stork Club again. Yvonne was there with somebody else, but I persuaded her to join me after they left, and took her straight home. I just had to have normal sex again. I've grown out of all that schoolboy stuff at last. Perhaps I'll go back to it when I'm old, but for now I prefer girls. I saw Al* this evening but I didn't tell him what was going on. The film world is different, I suppose. It's more exciting, and I've got a hangover to prove it!

MONDAY, 24 SEPTEMBER

Back at work in the hall set, taking it apart and putting it back again so we can film it from every angle. I have been having a feud with MM's stand-in. She and SLO's stand-in are always in the studio, on call every day, and they are meant to arrive at the same time as the stars. After a quick visit to make-up and wardrobe, they must be on the set by 8 a.m., ready for lighting to begin. It is a thankless task. They just stand where they are told and move where they are told, while they are lit as if they were the stars and their moves are 'plotted' by camera and sound. They never get the chance to perform, even if the star is ill, like an understudy does in the theatre. They are generally considered to be at the very bottom of the studio pecking order, only just above the 'extras' who make up the crowd scenes, and from whose ranks they have been drawn. I suppose I look at them the way Terry Rattigan looks at me – (which is also the way MM looks at Terry Rattigan!). MM's stand-in is a pretty little thing, but half MM's size and with none of her personality. Now she has

* Alan, my older brother.

taken to arriving late in the mornings too. Not as late as MM, of course, or she would be fired instantly, but 25 minutes late is a lot for a stand-in.

I am responsible to David for getting the right people on the right set at the right time. With MM this is difficult, but with the stand-ins it should be automatic. Indeed, they are usually so anxious to please, and be hired again, that they are early. The MM girl has not taken any notice of my stern rebukes. This morning she even threatened to get me into trouble for being rude – which I expect I was. I will have to investigate this a little further. When a girl like that starts getting cheeky, it usually means she has some powerful man to protect her – I have deep suspicions.

TUESDAY, 25 SEPTEMBER

I got the 2nd Ast Dir to cover me at the Star Dressing Room entrance after SLO had arrived, taking a fairly certain gamble on MM being at least an hour late. Then I went round to the main entrance and waited out of sight. Sure enough, at 7.30, Jack Cardiff drove up, and the MM stand-in hopped out of his car. She waved goodbye before she hurried inside, and Jack went off to park. There is no law against giving stand-ins a lift to the studio, but now I knew why she could afford to be cheeky. Jack, as lighting cameraman, is the most important man in the studio after SLO. It is he who is responsible for how the film looks, after SLO has decided what it should contain. Jack is also especially important to MM. It is he who makes her look so beautiful. She also likes him and respects him. He is indeed a very charming and likeable man, although I don't know him that well. It is not up to me to criticise him if he makes a friend. But it is my job to get stand-ins on the set on time, even if it is really Jack who will be kept waiting if they are not. David feels very strongly that just because MM is always late, the rest of the studio must not be allowed to get slack. I decided not to tell David what I had seen, but when the MM girl came on the set, late again, I gave her a pretty firm rebuke. I did it in front of Jack in the hope that he might realise that he must get her to work earlier. That was not a success. Jack was livid. He told me that, as lighting cameraman, stand-ins were his problem, and to mind my own business. David just blinked like an owl, and motioned me out of the studio. He didn't want to have a row in front of the crew, and told me that he would have a quiet word with Jack later. For the rest of the day, there was a considerable coolness between Jack and myself. I am sure he won't mention it to SLO, but I am only the 3rd Ast Dir; and 3rd Ast Dirs are not expected to upset lighting cameramen. Luckily Tony didn't notice anything. He never does, bless him, unless SLO is involved.

WEDNESDAY, 26 SEPTEMBER

Dame Sybil came into the studio again today. I was wearing her red scarf as usual, and she gave me a huge hello. It was nice to see her again and MM was thrilled – a visit from Grandma! Having been warned, MM was even almost on time. Dame S is now acting in a West End play, which means she doesn't finish until 11 p.m. at night, but there she was in her hire car at 7 a.m., beaming and smiling. We filmed her making the Grand Duke give Elsie Marina a Carpathian medal, the one which he had just given the Ambassador. ('Such quibbles,' when he objects!) We could not do it earlier because the hall hadn't been built. Her character in the film is as sympathetic as she is, deaf to anything she doesn't want to hear. When Elsie says 'Oui' she is quite convinced that she can speak fluent French.

MM was in top form, bouncy and jolly. Her appearance, off camera, changes with her mood. When she is happy she looks really attractive. One can see what all the fuss is about. She is only 29* and she certainly has a wonderful figure. She doesn't even need a bra in that amazing white dress. With Dame S she behaves like a schoolgirl,

---

* Actually she had turned thirty in June.

and an obedient schoolgirl at that. Jack has started to play up to MM much more too, which helps. Alas, it is too late for SLO to react. If he could only strengthen her confidence somehow, reinforce it when it is high. But Plod tells me that Lee Strasberg calls her every evening from the USA – reverse charge of course – and this undermines SLO a lot. I mentioned this to Milton. He also hates the Strasbergs but by now he seems powerless to prevent their influence. At least Milton's son, Josh, is OK after the accident. But MM seems to be slipping from his grasp.

THURSDAY, 27 SEPTEMBER

We continue with reaction shots of MM in the hall – her first impression of the Embassy, her meeting with the Grand Duke, and the scene where Dicky reassures her that he will save her from a fate worse than death. She seemed less clear in the head today and more woozy. I hope Milton isn't giving her too many pills again. It's one of the ways he can still control her. Milton now has an assistant called David Maysles.* David looks like a young American college undergraduate. He has a great deal of ambition and this makes him irreverent and mischievous. He frequently says what Milton would like to say but does not dare, and despite his appearance no one could describe him as 'nice'. Milton calls him a 'film maker' and says he is very good in his own right. But he spends most of his time running errands (like me) and chasing girls. He is flippant but cheerful. He is always playing with Josh, which gives Amy a break, and he makes Amy laugh, which makes me jealous, I'm not sure why. He told me that Milton orders the pills for MM from Amy's doctor in New York. There are 'uppers' for when she is down, and 'downers' for when she cannot relax. I gather that in America you can buy any pill you want. Don't they realise that nature has

---

* 1931–87. With his older brother Albert he went on to make a number of acclaimed documentary films (*Salesman*, *Gimme Shelter*, *Grey Gardens* etc.).

already worked out how to keep you balanced without uppers and downers? I know they think MM is a special case, and I suppose she does have unnatural pressures and demands. But now she is like a see-saw, forever being pushed up or down and never level. In the end she will loop the loop like her mum.

FRIDAY, 28 SEPTEMBER

More hall but no Monroe. Hedda called at about ten to say she wasn't well again. Plod had already phoned to tell me that there was no sign of life at 8.30 and I had warned SLO. Milton was caught unawares, and SLO despatched him to see if a doctor had been called, or was contemplated.

There is still plenty we can do without MM. After lunch we did the shot of the Grand Duke's arrival at the Embassy, just as Elsie has decided to walk out. She turns to the front door to leave, which we have already shot, and then we cut to the back of her head. The big doors open, she curtseys and her head disappears downwards to reveal SLO's grinning face.

'Good evening,' he says. 'How kind of you to come at such short notice.'

He really looked most alarming with his monocle and his patent leather hair, but he did several 'takes', until he was absolutely happy with this ghastly appearance. In MM's absence we did the shot with MM's stand-in bobbing up and down in one of MM's precious wigs. She was thrilled to be 'understudying' MM even if one couldn't see her face, and she has got over her anger with me.

All this made it clear that I had somehow to make it up with Jack. By pure luck I heard him talking enthusiastically about the Turner paintings in the Tate Gallery. He was sitting in a little circle of admirers – Carmen, Tony, Denys and Co – while he waited for the gaffer to do his bidding. I was standing (3rd Ast Dirs never sit, remember) on the edge of the circle, and I butted in.

'My father owns one of those paintings,' I said.

'No,' said Jack kindly, 'these are all in the Tate Gallery, and the ones I am talking about are very big.'

'Well, my father has the only one in the world outside the Tate,' I replied. 'Somehow it escaped and my father bought it nine years ago. It's hanging in the drawing room.' Jack had to look at me again. 'The drawing room' probably wasn't a concept he associated with 3rd Ast Dirs. They are meant to talk about the lounge. I'm sure that in his nice, easy-going way it has never occurred to him that I was of any particular significance (i.e. the son of friends of SLO and Vivien etc.). Why should it? I've never looked at the stand-ins like that, and I see them every day just as Jack sees me. But now he was curious. (Snobbishness, too, is a sympathetic human failing.)

'Is your father a collector, then?' he asked, prepared to be dealing with a lunatic.

'Yes, he is. He's an art historian actually.'

Jack's mind did a rapid search of his memory. Colin Clark?? 'Your father isn't Sir Kenneth Clark, is he?'

'Yes, he is.' No reaction from the crew. Carmen already knew this but none of the others had ever heard of art historians, let alone Sir Kenneth Clark. Jack is an artist with light who also aspires to be an artist with paint. Jack nearly jumped out of Jack's skin with excitement.

'Oh, how wonderful. I admire your father very much. I'd love to meet him and discuss painting with him. In fact he owns the picture I admire most in the world – the nude portrait Renoir did of his wife on their honeymoon.'

I was just warming up. 'Perhaps you and Mrs Cardiff would like to come down to the country one weekend. You could meet my parents and see the Renoir and the other pictures.' All this was out of the MM stand-in's earshot. (When you wield such flagrant power, you must be merciful!)

'Oh, that would be fantastic. I'll tell Julie' – for thus Mrs C is called – 'She will be thrilled. Perhaps we could drive down. It is in Kent isn't it?' Yes, and it's a castle as I'm sure you know, but I didn't say that.

'I'm going down this weekend and I'll arrange it,' I said. 'I'm sure my parents would be flattered to meet you both.'

Victory over stand-in complete. Indeed Jack went round telling everyone, whether they had heard of Sir Kenneth Clark or not. SLO took it calmly. 'You'll love K and Jane. Gorgeous house, too,' he said without taking much notice. Poor man has other problems right now. But I'm very happy. Jack is a nice, interesting and enthusiastic man and I'm sure my parents will like him and his wife.

Mr P came into the studio at the end of the day, delightfully gloomy as ever. He has already had to put his Number 2 cross-plot into effect, but for some reason he blames AM and not MM. The demand for a Jaguar was seen as a last straw. He also has suspicions that Paula Strasberg is fleecing us and that Milton is fleecing MM.

'So who do you trust?' I asked.

'No one, Colin – including you.' Grin, grin.

MONDAY, I OCTOBER

MM had been told she need not come in today or tomorrow. It's very doubtful if she would have turned up anyway. Once the word 'doctor' has been mentioned, it usually takes three days for her to recover her stamina and her will power.

We have two days in the Foreign Office set, which has been built in Studio A. It needs its own studio because film we shot on location two weeks ago is projected onto a screen outside the windows, to look as if the carriages are going trotting by in the background. We filmed the coaches from the actual Foreign Secretary's office, looking down on the road round St James's Park. The carriages were so far away that we used the stand-ins, dressed in the stars' costumes. We will film the stars themselves in close-up later, in the studio.

The BP* needs a long throw and powerful arc lamps. These are noisy. They hiss away and get extremely hot. If you even glimpse

* i.e. back projection.

one straight on you are blind for half an hour. So they have to be quite far from the camera and the microphone. Setting them up is a complicated business, and so is the art of balancing the light between the actors in the room and the light projected on the screen behind them. There were considerable delays while adjustments were made. Two totally competent actors (Dicky Wattis and David Horne) went through their lines again and again. Sounds familiar? Of course this is what happens every day, but for once it was not MM's fault. It was a piece of antiquated lighting equipment, which makes a pretty unconvincing picture at the end of the day. Does anyone complain? Not a soul. Just because the antiquated lighting equipment didn't flounce off to a mobile dressing room, shaking its fingers? Technical matters, and especially lighting matters, are above criticism – out of bounds. If you dare question what is going on you get dark looks, scowls and murmurs of union displeasure. It is as if we were ruled by some secret society, with its own rules into which we must never enquire. And indeed that is true. The Electricians' Union is above any question or criticism, yet it can bring the whole studio to a halt at a moment's notice. Everyone behaves as if technical mysteries are so mysterious that only technicians can understand them. Absolute nonsense! It is all simple and basic. All this mystery is just to hide laziness and incompetence, to make sure that three men are hired to do the job of one. The art of acting is far more mysterious, yet every technician feels free to criticise MM. They damn her every time she has an attack of nerves, as if it was *she* who was lazy and incompetent. It is MM who really lights up the screen, and not some engineers fiddling with switches. But of course I could never say this in public, not even to David.

TUESDAY, 2 OCTOBER

More Foreign Office. The scene seems dry as dust. This is partly intentional – the stuffy old Foreign Office having to cope with exotic Balkan Grand Dukes. But the main problem is that the scene does not contain MM. SLO playing Oedipus and Hamlet simultaneously wouldn't generate as much excitement as MM on screen. Drugged, confused, frightened, late, vague, maddening as she can be, she changes any scene from night to day. Without her, we are all just technicians arguing about our unimportant little problems. Even dear Dicky W can only add to a scene, not create one.

There is no denying that MM has problems. She is herself one gigantic problem. But she is also the solution! As long as she can get to the studio and walk onto the set, it is worth everything to film her. This plump, blonde(?) young lady with the big eyes is certainly very hard to control. Right now she is almost too much for a young, smart producer (Milton), a top playwright and intellectual (AM), America's foremost dramatic coaching couple (the Strasbergs) and England's best actor/director (SLO). MM is just a force of nature. That is sort of wonderful for us, to watch and be associated with, but it must be very uncomfortable for her. I wonder if Garbo was like this, or Chaplin. Vivien is a force of nature too, but she is so formidably intelligent that, to some extent, she can control it. MM does not have that power – and even Vivien can lose it sometimes, come to think of it.

WEDNESDAY, 3 OCTOBER

Plod called first thing. Lee Strasberg had arrived yesterday from New York, to take personal charge of MM's performance in the film. MM wasn't coming in today, but Lee Strasberg was!

'Well done, Plod.' Spies are useful. Even half an hour's warning is better than total surprise. I ran to SLO's dressing room with the news.

Predictably SLO exploded. 'Paula's bad enough. I'm the f—ing director of this f—ing film. Call Milton. I'm the f—ing producer too. I won't allow Lee Strasberg on the set. Call the studio police, and have him stopped at the gate. F— him.'

I had already squeezed in a call to Tibbs, and Milton was on his way.

'Send him in here as soon as he arrives. He can go to the main gate and explain. Why is Lee here, for Christ's sake?'

Me: 'Perhaps MM has asked him to come.'

'Well she can't have him, at least not in my studio.'

This was not the moment to remind him that MM was an equal partner.

'We are only halfway through this f—ing movie. This will make it impossible to finish. I can't direct with so many people interfering' etc., until Milton arrived.

'Milton, dear boy, this is a very expensive film we are making. We aren't a bunch of psychoanalysts trying to sort out Marilyn's mental health. WE ARE MAKING A FILM. I can't work with Lee Strasberg on the set. I can't even work with Paula Strasberg on the set. We agreed she would stay in Marilyn's dressing room, if you remember. I am the only director allowed on the set. Understood?' Milton shrugged gloomily. 'Well, dear boy, run along and explain that to Lee. He'll be arriving at the main gate any minute – COLIN!'

'Yes, Sir Laurence.'

'Oh, there you are.' I'd been making myself as small as possible about three feet away in the same room. 'Go and get Jack and Tony and David. We'll plan the day without Marilyn. It's just as well she isn't coming in. Then Lee can't interfere.'

I rushed off. I have to be very careful with these messages. It is *not* a good idea to arrive on the set, out of breath and clearly in possession of important news no one else has. I have to sidle up to each recipient in turn, tell them the message as if it was specially sent to them alone by SLO. Each one says: 'Have you told Jack? or David? or Tony?' and I indicate that they will be next on the list, even if I've already told them. Only when all of them know can I dash over to Dicky and Paul and burst out with the latest gossip.

Today we have a new set in Studio B – a small sitting room of the Embassy, downstairs, leading off the Grand Hall. It has an attractive garden at the rear, completely false, of course, with a summer house. There was a lot of preparation going on. Carmen and Dario like to keep adding things up to the last minute, thereby driving Elaine crazy. Elaine actually never loses her cool manner (but she does get very severe).

By lunchtime SLO and Tony B were quite cheerful. Milton had warned Lee, and Lee had been upset but contrite. He had rushed across the Atlantic at MM and Paula's frantic bidding only to realise, in the cold light of an English October morning, that there is no magic wand where MM is concerned. The truth is that MM is unhappy here. She no longer thinks that the film will transform her career from dumb blonde to serious actress (as if . . .). She doesn't trust SLO, or think that she can learn anything from him (this is probably true). She has mixed feelings about Milton, and suspects his motives (wrongly I think). She is not even that happy with AM and looks as if she thinks he isn't really in love with her (also probably true). She does not even know what she does want, so how can Lee give it to her? Lee is a really clever man. I met him outside the star entrance and we had a long chat while he was waiting for the car (which had immediately returned to Parkside, like a brainless homing pigeon). I asked him about Susie and told him what a fan of hers I was. (She came over with him and is staying at the Dorchester.)

I said if he could just persuade MM to finish the film, which is halfway through, then everyone could relax and be happy again. Luckily he agreed. Seven more weeks of hard work seems a lot, but he is sure MM will do it. He is only staying two nights, but Susie is staying two weeks, so I am sure to meet her. (Currently one of my life's ambitions!) I think Lee's visit has been 'cathartic' and may actually help quite a lot. It has allowed everyone to put their cards on the table. He is one of the few intelligent people who can get through to MM, and he doesn't have an axe to grind. We'll see.

THURSDAY, 4 OCTOBER

MM did come in this morning, and quite bright and cheerful she was, if a little forced. So far so good. She always likes a new set too.

Today we were out in the garden, with Jeremy whom she still (just) gets on with, so we were all full of fresh hope. The garden has a nice sunny feel to it when the lights are on, but to achieve this effect means more light than usual and therefore more heat. MM had to wear the raincoat over her dress in these scenes, and that meant she perspired a lot, and had to change clothes a lot,* with consequent delays. Nothing is easy in the film business. But MM's nerve held. Jeremy was as charming as usual and SLO was in a more confident mood. He felt he had achieved a victory over the Strasbergs, and this he badly needed. He became more avuncular with MM, and not so tense and tetchy, which I am sure she appreciated.

After lunch, who should appear but Susan Strasberg. I have always been looking forward to meeting her more than meeting MM. Even seeing MM in the nude had left me cold – well not exactly cold, to be honest, but not in love. But Susie had stolen my heart, in her movie. Susie is not exactly pretty, but she is luminously beautiful. She has huge brown eyes, a very full mouth with a wide grin, and skin so pale that it is almost translucent. She arrived on the set with Paula, looking like a real little star. Luckily Paula and I have always got along – I've made sure of that – and I've made no secret of my admiration for Lee, so I got a very good introduction: 'This is Colin, who has been so helpful. He's the son of the Lord, Kenneth Clark.' (Americans never understand English titles.) I was completely tongue-tied and could only gulp, as usual. Susie was enchanting.

'I love film studios. Do show me round. Marilyn won't be ready for ages.' (True.)

The film crew watched in amazement as their 3rd Ast Dir gulped off into the distance with this ravishing little creature. In fact she was so nice to me that by the end of the day I had bucked up courage to ask her to have dinner with me, and been invited to come to the Dorchester next Tuesday evening.

Having said all this, I have to admit that Susie is out of my league.

* Bumble Dawson had provided three identical white dresses.

She's a Star. She's used to mixing with Stars, like William Holden, and although she is no older than me (or younger?*), I can only relate to her the way I do to Vivien. Adoration and devotion, but embraces are unthinkable. Even so, I am very excited. I can dream of it even if I can't think of it.

Jack and Mrs C are invited for the night at Saltwood this weekend, so I will drive down there immediately after work tomorrow.

RUNNYMEDE, SUNDAY, 7 OCTOBER

I got to Saltwood too late for dinner on Friday night and had to go to the pub for sausage rolls. The Castle Arms is not to be recommended for its food, but if I asked for a late supper at home the servants would all give notice. M and D were very sweet and understanding about the Cardiffs' visit. Papa even said that he had heard of Jack (from *The Red Shoes*) and was looking forward to meeting him. When they arrived on Saturday at noon, they were immediately taken round the garden by Mama. Not many flowers, but the roses are pretty on a good second showing. It was sunny and the castle always looks impressive in the autumn. Jack and Mrs C are really charming. They were both very appreciative and Mama was delighted. Then we had drinks in the drawing room and Jack waxed lyrical about the Renoir until lunch. I could see Mrs C was more taken with the idea of our own cook and butler. M and D, who usually only have guests as sophisticated as themselves, enjoyed the visit thoroughly. In the afternoon, I took the Cardiffs over to Canterbury, which they had not seen. Then in the evening Papa took Jack round the other pictures and over to the Great Hall, while Mama had a good heart to heart with Mrs C. (I dread to think what she told her about me!) After dinner, when Papa had announced 'Bed for all' and started turning off the lights, I held Jack back and we both stayed in the small library for a whisky and soda. Jack was extremely mellow and

* In fact she was only eighteen. She had appeared with William Holden in *Picnic*.

we had a long chat about work. Naturally he is worried. He can see that MM is driving SLO nuts, and this is having a bad effect on the production as a whole. This is a very important film for him.

Then Jack told me a secret. Evidently, a couple of weeks after filming started, MM found an open notebook on AM's desk at Parkside. In it, AM had written some pretty bad stuff about MM – how disappointed he was by her etc. MM had been absolutely shattered. No wonder she took pills and came on set as Ophelia instead of Elsie Marina. I guessed that AM didn't love her enough. Whatever he felt, he shouldn't have written it down and left it for MM to discover like that. Jack had comforted MM as best he could.

Jack told me this to show how deeply he was in MM's confidence. I wish she could have told SLO. It might have made it easier for him to understand her behaviour. But now it is definitely too late. If SLO heard what AM had written he would just say 'She's a disappointment to me too!'

Nevertheless I did ask Jack to share everything with me in the future. I am the only person who picks up all the little bits of information and can put it to SLO when I know he will listen. If he explodes at me it doesn't matter. He never stays angry for long. Of course I will never tell SLO anything unless Jack agrees, but at least he and I can talk over the problems. I only have SLO's interests at heart. Jack is more concerned with the film, but it is SLO's film, so we all have the same purpose in the end. Jack and I went to bed firm friends and that must be a good thing.

When I got back here, Tony broke it to me that he and Anne are giving up this house in two weeks' time. Somehow I had assumed that they had it for the duration of the film, but they don't want the responsibility in the winter. I can't blame them.

They have been wonderfully tolerant of me. I have used their house like a hotel – and I haven't shown them enough gratitude. Evidently Anne's grown-up son (Ned, I think) is coming back, and they have to be in London. I must find somewhere else round here. I could not do this job if I had to commute from the West End.

MONDAY, 8 OCTOBER

MM arrived quite early this morning and completed a long scene with SLO before lunch! In fairness to her, I must record that she did it well and was really quite professional. This was partly due to her being clear in the head for a change, and partly due to this bit of script being much more suitable to her talents – also for a change. I've always thought that this was a lousy vehicle for MM as well as for SLO.

Rattigan couldn't write the menu on a fish and chip shop blackboard. *The Prince and the Showgirl* is all so light, it's like a sort of 'in-joke'. If it's Larry or Vivien in the theatre, the audience can join in. But for the film-going public? I very much doubt it.

Today MM had something she could get her teeth into. She had to tease, and she had to control. When the Grand Duke lost patience, and swore in German, she had to slap her hand on the table and cry: 'Well done. That's the best yet!' She clearly enjoyed it and it showed.

SLO thinks that all the top stars should be able to act anything. Actually everyone else in the film has been carefully chosen to match their roles – Dicky W and Dame S are obvious examples. Did he ever think if this was the *right* role for MM? Did Milton? Was MM consulted on that, or did they all think that as MM was an 'actress', she could easily play a song and dance girl? That is what she is acting, of course, but what she is *meant* to act is Elsie Marina as created by Rattigan. Where her concept and Rattigan's concept don't fit together the friction causes her (and us) pain. I suppose they all leapt at the chance of Olivier and Monroe in the same film, and then slotted in a script that seemed suitable. There were similar-ish roles for SLO and MM, and only four major sets so it looked quite cheap to make. Olivier also knew exactly how to play it and on whom he could rely to make it work. Roger, Bumble, Tony, and Rattigan himself, Billy Chappell and Addinsell. But did MM read the script and think 'This is me' or 'I can impersonate this girl' or 'I have a deep feeling for this character and long to portray her on film' or indeed anything at all? Whenever there is a scene which suits her mood, she can do more than we expect. Even in the love scene this afternoon, she surprised us by how well she performed. But if she had spent a few days going through the script before we started with a really sympathetic director, things might be very different now. Those rehearsals were really only for her. The other actors don't need them. It was a smoke screen put up so she wouldn't feel singled out. But in the event, and because the others were so professional, she was made to feel uncomfortable, and the rehearsals had the opposite effect to that intended. It's easy to be wise after the event, but I don't think SLO *thought* enough!

TUESDAY, 9 OCTOBER

A series of 'tender' scenes between SLO and MM made for a gradual deterioration of MM's morale and confidence level, and a consequent shortening of SLO's fuse. MM doesn't seem to mind the actual kiss as much as SLO does. It was shot over SLO's shoulder, to favour MM, and SLO does not actually kiss her lips. In all the embraces, he just kisses her between the lips and her chin. (This is a theatrical trick, I suppose. SLO is not the first leading man who cannot stand his leading lady!) MM has probably had more experience of being kissed by someone she doesn't like, or even doesn't know. But SLO gets completely rigid, as if it is agony for him to get so close to her. His performance has been too severe, for my taste, all through the movie. I'm sure royalty were like that in 1911, autocratic and self-centred, but this is a Fairy Story, for heaven's sake, not a historical drama.

I had a long discussion about this with Susie S tonight. She invited me to the Dorchester and when I got to her room, she announced that she didn't want to go out for dinner, and we would eat there. This sounds like a cue for romance, but alas it was not. Susie is a beautiful person – intelligent, sensitive, full of life and fun, but her heart is more mature than mine. It has probably been broken a few times already, and it works on a different level. So we ordered dinner (the waiter was incredibly rude; so much for the Dorchester) and chatted about the film, and her parents, and all the problems in between. Susie has great insight into MM. She is nearer to MM's age than the rest of them, and must face many similar challenges. The two 'girls' obviously get on very well. Of course Susie doesn't see the desire for control in her own Mum that drives AM and Milton to distraction. The trouble is that MM simply cries out for someone to control her, and no one can resist trying to do so. She dumps her problems in Paula's lap, and then while the wretched woman is trying to sort them out, MM goes and dumps them on someone else, and they start working on them, and so on.

Susie says that Paula is going back to NYC in a week. Her permit to stay in England will expire soon, and anyway she needs a break. Then all MM's problems will be our problems. Hedda is going back too, but she has never been much help. Susie has promised to come down to Saltwood for the night next Saturday. I feel thrilled. I know I can't remotely possess her but I still can't resist her charm. I stayed up too late tonight but I'm happy. It's my 24th birthday. I didn't tell Susie, though. I want her to think I'm older.

WEDNESDAY, 10 OCTOBER

MM was very troubled today. She had the greatest difficulty remembering even the simplest line – again. We were shooting the continuation of the farewell scene and there were some long takes.

'Oh dear. This time it is up to me to be grown up' gave her a lot of difficulty. She got it in her head that the scene was tragic, and it really isn't written that way.

At one stage, she had to ask: 'Poor darling, do you feel terribly disconcerted?' This was said tenderly but lightly by Vivien in the play. It is a sort of Rattigan joke because 'disconcerted' is one of the Grand Duke's favourite words. Poor MM could not get the point. Because she wasn't allowed to play it as a tragedy, she simply failed to remember it. Her frantic hesitation, as she searched her memory and grabbed the line out of the air, may look like passion. We will see at 'rushes' tomorrow, but it was the best we could get.

THURSDAY, 11 OCTOBER

Dame Sybil back, punctual as ever despite her play. It is pitch dark at 6.45 a.m. now and very cold, but the red scarf is still all I need over my jacket.

Dame S had a great scene, sweeping in to the downstairs sitting room, giving MM a photograph and a medal and lots of advice before sweeping out again, with Dicky Wattis and the ladies-in-waiting in her wake. Her line 'You may kiss me, my dear' reminded me of Papa's story about Empress Eugenie in Menton.* MM looked as surprised as Papa had been. I think she'd forgotten about that bit, as she had no line to speak, but she managed it well. She still responds to Dame S's uncomplicated warmth of character. After lunch we did Elsie Marina's farewell to the Grand Duke in the hall. She is standing alone in the doorway of the sitting room, and she looked a forlorn figure. I wish we could have ended the filming then. It would have made a nice memory. But there is still a long way to go. The coaches, the Abbey, the Grand Ball and the theatre, not to speak of the exteriors on the 'lot'.

At least I have found somewhere to live. It is just a room over the pub a couple of miles from here, but I can get supper there too. They've asked if I can help behind the bar! Free beer?

FRIDAY, 12 OCTOBER

There are two separate sets of scenes in the coaches – each with a back-projection screen to make them look as if they were going along

---

* In 1911, when my father was eight, he met Empress Eugenie in Menton. She invited him to kiss her, but since he had never kissed anyone in his life, including his parents, he turned and fled.

the road. The first were done in the morning, while MM was getting ready. SLO, Dame S, Jeremy and the Ambassador (who only appears once again and never speaks, poor man) took turns to feature in close-ups which will fit into the stuff we shot outside the Foreign Office. The coach party salute and bow gravely to non-existent passers-by, but of course they do not speak. No sound always makes for a very easy shoot, even though we all stay quiet as mice. It means that Mitch doesn't have to fuss where his boom can go, without it casting a shadow on the stars. Then the BP film was changed from St James's Park to the crowded stands of cheering people on the way to the Coronation. In squeezed Dame S and MM on one side, SLO and Dicky opposite them, prepared to be rocked gently up and down and cued to react as ordered. Dame S had a funny speech about her last coronation: 'Happily no fatalities – except in the crowd' – turning to wave to them. MM had to 'silent act', or react, a lot, which is not her 'forte'.

I'm not surprised she was a little hysterical. She went to the first night of AM's play – *A View from the Bridge* – last night and she must be exhausted. The papers are full of her 'low-cut crimson dress'. Evidently it brought the house down more than the play. Plod said AM didn't mind a bit. His ego is impregnable.

I dined this evening with Al at the club. Quite a relief to feel civilised again. Al takes a pretty jaundiced view of 'Showbiz' and is not too sympathetic when I describe my lack of love life either. 'You should be tougher, old boy.'

I know he is right. He is wonderful company, much cleverer than I am, but that's what's great. Talking of unsuccessful love life, I am driving Susie down to Saltwood tomorrow morning. At least I have the new Lancia Aurelia GT to take her in, but I don't expect she'll notice.

CARPENTERS' ARMS, SUNDAY, 14 OCTOBER

Susie was a magical weekend guest. She chattered away merrily on the drive and enchanted Mama and Papa as soon as she arrived. She is a good talker but also a very good listener, and there is nothing Papa likes more than a pretty girl who listens.

After lunch I invited her for a walk along 'the white cliffs of Dover' in the sunshine. As we were whizzing in to Folkestone an elderly car in front of us pulled over to the right, signalled a right turn by hand and indicator and then turned sharply left. Only the Lancia brakes saved me from the dubious distinction of putting Hollywood's most promising actress straight through the windshield. Even so, we banged the left side of the other car. A policeman on a motorbike actually witnessed the whole event from the other side of the road and came over. It turned out that the combined age of the four occupants in the other car was over 320, and the whole thing quickly developed into a farce. The driver, who was not the youngest, started to explain to the policeman. 'I'm just a silly old fool,' he said. The policeman had his crash helmet on and misheard. 'Who are you calling a fool?' he asked menacingly. But the driver was deaf too and persisted. Cross purposes set in all over the place, and Susie and I quickly left before we got complete giggles. But up on the cliff, Susie suddenly went silent and preoccupied, and we hardly spoke until we got back to the castle. Perhaps it was the shock.*

She recovered during dinner, and by the time I dropped her back to the Dorchester this evening we were the firmest of friends. I do hope to see her again, but I somehow doubt it. She will marry some super star and that will be that. Is there nothing for me between a little Wdg and a Hollywood star?

MONDAY, 15 OCTOBER

The coach was a lot easier to work with when it just sat on rockers in front of a BP screen. As soon as horses were attached it became

---

* I later learned that Susan had just been jilted by Richard Burton, who had been her lover. She wrote in her autobiography that she had been thinking about jumping off the cliff. Quite a compliment to my company!

unpredictable, no matter how many grooms were standing by. We started the day with it actually in the studio, outside the front door of the Embassy. SLO, MM, Dame S and Dicky had to walk out of the hall and get into it, on their way to the Abbey. A seedy bunch of extras stood around outside, hiding the fact that Belgrave Square was missing. There was no dialogue, so getting into the coach was not much problem, but each time it set off, it was with a mighty lurch.

This did not look good, so the coach had to be backed up, and everyone extricated before we could try again. Tony B was directing – since SLO was in the blooming thing – and he could not be satisfied. These repeated neck-snapping departures were quite trying on the nerves of the passengers, and also on their costumes, wigs, monocles etc. In the end, SLO had had enough. 'Print the bloody lot,' he said. 'We'll choose the best at rushes. One of them seemed OK to me.' Tony pretended to be angry, but he was secretly relieved. He can never be angry with 'Laurence' for more than 10 seconds, anyway.

After lunch, we took the coach and the stars and about 150 extras onto a windy 'lot' to do a little trotting about. It was extremely hard for Jack to light, even with arc lights. It isn't meant to be sunny, after all. They went under a false Admiralty Arch with MM getting very excited and Dicky W looking nervous (real-life nervous). Then they reached the theatre in which Elsie Marina was performing. In front of it was a stand, packed with the cast of Elsie's musical comedy, *The Coconut Girl*. Tomorrow this group will have dialogue, but for today they only had to cheer wildly, toot horns and wave flags. They are a lovely bunch of actors and actresses, very good hearted and jolly, despite the weather and the delays. They know they aren't at the centre of the film but this doesn't seem to worry them a bit. For them, any work is better than nothing. I hope MM doesn't have to learn this hard lesson one day.

TUESDAY, 16 OCTOBER

No more coach and horses and no more MM either. She had a day off. The weather is cold and grey so we had arc lights on the lot again. At least it didn't rain. One never films in the rain, David tells me. 'Film rain' is always carefully directed from a special hose pipe. But the lack of rain clouds worried Jack Harris. There is no pleasing a film editor!

The theatre cast did their dialogue in medium shot, so very few extras were involved. Jean Kent* is 'the star' and she looks lovely. I fancied her like mad when I was a teenager and she was a heroine of B movies. Gladys Henson** is the dresser, and she reminds me of the little Wdg's boss (who now disapproves of me so much). There are three super girls who play MM's special friends – Vera Day is very cute and cockney, Gillian Owen is dark and quiet, and Daphne Anderson is just lovely. She has generous smiling eyes and a wide mouth – the sort of big-sister friend any actress would dream of having in real life. She shares 'digs' with Elsie Marina and there will be a scene there later. And of course they all feature in the back-stage action, which we will film last of all. For now, Daphne has a trumpet which she blows mightily to catch MM's attention. (It doesn't really make any noise at all. The 'toots' will be added later.) Then we 'shot' the girls on the pavement outside the Embassy; waving and tooting again. Beside them was the barrel organ which is meant to be making the music which Elsie is dancing to when Jeremy comes into the purple room. Naturally, it too doesn't make a sound. My goodness, what a long time ago that purple room seems.

Incidentally we saw the 'rushes' of our efforts yesterday and the coach does seem to jerk mightily on departure every time. It is always

* b.1921. Her many films – not all of them 'B's – included *Fanny by Gaslight*, *The Wicked Lady*, *The Rake's Progress* and Rattigan's *The Browning Version*.
** (1897–1983). Irish actress who specialised in warm-hearted maternal characters.

doubtful when you insert a note of reality into a fairy story but I think it will work. In fact it looked quite amusing to me, if not to Tony.

WEDNESDAY, 17 OCTOBER

Paula has gone back to NYC, taking Susie with her. This is seen as a great victory by the anti-Paula brigade but it is bound to put an added strain on MM, and indeed on AM. Luckily, it coincided with her getting very good reviews in all the papers for her latest film, *Bus Stop*. Josh Logan, the director, told a different story, but as usual the only thing that matters with a film is the final result. So MM was full of the joys of spring on a cold grey morning. Just as well. We are still on the lot, and this scene follows her dance. She was happy when she did the dance, so she has to be happy now. And that isn't easy when you are perched up behind a fake window in a long white evening dress. There wasn't any serious dialogue to remember. The first time she looks out of the window – or through it, since it is out of doors, there is only a crowd of extras beneath. The second time she sees her friends and waves. Then she has to hush them, as she pretends that she is listening to Jeremy on the phone. This was a little hard for her. 'Listening Intently' does not conjure up any particular expression. MM chose anxiety – not a difficult one for her to choose, given the circumstances. Then Elsie moves out onto the broad balcony over the front door, to reassure her friends and talk about the Grand Duke. The final shot was of the Grand Duke, standing in front of another fake window reacting to her description of him. In these window shots, SLO always exaggerates and stands too close to the edge – both of the window frame and the camera frame. I know he wants the audience to be sure to see MM in the background, but it looks artificial. He did just the same in the purple room, but if Tony doesn't see it there is certainly nothing I can say.

THURSDAY, 18 OCTOBER

We are back in the studio to film the interior of Westminster Abbey. Roger has built two sides of the nave with an arch in between. As usual with film sets, when you first see it you can't believe it will work, but it always does. The angles have been worked out long in advance. SLO and Dame S are on one side of the Abbey, and the arch, and MM sits next to Dicky W on the other, but they can see one another. By now we all assume MM will be late (I wish we'd done that from the beginning), so we started with Dame S and SLO, sitting among a group of the most distinguished-looking extras we could find. These were dressed as other minor royalty and ambassadors and they looked pretty good. Everyone stood up and bowed as a row of even more elderly extras trooped past, dressed as 'serjeants at arms' or whatever, escorting the royal couple. Rightly King George V and Queen Mary were left to the imagination! When MM arrived, we did the same procedure with her and Dicky. MM looked suitably awed and was on best behaviour. She's always more relaxed when there is no dialogue (who isn't?). She had a very pretty headdress and necklace on which the Queen Mum (Dame S) had lent her earlier on.

After his usual conference with SLO, Milton asked me to go back with him to Tibbs. He and Amy then invited me to move in to the spare room at Tibbs and stay for the rest of the movie. I was overwhelmed.

'When?' was all I could say.

'Tonight if you want to.' It's true that I don't have much luggage, but I must say goodbye properly to my friends at the pub so I am back here for another couple of nights.

'Can I come on Saturday afternoon?'

'Whenever you like.' That open hospitality, with no strings attached, is absolutely the best side of the American character. Milton and Amy have always been so easy-going and friendly and I am absolutely thrilled. I suddenly realise how lonely life has been here. Now I feel back in the family again.

FRIDAY, 19 OCTOBER

Today was MM's big day. At last she really had to act in a 'method' way. She had a chance to put all she had learned from Lee Strasberg into practice. No song and dance, no flippant chat. She had to feel emotions and convey them to the camera with nothing to help her other than her own face. She is in the Abbey; she is in close-up; she is in the midst of a solemn and historic occasion. The Monarch of England is being crowned. Now that is pretty strong stuff for a showgirl. Of course to act in a conventional SLO way would have been easier. But MM had been determined to do something the 'method' way or bust in the attempt. The problem is that with the crew all round – and there are often as many as 60 people behind the camera* – it is very hard to sit and *feel* anything. It must be easier to pretend you feel them, but that would be cheating! Elsie was supposed to be so overcome with the drama of it all that tears spring to her eyes. Evidently MM has done the tears trick in previous movies, and she is rather proud of the achievement, so she had told SLO that it would be no problem. She had been powerfully briefed by Paula before she left. 'Think of Frank Sinatra. Think of Coca-Cola,' Paula had said. (I swear that is a direct quote.) But in the event, poor MM could not manage to squeeze a single tear. Loud Handel ('Zadok the Priest'??, I think), played on a tape in the studio, meant nothing to her. (Why should it?) Her lips parted and quivered and she seemed to go into a trance. The camera rolled away a lot of very expensive film, but no tears came. Glycerine was produced to make fake tears but she refused it. She flushed an unmakeupable rash and we all settled down to wait some more – while she went back to her dressing room.

I fancy she had a couple of glasses of champagne to steady the nerves, but for whatever reason, when she came back to the set, a real tear did indeed trickle down her cheek. A triumph for the Actors Studio indeed, but glycerine would have been much quicker!

* Nowadays it would be more like three hundred.

This is my last night in the pub. They were all very kind and gave me a jolly evening. Funnily enough I found that I have drunk much less in the evenings than I usually do. Perhaps after the film is over, I should get a job working behind a bar instead of sitting in front of it!

TIBBS FARM, SUNDAY, 21 OCTOBER

It is simply great to be at Tibbs. What luxury after the pub, and even dear Runnymede. There is nothing like deep pile Wilton underfoot in the bathroom. Milton and Amy run an open house, with drink and food always available. Milton's assistant David Maysles is very 'laid back' and easy-going. I suppose he and I are a bit too alike to be friends. He is to Milton what I am to SLO, and so we both know what makes the other tick, and how much ambition lurks beneath the surface. David has an incredibly pretty girl friend, an English actress called June Thorburn.* (There he is definitely one up on me.) Both of us are 'gofers' for now, and no gofer likes gofering in front of another gofer, which makes us wary of each other. In his case, he is forever running down to the shops (on a motorscooter) to get Milton and Amy fresh supplies. I think Amy is taking Josh back to USA soon, and then life will get even more relaxed. There is only one problem. It is going to be very difficult to go up to bed at 9.30 p.m. I have found that if I want seven hours' sleep, from 10.30 p.m. to 5.30 a.m., I have to be in my room by 9.45 p.m. I need the time to write this diary, and to compose myself. Milton likes to start to eat dinner at 9 p.m. One thing is certain, I still have to be at Pinewood by 6.40 a.m. each morning if I want to keep my job.

MONDAY, 22 OCTOBER

Plod called up, early, to say that a new 'shrink' had arrived from the USA to see MM, a Doctor Hohenberg I think. Just what MM

* (1931–67). Her films included *The Pickwick Papers*, *The Cruel Sea*, *Tom Thumb*.

needs – another daft piece of advice from someone with instant solutions! He* may hold her hand and calm her down temporarily but it would take years to cure her problems permanently. His arrival definitely means MM will not be in today.

We have moved into the Grand Ballroom set. SLO and Dicky had a nice scene with Maxine Audley.** Maxine is Lady Sunningdale, an old girl friend of the Grand Duke's. (Her name is a typical 'in joke' of Rattigan's. He lives in Wentworth, which is just down the road from Sunningdale, and people who live in Wentworth look down on Sunningdale.) The Grand Duke is setting up a date for later that evening, because Elsie Marina had passed out on him the night before. She had drunk 'an amount of vodka which, in Carpathia, you would add to the morning milk of a two-year-old child' – in reality about six glasses, plus champagne. Naturally SLO and Dicky and Maxine played the scene impeccably. They have all acted together many times. It was only the 'extras' and the lights which needed attention. Maxine used to be a great beauty on stage. She is still very handsome (and sexy), but compared to MM she looks tired. SLO and Jeremy have very fine matching white uniforms, with red sashes. A ball scene really brings out the best in Bumble (and Cecil Beaton), and the ladies' dresses are equally sumptuous.

My main task was to look after the horde of extras, mostly members of old-time dancing clubs, who will fill the ballroom tomorrow. They have to be carefully shepherded between wardrobe, where their costumes are fitted, to dance rehearsals with Billy Chappell. Unlike regular FAA extras, they must not be yelled at and ordered around. Our regular extras are still here, of course, as guests and servants, and anyone else who doesn't speak or dance. They will all be on camera tomorrow. It is going to be a hectic week. At least

* Actually Dr Hohenberg was a she.
** (1923–92). Distinguished stage actress whose occasional film appearances included *The Barretts of Wimpole Street, Our Man in Havana, The Trials of Oscar Wilde*. She was a great friend of Vivien Leigh.

Milton had no one to dinner tonight so I could slink up here early with a sandwich from the 'fridge'.

TUESDAY, 23 OCTOBER

The dancers looked fabulous as they swirled round the studio floor. There are real crystal chandeliers, and Roger has included a magnificent carpeted staircase with a full orchestra at the bottom of it. Roger, Carmen, Bumble and Dario all fuss around until the camera is actually running, and Elaine has a terrible time trying to keep track of such complicated continuity. The band plays the Sleeping Prince Waltz, while the couples all revolve under the watchful eye of Billy C. Even MM was exhilarated and gave a sparkling performance when she finally arrived. (Music and a new set – both always cheer her up.) We have finished on the gallery and moved to the staircase. The first shot with MM was of her and Jeremy sitting in the middle of it, blocking the paths of the other guests. Lady Sunningdale is stuck behind them and we hear her say, acidly, 'Excuse me, please.' Then we cut to Maxine and see her walk, disapprovingly, round Elsie, and down to the dance floor. It was a good moment to compare the two, one a fading beauty and the other so young and fresh; one so British and one so American. For all the pills and problems, MM looks so full of life and *joie de vivre* in comparison.

The Grand Duke enters the shot from behind and Jeremy persuades them to dance. They went out onto the crowded dance floor, and it was quite a touching scene in a way. MM is a good dancer, and for once SLO's ultra stiff posture made a moving contrast. Our problem was that the extras tend to slow up. They are not as blasé as our regulars, and they all want to be in a close-up shot with SLO and MM. But one can't blame them.

WEDNESDAY, 24 OCTOBER

The good news came at the end of the day. The 'rushes' looked fabulous and even MM, who came to watch for a change, was very impressed. She looked great, the dancers looked great, the set looked great, even SLO looked quite handsome. During the day, things were not so good. For some reason, MM was in a bad temper, so everyone suffered. She was curt with Milton, abrupt with SLO and even snapped at her dresser and her make-up man, which is extremely rare. Plod says that she suspects Milton of some sort of knavery. He also said that she grumbles at AM all the time now.

Even so we managed one very long take in which Elsie and the Grand Duke start to dance. Elsie tries to persuade the Duke to make peace with his son and, as they swirl around, she reads out the young King's conditions. She seemed to forget the last one for a second – genuinely or not I don't know – and then blurted out, 'Oh yes, and he wants a general election.' Strangely enough, it actually worked quite well.

The Grand Duke is dismissive of her attempts to play politics. 'Madame de Pompadour is beyond your range, my dear.' Then he asks 'Do you reverse?' meaning the waltz. MM gave a wild laugh. 'Just try me!' she cried and off they both swept into the crowd.

Only in fairy tales, and films, alas, does such a large crowd dance in such perfect harmony.

But that was all we did get today. The other dancing shots will be done tomorrow, as each requires a new set-up down on the floor. Lots of work for Jack and the stand-ins to do first thing. When MM arrives at her usual hour (8.30), three set-ups a day with her are the best we can hope for. Thank goodness this is such a simple, studio-bound film to shoot.

THURSDAY, 25 OCTOBER

Another day of MM dancing with SLO. The two-shots aren't too bad, but the close-ups are technically very tricky. The cameraman has really to dance with them, and the lighting is critical. In his close-up, SLO had to show that he now realises how delightful this showgirl is, no matter how headstrong and 'disconcerting'. In MM's close-up she had to make it clear that she is now ecstatically in love with the Grand Duke. This was asking quite a lot of both of them. MM was clearly the subject of a technical debate most of the morning, and anyway she was still feeling pretty bad-tempered. Added to that she clearly loathes the man she is meant to be in love with. I think the final – and successful – result was more the result of self-hypnosis than great acting, but perhaps there isn't, or shouldn't be, much difference between the two. In the end we managed four set-ups so we should be out of here by the end of the week.

I had a total surprise when I got back here to Tibbs tonight. Waiting on the doorstep in a hire car were Little David Tennant and Dommy Elwes.* I knew at once that they must be desperate for money, and couldn't but wonder which of them would end up paying the fare! They had found out where I was through Lockhart and Mr Cotes-Preedy at the Club. It turns out that they want me to share a flat with them when the movie is over, and they want to take the flat right now. It is at No 3, Mount Street and has a drawing room overlooking Berkeley Square. It sounded terrific but of course there was a catch. It is quite expensive – £24 per month (£8 each) – and I have to sign the lease, and I have to put up £300 for the privilege (to own the lease). David even insists that he has one of the bathrooms to himself, and Dommy and I share the other one. Dommy has to take what he can get of course. He hasn't got a bean and, I suspect, has no intention of paying the £8 per month either. It seems a bit hard on me but David is so arrogant that one can't argue with him. *He* found the flat, he is doing me a favour etc. Well, I have to live somewhere, and David and Dommy are very stimulating company. Also it is the only offer I've had, and I hate living alone. So I said 'yes' and duly wrote out a cheque. Dommy is going to start

---

* Dominic Elwes is now dead, alas, and did indeed turn out to be an expensive flatmate. I was entirely mistaken about David Tennant, however. He more than paid his way before he sold me the lease of the flat and left for the USA. (They were both actually quite big – 'Little' was a nickname.)

---

redecorating right away. He is very good at this, but he has very expensive tastes. Right now he tells me he is involved with the two 'geniuses' of interior decoration – a Mr Bonsack and a Mr Fowler.* He says he will make the flat so beautiful that no girl will be able to say 'no' at the crucial moment! I gave him an absolute spending limit of £400, but limits mean nothing to Dommy. He can charm credit out of a stone. I have lived rent-free for most of the film, and I've spent very little of my wages. Even so it means dipping into GrandPapa's trust – again.

FRIDAY, 26 OCTOBER

We are now at the exit of the ballroom. Elsie is scared of losing her love, but the Grand Duke has his mind firmly set on Lady Sunningdale. The little Ambassador re-appeared for this scene, talking to Lady Sunningdale in the background. I thought he only featured in the coach and the Embassy so I'd forgotten who he was and mistook him for an extra. Luckily I just stopped short of demanding his card when he did not immediately do what he was told. Then MM and SLO did a long scene together – one of the many 'goodbyes' that run through the script. I suspect MM cannot remember which is the last goodbye or which is the important one, so she tends to give them all a lot of heartfelt drama. In today's, Elsie is meant to know that she and Jeremy are only going for a jaunt and that she will soon be back at the Embassy, so they are not saying goodbye for long. But that did not enter into her performance.

'Oh, your Grand Ducal,' she sobbed. 'It's been a great, great . . . well . . . goodbye.' Luckily one forgets the script where MM is concerned, and it works. 'She's the only one the public will be looking at,' Dame Sybil had said. 'She's really giving everyone else lessons in acting for the cinema.' Nine weeks ago this observation

---

* Mr Bonsack had a very expensive bathroom shop, and Mr Fowler was the partner in Colefax & Fowler.

made SLO cross enough. Now it might make a murderer of him, but it is still true.

Talking of Grand Dames, I hear that MM is going to see Dame Edith Sitwell* tomorrow. I could hardly believe it, but Edith is as eccentric as they come and she also adores the limelight. I met Edith with Osbert** at Rennishaw when I was in the RAF. She was hilariously funny and witty and I was in stitches all through lunch. She told how she was on a driving tour of Italy, when they came across a herd of bullocks in the road. 'Drive on' she ordered. Then one bullock stuck its head through her open window, just as the car began to accelerate. 'Stop!' she shrieked, but the driver could not hear, and the bullock had to gallop alongside, its big frightened face an inch from Edith's. Luckily it wasn't a very fast car. I do hope she tells stories like that to MM. It will cheer her up no end.

I didn't say anything of this to MM, or to Milton. Indeed, SLO looked grimly at me as if to say 'Don't you dare.' He knows Edith is a great friend of Mama's, but he clearly conveyed 'Don't get involved, Colin,' and I'm sure he was right. Those two ladies can be as crazy as they like to each other. Neither will understand a word the other is saying, that's for sure, and probably neither will even listen. A highbrow MM is not.

MONDAY, 29 OCTOBER

MM was given the day off today, and quite rightly so. She is going to meet the Queen. First Dame Edith Sitwell and now the Queen! Not bad for a little girl from California. She will be at the first night of *The Battle of the River Plate**** at the Empire Cinema, Leicester

---

* (1887–1964). Poetess, public figure and celebrated English eccentric. She had met MM at a Hollywood tea party in 1952, and invited her to come to tea in London.
** Edith's younger brother (1892–1969). Poet, novelist, biographer, autobiographer. Rennishaw Hall was the Sitwell family home in Derbyshire.
*** Directed by Michael Powell and Emeric Pressburger. It was released in the US under the title *Pursuit of the Graf Spee*. Tony Bushell was one of the principal actors.

Square. Naturally she needed the whole day to get ready for this momentous event and I expect the Queen did too. (They are the same age, actually. The Queen looks a little older, but healthier.) Bumble helped MM to choose a suitable dress and was at Parkside all day overseeing preparations. Bumble is actually a very calming person. She always seems to be so wrapped up in her own nervous twitches that she doesn't have time to take any notice of yours. The effect is very endearing and MM likes her. Plod is very thrilled about the whole affair. His protégée, as he thinks of MM, is going to meet his monarch. Of course he will be there in the car, protecting MM just as his friends protect H.M. If Plod is excited, MM is in a complete spin. Plod said she has been curtseying all over the house and even trying to talk in an English accent, goodness knows why. I suppose that meeting the Queen is a wonderful sign of success for every actor and actress. Even MM can't ignore that, and any encouragement is so good for her soul that I am happy for her. More than anything, MM wants to feel accepted, and to her the invitation to a great Premiere like this, and shaking hands with Royalty, means that she has been accepted as one of the great actresses of her time. She is no longer just a sex symbol or a calendar girl. She is making a film with Sir Laurence Olivier. The Queen is not to know that the film is on the verge of falling apart because MM is always late and cannot remember her lines. Indeed, I'm sure that the Queen wouldn't care two pins even if someone had told her. Film-making is as much a mystery to H.M. as it is to most people. It is only the finished movie that matters. All actresses throw tantrums and have done since time began. If the Queen did but know, MM throws fewer than most. Only someone very unkind would suggest that it is the Queen's advisers who choose the latest Hollywood freak to amuse their mistress. Certainly not me.

TUESDAY, 30 OCTOBER

MM got rave reviews for her appearance last night. 'MM Captures Britain' was one headline. But in Studio A the drama continues.

I suppose MM stayed up very late and so was extra tired today. The trouble is that she takes extra pills when she doesn't feel 100%, without really knowing what effect the pills will have. If I take a pill and it makes me feel lousy, I don't take it again. Not MM. She just takes another pill to counteract the first one. As a result she was at her most distant and remote. When she is like that, no one can talk to her. It just isn't worth the effort. This is so sad, because she should be on top of the world. Drugs just spoil everything. I know how tempting they are and goodness knows I can't preach. I take too much alcohol, and too many cigarettes. MM looks more and more vulnerable and I am sorry for her. But when a whole studio is waiting to do an expensive and complicated shot, going ga-ga is not the way to be popular.

This morning, during one of the inevitable long delays, I went up into the lighting grid. I was invited, I hasten to add. You never *dare* to stray into anyone else's little kingdom here without being invited, especially the Kingdom of the Sparks. It is incredibly hot. All the heat of the studio lights is trapped up there. The extractor fans are turned off during filming, and then the place is airtight. There are far more men up there than I realised, mostly in string vests. I never thought they took any notice of what went on below them on the studio floor, but they know everything and everybody. They cannot stand MM. Even *they* get frustrated, waiting around for her to start work, and to remember a single line. They are real old pros, veterans of countless Rank films, and they think of MM as totally unprofessional. I tried to explain that it wasn't fair to expect MM to be like Norman Wisdom,* but they weren't having it. 'If it wasn't for our loyalty to Sir Laurence,' said one, seriously, 'I'd have edged a spanner off the grid and onto her head.' I'm very glad indeed they haven't gone that far.

When I went into SLO's dressing room with the whisky and cigs this evening he was alone. Tony goes back to London now and

* Durable British comic actor, 1918–2010.

Milton had dashed home with MM. SLO wanted to chat and even offered me a drink.

'Can you believe it Colin? Am I doing such a bad job? Anyway it doesn't matter.' The poor man slumped in his make-up chair, wiping his face. 'The bloody Strasbergs have won the day with Milton, and Paula will be back tomorrow.'

'Maybe that will put MM in a better humour,' I suggested.

'I have never been in a situation like this before, Colin and you can be bloody sure I never will again. It's a f—ing nightmare. I thought this would be an exciting challenge, a renaissance, I thought Marilyn would make me feel young again. Some bloody hope. I feel dead. I look dead in the bloody rushes. It's killing me.'

'It won't be long now, Sir Laurence,' I said. 'We must keep our nerve.' He grunted.

I can see he feels completely smothered. If only he'd stuck to acting. He thought his role as Grand Duke was so easy, especially after the theatre, that he might as well direct too, and of course get the extra money. Little did he know what went on beneath MM's famous bosom!

WEDNESDAY, 31 OCTOBER

SLO was late. He even arrived after MM for once. ('F— her' he said when I told him.) But he was still on the set long before MM. He is so professional that he can easily get made up and dressed in half an hour if he wants to, just as he does in the theatre.

MM's retreat into a fantasy world is getting more common every day. It is both the cause of, and is caused by, MM's growing unpopularity. If any of us talk to her she looks at them as if they belonged to a different species, and this does make it very hard to like her. Even the most kind-hearted members of the crew, who understand some of MM's problems – and I like to think this includes me – still get frustrated and fed up.

The Digs scene we shot today should be a very nice one. Dicky W is sitting behind a screen – all elegant legs and blasé voice – while Elsie dashes round, choosing a dress. She is helped by her roommate, the divine Daphne Anderson. It is at the beginning of the story, and Elsie clearly thinks that she is invited to a big Embassy reception, even though she can't think why. Daphne – who does know why, or at least can guess – clucks round with sisterly concern. Elsie didn't seem to need any special 'motivation' except the obvious one of a girl trying to get the right dress on. But soon MM was dashing backwards and forwards to her recliner, shaking her hands like a dervish, even though you can't imagine two more sympathetic professionals to act with than Dicky and Daphne.

THURSDAY, I NOVEMBER

Winter is almost here, but the film seems to go on and on. Are all films such agony? Those balmy summer days with my little Wdg seem literally years ago. But showbiz has its compensations. Tonight Milton had a wonderful dinner party. It is already 11.30 but I must make a note of it before I go to sleep.

The main guest was Gene Kelly, and he is quite incredible – friendly, positive, unassuming and fantastically witty. He can mimic anyone, dance on a sixpence, sing like an angel and tell endless jokes. At one stage I remarked to him how much I had enjoyed the Bolshoi Ballet* – I was trying to impress him I suppose, since only a few people have been able to get anywhere near Bolshoi performances. He immediately jumped up and did an impression of Ulanova which was devastating – but also touching. After all she is about 45 and

---

* The Bolshoi Ballet was visiting London for the first time since the war. My father had a box for the opening night as he was on the Board of the Royal Opera House. I had taken a beautiful young actress called Maureen Swanson (now Countess of Dudley) but it had been a total failure, which is why I didn't mention it in my diary.

still dancing Giselle, albeit magically well. Gene Kelly managed to convey all this as he danced in the dining room of Tibbs Farm, humming his own rendition of the music. Most impressive, and there is no doubt what got him to the top – talent. The other star guest was a glamorous star*let*. She is an Italian girl called Elsa Martinelli* and she has had a special place in my affections ever since I was 15. I had a colour photograph of her pinned up inside my 'bury'** at Eton. In it she had on very short jeans and a revealing wet shirt. Attired thus, she alternately drove me crazy and stimulated me to action for two years. I suppose the 'real thing' could never quite match a posed pin-up. Miss Martinelli is still beautiful, but eight years older now of course. She is also very unpleasant. She is gratuitously nasty; she rarely smiles, and she loves to put people down (especially me), so that's the end of that love affair! I'm certainly glad we aren't making *The Sleeping Prince* with *her* playing Elsie Marina.

Even so, Milton is a wonderful host, and David Maysles is an excellent foil, so the whole thing went really well. It was almost impossible for me to get up and leave the room. GK and EM are staying the night. EM has a near perfect figure – or at least she had in that picture. Even so I didn't want to sleep with her. Poison is poison, no matter which bottle it's in.

FRIDAY, 2 NOVEMBER

Usually Milton controls his energy much better than I do. That is possibly why he is so successful. But today he looked very grey. Alas it looks as if he has finally fallen out with SLO. He – Milton – is fed up with being responsible for delivering MM to the studio every morning, and taking her bad temper all day. 'I'm not her nanny,' he said plaintively this evening. 'Olivier should scream at Paula. She

* b.1933. Her English-language films included *Manuela, The Trial, Marco the Magnificent*.
** Eton slang for desk ('bureau').

has more influence than me. Tell him to scream at Arthur, Colin. See if that helps.'

We all know that it is no good screaming at any of them. SLO is getting very frustrated. After all Milton *did* promise to get MM to the studio for work. He did assure SLO that he was in control. He did promise to restrict Paula to MM's dressing room and so on and so on. Milton is the only person SLO can scream at (except for Tony and me), and when SLO has to scream, he screams.

And Tony is being really short with Milton, which is a sure sign that SLO is being very rude about Milton behind his back. Tony would never dare to do that off his own bat. If filming goes according to plan – the new Mk III plan, that is, not the original Perceval cross-plot – then we will be finished shooting in two weeks. Surely we can last till then.

We were in the Elsie's dressing-room set today, and MM was being very erratic. She grabbed a huge powder puff and covered herself in powder, and then she rearranged her hair in the mirror. This sort of behaviour is fine in a real music-hall dressing room, but on a film set it gives hysterics to make-up, wardrobe, wigs, continuity (Elaine), camera (Denys) and sound (Mitch). I suppose it did make a bit of a mess but the effect was like that of a hand grenade.

We had just finished a scene with old Gladys Henson as the dresser. She and MM had both got so nervous that we nearly gave up and went home. 'My shoulder thing is busted' was the best we could get for the essential reference to a pinned strap which will break again in front of the Grand Duke. We are saved by the fact that all the other actresses are absolute stalwarts, who never panic, no matter what. Take after take they produce the same flawless performances, as if it was the first. I suppose if they were all nervous Americans they could all have hysterics together, and get it over and done with. A sort of camaraderie might have grown up which would embrace MM instead of excluding her. These people would love to include MM, but they just do not speak the same language.

The result is that she feels, and becomes, more and more remote. We all feel helpless and frustrated.

I must get some sleep. Stars can afford nervous breakdowns, senior crew are allowed to have a headache, 3rd Ast Dirs must stay in rude health. No energy, no job.

MONDAY, 5 NOVEMBER

Guy Fawkes night, and no prizes for guessing where we would like to plant a bomb. But she didn't turn up at all this morning, so we had a relatively peaceful day.

Milton is not quite so quick to go to SLO's dressing room after 'rushes' these days, nor quite so welcome, and Tony heads off for London. This means that I can usually stay for a chat and a drink. SLO likes to unwind with big whiskies and Olivier cigarettes for half an hour before going home to Vivien. Tonight the poor man was already worrying about what he will do next. He has to continue working on the film – editing, adding music, special effects etc. until after Christmas – but then he wants to find a new challenge. He is obsessed with the fact that he will be 50 next year, and sees this as a big turning point. Famous as he is, he is not interested in the successes of the past. He feels he has a far greater contribution still to make, and is not prepared to rest on his laurels. All the trappings of being a star he sees as hindrances – Notley, the knighthood, even, to some extent, Vivien. It is wonderful to be so ambitious – at 50! He very kindly said that he hopes I will stay with him, whatever he does. Of course he cannot guarantee anything. He may accept a job working for somebody else. That would probably be a relief to start with, although he is too experienced to be told what to do except by a very few, brilliant directors.

'But you are part of the family now, Colin,' he said, and that is what I wanted to hear more than anything else. Loyalty is what he demands and then he is fiercely loyal back. He certainly won't go straight into another film – he couldn't stand it – so that means the theatre. But which play? And for whom?* Right now he has to get this film finished somehow. It's much too late for him to find a new approach – to MM or to anyone else in her group. He does realise that Milton is trying his best, but he has lost some of his respect for him. He knows that AM is only too keen to get MM out of the house in the mornings, and for this reason alone is an ally. He can see that everyone else in the film is rooting for him, and giving all the help they can. But still: 'Frankly Colin, I've had it' is his constant refrain. 'Vivien is being very difficult. She is clearly fed up with the whole thing. She never liked the idea – hated it in fact. She was jealous, I suppose, although she'd never admit that.' Now she is bored. Doesn't want to listen to SLO's moans any more. She always hated early nights. She won't respect film discipline. She's started the old round of house guests and dinner parties and late nights at Notley. 'I don't like that, Colin. In fact I hate it.'

(I haven't bothered to put in all the swear words, but there were plenty.) The truth is that, once again, Vivien doesn't let him get enough sleep. Fancy being tormented by both these women at once – Vivien Leigh and Marilyn Monroe. And I get the impression that he isn't having sex with either!

TUESDAY, 6 NOVEMBER

We are still in Elsie's dressing room at the theatre. The 'girls', Elsie's companions, with minor roles to play, are what keep us all going. They are completely unspoilt, and are thrilled to be working with MM, which makes them a joy. MM is so famous that any actress could be forgiven for thinking that a little of that fame must rub off. Vera Day plays, and is, a cheeky Cockney. Her husband came to collect her this evening and we met in the long corridor. I soon

---

* In fact his next project was to be one of the most unexpected and significant stage performances of his career – as Archie Rice in John Osborne's *The Entertainer* at the Royal Court, directed by George Devine.

found out why she bothered to introduce him to me. 'I wonder if you could do me a favour Colin,' he said immediately. I murmured that I'd be delighted to try. 'Right then. Go to the editing room and get a few frames of film with Vera in the picture with Marilyn. I'll see you all right,' he added, and pressed a 2 shilling piece into my hand. 'There's another of those for you when you get the film.' That was more naive than I thought.

'No, no, that's frightfully kind of you,' I said, 'but I can't take it. I'll certainly try to find the film, but Sir Laurence would never allow me to accept a reward. Thank you so much for such a generous offer.' He looks like an Old Kent Road bruiser, and he wasn't too pleased to have his 'generous' tip returned. I wonder what I would have done if he'd offered me a 'fiver'? Actually it won't be too easy to do what he asks. I'll have to ask the ast editor for a trim. He will only let me have something shot before the clapper or after the cut and I don't think Vera is in shot with MM very often, except in the middle of a scene.

WEDNESDAY, 7 NOVEMBER

A new film has started shooting at Pinewood with Bob Hope and Katharine Hepburn. It is a comedy called *The Iron Petticoat*. Everyone was dying to meet Hope and dreaded working with Hepburn. Needless to say Hepburn is *divine* and BH is arrogant and unpleasant.

Hepburn says hello to everyone while Hope remains totally aloof. I met Hepburn today when she came to visit SLO. She is as gorgeous as Dame Sybil, only much younger, all red hair, and freckles, and a huge smile which she turned on me as often as on SLO. SLO did have a point when he said later: 'Why couldn't MM have been like that? What a lot of fun we could have had, making this film.'*

* Katharine Hepburn had been a witness at SLO's secret marriage to Vivien in California in 1940. In 1973 she and SLO made their only acting appearance together, as the ageing couple in *Love Among the Ruins*, directed by George Cukor for American television.

'Yes, but MM's had twice the publicity and half the training as an actress. That would derange anyone.'

'No training as an actress at all,' said SLO gloomily. And yet he is forgetting what Dame Sybil said about who the public will be looking at when the film comes out.

My main goal now is to keep SLO cheerful. But I have a dilemma. Do I stick to SLO when all this is over, and hope that he will take me to the theatre with him? Or do I stick to David, and the film gang, and try to get a job as a 2nd Ast Dir with them on their next movie? I haven't talked it over with David yet and that is going to be hard to do without seeming to presume that he would help me.

David can be very touchy and he has always been ambivalent about having a 3rd Ast Dir with 'connections'. I'd really have to dump those 'connections' completely to stay with him. The film world is '*sauve qui peut*'. It is dangerous to presume too much, even though David and Mr P are two people I really feel I can trust to help.

THURSDAY, 8 NOVEMBER

We are now back-stage at the Gaiety Theatre. The Grand Duke is making his visit to the cast in the interval, and they will all be lined up to be introduced. In the 'rushes' of yesterday's footage, MM looked really embarrassing, as if she came from a different production altogether – the mad woman of Chaillot.* Her hair was down and her eyes were wild. Her line 'Oh gosh! I don't have a thing to wear' came out like the cry of a drowning woman – and, come to think about it, that's really what it was!

Today she was more cheerful. She was among a whole group of actors and actresses who treated her pretty much as one of them – a bunch of players thrown together in minor roles in a musical comedy. As they all jostled round, pushing and chattering, she must have felt

* Play by Jean Giraudoux (1882–1944). It was filmed in 1969 starring, coincidentally, Katharine Hepburn.

like she did in the Actors Studio, but tonight MM complained to Paula that she was feeling ill. Paula can no longer speak to anyone English but me, so I act as interpreter. I rushed the news to David first this time, so he could warn Jack and the crew. An early warning like this definitely means that she will not be in tomorrow. Then I went to SLO's dressing room to break it to him gently over a whisky.

'Quick. Warn the crew before they go home.'

'Done.'

'Well try to find Milton, and see if she'll see a doctor. She might be off for five days.'

'Milton's already gone to Parkside to see what he can arrange.'

'Oh. Good,' SLO said doubtfully. He likes me to think for him, but I suppose sometimes it makes him feel old.

'I'm afraid MM is a very healthy young woman,' I said. 'She's just in bad condition. No regular meals, sleep or exercise. Pills one day, champagne the next. No wonder she feels ill but I don't think she *is* ill.'

SLO growled. 'Discipline is the most important thing for an actor. An actor can be permanently drunk, like Bob Newton or Charles Laughton, so long as they have discipline. Without it any actor just falls apart.'

'MM is too spoiled now,' I said. As long as everyone keeps telling her she is a genius and can do no wrong, she won't understand why she should go to sleep, or eat, or turn up at the same time as normal people. It's no good saying 'Marilyn, you are a normal person underneath.' She is completely convinced that her extraordinary fame exempts her completely. What no one dares to tell her is that her fame springs mainly – but not entirely – from her appearance.

'You know, I actually fancied her when I first met her,' said SLO. 'She's a freak of nature, not a genius. A beautiful freak.'

FRIDAY, 9 NOVEMBER

Since we knew MM wasn't coming in, we were all prepared. Everyone is sympathetic to SLO, and tries to help if they can. He looks pretty gloomy all the time, and his performance gets less and less appealing. This is a special pity because what we are shooting now is his first appearance in the film, apart from his arrival in the coach.

MM's first appearance was the mad scene with the powder puff, so they are a pretty sorry pair. (I wonder if that is why she was so nervous then. I hadn't thought of that – but maybe, just maybe, she had.)

Tony B is not as friendly to me these days. That's sad, after all the happy times we had together at Runnymede. I hope it doesn't reflect something that SLO has said to him. Actually I think it is because he is slightly jealous. He is so very possessive of 'Laurence', as he calls him sternly. But he is still a lovely man, and mellows quite quickly when I pretend I haven't noticed him being cool. I don't know if he also expects to move on with SLO. Perhaps SLO has told Vivien – just to please her – that he is taking me with him into the theatre. Vivien's world is built on 'Chums' or – in my case, as with Gilman – adoring slaves. Tony is a SLO man, not a Vivien man. He likes to go off with SLO while Anne stays with Vivien. Now the film is ending, Vivien's influence is growing stronger every day. We will know in 10 days' time.

SATURDAY, 10 NOVEMBER

This morning I just couldn't resist doing a practical joke on Milton and David. The phone rang when we were all having drinks at lunch-time. I was sitting beside it so I picked it up.

'Does Mr Greene need a car over the weekend?' asked a voice. 'Now, listen here Marilyn,' I said crisply. 'I've had enough of your bad behaviour. You're late, you're rude and you don't learn your lines . . .'

By this time Milton and David M had both reached the phone, arms and legs flailing wildly.

'Marilyn, Marilyn, we love you!' they screamed at the startled hire car company. 'Don't listen to him. It was Colin. He's gone crazy. We love you!' I was laughing so much that they began to smell a rat. 'Marilyn? Marilyn?'

'Is that the Greene residence?' said the chauffeur at the end of the line.

I don't know if they will forgive me. I suppose it was cruel of me after so much hospitality. They pretend to see the funny side, but Milton was badly shaken. Even David M 'lost his cool' for a minute or two. At dinner tonight Milton looked at me strangely.

'I didn't know you Brits had it in you,' he said, whatever that means.

MONDAY, 12 NOVEMBER

Seven more days, and then we will all have to go back to the real world. For 15 weeks we have been hermetically sealed in a huge concrete box, like animals in a zoo. We are almost completely cut off from life outside. We arrive in the dark before anyone else is awake and leave in the dark after they are back home again. The average is 13 hours a day. Somehow we have all managed to get along, except, I suppose, for poor MM (and the little Wdg). No one can approach MM now. If you address her directly, you might as well talk in Swahili. She is, no doubt, more desperate to get out than we are. That, however, was not 'motivation' enough to get her to the studio today. Plod rang early – 'Not a chance.' SLO was in a towering rage. The whole cast of *The Coconut Girl* had been called, and there was only one scene we could shoot with them. This consisted of Jean Kent – the leading lady – lining up everyone back-stage ready for the Grand Duke's arrival. As she is finishing she has to ask 'Now. Who's missing?'

'Elsie Marina,' calls Daphne.

'Oh, can't that girl *ever* make an entrance on time?' Miss Springfield replies, crossly. The irony was lost on nobody.

After lunch we did the part of the Grand Duke's progress down the line where he meets Vera Day. Up until now the film has only had one female in it – namely MM, if you don't count old Dame S. I think SLO sometimes forgets what real girls are like. Little Vera Day gave off more energy than SLO expected. He seemed taken aback and almost forgot his lines for a moment – unheard of for SLO. Of course he is very tense, and perhaps he is so brainwashed by MM and Vivien that he expects all women to be difficult. Vera is simple, direct, and sexy. She radiates a different sort of life force to MM. It is lower voltage – and not so far reaching – but it is strong enough to give you a jolt. SLO is normally so wooden, Dicky so dry and Jeremy so discreet that it is little wonder that MM jumps out of the screen every night in 'rushes'. She really has had no competition at all. No one could deny MM's natural talents, and I'm not suggesting that Vera Day could carry the movie, but even so, SLO got a surprise. It was like a man who works in a power station getting an electric shock from his car battery.

I have certainly missed female company over the last 15 weeks. I suppose it's not until you get to be a producer that you sleep with the starlets. I hope there are more opportunities in the theatre. If not, I have a dangerous tendency to fall in love with other people's wives.

TUESDAY, 13 NOVEMBER

At last we have done MM's entrance into the line-up. As the Grand Duke enters through the fire doors and walks onto the stage, Elsie Marina can be seen joining the line in the background. She is in full stage make-up with a feathered hat. MM had bolted in from her recliner next to her portable dressing room in such a hectic flurry that most of the cast, who were agog to see this incredible creature at last, were disappointed. Then the whole apparition vanished again just as quickly when Tony said 'Cut.' Up until now, the timing of her performance has been set throughout the film by her, and this is by design. SLO saw that was something that you could not alter. Today's entrance required split-second precision of the kind she absolutely hates. There were many false attempts and too many people trying to 'cue her in'. We only just had time to do the two-shot where Daphne tries to calm her down – on screen and in real life. MM looked over-excited to meet the Regent. It was as if Elsie was already wondering if he would be attractive and whether she could seduce him, and this is not the way the plot works. But SLO could not throttle her back. Perhaps she is happier hiding behind the heavy 'stage' make-up; perhaps she feels that the end is nigh; or perhaps she had had an extra glass of champagne. (It is not that MM drinks too much, but sometimes at unwise times.)

WEDNESDAY, 14 NOVEMBER

One last big scene with MM. The Grand Duke is coming down the line. MM is in the foreground. She is panicky.

'What do I do?'

Daphne consoles her. 'Just say "How do you do?"' etc.

The manager of the theatre says 'Miss Elsie Marina.'

Grand Duke: 'And the little American friend of our heroine. How do you do?'

By this time MM is desperately trying not to anticipate what is about to happen. 'How do you do, your Regent,' she says. 'Oops,' and her shoulder strap breaks. As she nearly popped out of the low-cut dress, she instinctively turned from the camera, as if from a prying eye, but it worked well.

'The damage, I trust, can be retrieved,' says a delighted Grand Duke.

Elsie, panting for breath: 'Oh yes, I can fix it with a pin.'

The GD looks round. 'Has no one here a pin?' All the men feel their lapels, where flower girls have pinned carnations on them in the past.

GD: 'I would be most happy to assist you.'

Elsie, still confused (and MM even more confused!): 'No, your Regency.'

Pause while she scrabbles to fix the dress.

GD: 'Charming.' He goes to shake hands. 'Better not tempt Providence again.' Laughs. 'Charming. Good night!' He exits.

Actually it is the same stunt that MM pulled at her original press conference with SLO in the USA and one that I expect she has often used to get attention. The hard part was to include it in a pre-rehearsed scene for the camera. But it's all done now, and at one stage that was more than we dared hope. Of course this isn't the end of the job, for us or for MM. She doesn't fly home for a week. We have two days of 'post-syncing' in which MM will re-do her voice for the sound track. She must record any lines which were said off camera, and re-record sentences where her voice wasn't picked up clearly enough. (There hadn't been anywhere suitable to put a microphone when she was face down on the sofa etc.) But at least this means that she doesn't need to be in until 9 a.m. – which she hasn't been for a couple of weeks anyway – and she doesn't need make-up and wardrobe before work. Having said this, Monday and Tuesday have been set aside for possible 'pick up' shots, and for those she will need to be dolled up exactly as before. Elaine will see to that. Jack Harris and his assistant are frantically assembling a 'rough cut' to see which shots need covering. There is no question that we might have missed a shot by mistake, but it is extremely hard, over all these weeks, to make a seamless pattern and overlook nothing. So they will work tomorrow and Friday and all weekend. One thing is for sure – once MM has caught that plane back to the USA, that is it. No chance for one more frame of film of her, no matter how great the crisis.

So there were no celebrations. Milton says that he has arranged a party for Tuesday afternoon, after the last retake. But actually David

Maysles tells me that he has been left to organise it. And quite frankly he couldn't care less.

FRIDAY, 16 NOVEMBER

It was as if a great weight had been lifted off everyone's shoulders. SLO was looking relaxed and years younger. MM was cool and efficient. She never looks at SLO these days, or talks to anyone, but she listened intently to the sound editor's instructions and obeyed them to the letter. As a result she got through far more than we could have imagined, and, I must say, did it extremely well. Post-syncing is a knack, like formation-flying or dancing the tango. MM picked it up immediately, and even seemed to enjoy it. Her face and her voice would appear on the screen and she would watch intently, two or three times. Then she would wave her hand and her face would appear without the voice. She put her words in so exactly that we couldn't tell, in the director's booth, that it wasn't prerecorded. The song was the same. MM always enjoys music scenes and in the end we were all rather moved by this quiet, shy, firm voice. Just for once, MM could go back to Parkside feeling good about herself, but I don't think that is the memory which will endure.

TIBBS FARM, SATURDAY, 17 NOVEMBER

This evening we had a long post-mortem. I was surprised by how much the Americans resented us. I have to admit that I had always assumed that we were the charming well-behaved ones, and the Americans were the trouble makers. Of course they see things quite the other way. They think we are cold, unwelcoming and clique-y. 'Not you, Colin,' Milton put in, with a laugh, 'or we wouldn't have let you in the house.' By and large, we have been as disappointing as hosts as they – well, some of them – have been as guests. In the end I felt sad and apologetic. We haven't exactly behaved badly, but we have been very blinkered to other people's needs – to Milton's, to Paula's, to Arthur's and especially to MM's. It's not as if they had all been monsters in the Arthur P. Jacobs mould. Stupidly, I had assumed that we all had the same aim – to make a good film, on time and on budget. I see now that life is never as simple as that. Everyone, me included, has many other reasons for doing what they did. I really want to start a career, to make a good personal impression even if the film is a flop. I want to persuade SLO that he can't do without me and that he must take me into the theatre with him. MM wanted to change the direction of her career, to be taken seriously in a 'classical' acting role, with a great 'classical' actor. She couldn't expect to play Lady Macbeth straight away, but she wanted something that she could handle without relying solely on her sex appeal. For Milton, it was his first motion picture, his chance to prove to Warner Bros that he could deliver a film as executive producer. It was also a chance to make money. Being a photographer clearly hadn't made him as rich as he'd like.

What a pity that they didn't all sit down and work out what they wanted before the filming started. But then everything was excitement and optimism, and publicity. Serious thought was not encouraged. I understand why Mr Perceval was so grave, but he was the only one. SLO could claim that he'd scheduled rehearsals to be as well prepared as possible, but he and MM were both so on edge that a genuine dialogue was always unlikely. They should have had a quick affair together, and got onto each other's wavelength, at least. There certainly isn't going to be a 'next time'. All that we can hope now is that we've produced a good film. At the moment it is impossible to tell.

MONDAY, 19 NOVEMBER

Surely this was the hardest day of all. After lengthy conferences on Sunday between Jack (editor) and Jack (cameraman), Milton, SLO and Tony, they decided to do two more shots of MM, one more shot with SLO, and, if possible, one shot of both of them together. We started with MM. Make-up, Hair and Wardrobe had all been called for a normal studio day. In a way they were pleased. It is so hard to change the habits you have acquired over 100 days of doing the same thing – we were like patients in a mental hospital when the front door has been left open. Carmen and Roger and Dario had been running round to find the right pieces of set. Jack had to match up the lighting, Elaine was at her strictest, scouring her notes and peering at frames of 35mm film through a magnifying glass. I wonder if anyone explained to MM that these shots are not to correct failures on her part, but to fill in gaps other people may have left. I doubt it, by her behaviour, but then it is pretty hard to explain anything by now. She turned up later than ever, fretted terribly and retreated again and again into her dressing room. All Jack (Harris) really needed were two shots of MM for insurance – one in her white dress against an out-of-focus purple room; and one in her dress and frilly coat in an equally out-of-focus hall. There is a piece of purple wall still existing (thanks to the foresight of Teddy Joseph), and many bits of hall, so that was all right. But MM behaved like a drugged prisoner of war. We did get both shots but goodness knows if they are remotely usable. I suppose they might be better than nothing. We will watch them in 'rushes' tomorrow – in the morning for a change so – theoretically – SLO can ask MM to do them again if necessary. We also filmed SLO going to a window in the purple room, and looking back at camera. None of this seemed to harmonise too well with the original stuff, at least to my eye. It will depend on the skill of the two Jacks.

When MM left the studio, she did so quickly and furtively. She is supposed to come back tomorrow but we all know she won't. She didn't say goodbye to anyone, not even her personal dresser, who has been so loyal and patient, or to Gordon, her hairdresser.

We knew we would never see her again and, sad to tell, it was an immense relief. Poor Milton is very depressed. He feels a failure, but he would have needed the strength of ten men to have succeeded in all his roles. He had been warned about what he was taking on by other producers of MM's films. But her appeal is so great that he shrugged them off. Even MM is not to blame. The great engine of publicity that surrounds her is unstoppable. Like some awful curse of the gods, it stalks her every moment, and one day it will crush her.

TUESDAY, 20 NOVEMBER

Back at Pinewood for the last time.

Another shot of SLO, this time with the camera looking up at him from the floor – the point of view MM would have had when she slid to the ground after too much vodka. No one can find the ceiling piece, painted with cherubs, to which MM refers, so we had to go without it. SLO was stony-faced. He is not a happy man at the moment.

By lunchtime it was crystal clear that we wouldn't see MM again.

Mr Perceval came in to supervise the winding down of the production. He has asked me to help him clear up in the London office for another 10 days, but he still has Vanessa, so he is just being kind. Then the production office will be closed and LOP will vanish, I suppose. SLO explained that he will start editing next week. To my great relief, he did make a definite date for me to come to see him in London at the end of January. 'Don't worry, Colin. We won't let you starve. We'll find something for you to do.'

This is just as well as I got no encouragement from David at all. He sees me as part of SLO's team now – about to disappear with the rest of them. After lunch we did a shot of Dicky Wattis's stand-in's legs behind a screen – supposed to be in Elsie Marina's digs, while Dicky is waiting for her to get ready to go to the Embassy. MM had had a struggle to get into that tight white dress at the best of times. On camera, and helped only by Daphne, it had proved impossible. We desperately needed the 'cut-away' to cover Bumble and the dresser going in to help sort it out. It was very sad not to see Dicky himself. He and Paul became great friends and I will miss them.

After the last shot was over, there was a great sense of let-down. Milton and David Maysles appeared and invited us all into the next studio, which is not in use. At one end there was a large trestle table covered with packages.

'Men on the left, women on the right,' they called. 'A parting gift to each one of you – from Marilyn.'

Everyone pressed forward to look. At the men's end the packages were obviously bottles – identically wrapped. At the other end were smaller objects which turned out to be identical leather purses. Each item had been labelled with the name of someone on the crew. People rummaged around, finding the present with their name on. Then one man, I didn't see who, walked across the studio to one of the huge round rubbish bins. He stood there for a moment, and then he just threw his bottle in. Immediately one of the ladies followed and threw in her purse. There was a sort of rippling murmur of anger and assent, and then everyone followed suit. Quite soon the bin was literally over-flowing with bottles and purses, still wrapped and labelled – 'Thank you from Marilyn Monroe' in David's handwriting. For Milton that was too much; he shrugged and grinned and left. I had already said my goodbyes as I loaded up the car this morning. I expect we will all recover. But it's going to take a long time.

POSTSCRIPT

We never saw Marilyn again, but we knew exactly what was going to happen. She would fall out completely with Milton Greene (she did, in 1957), and Marilyn Monroe Productions would never make another film (it didn't). Her marriage to Arthur Miller would collapse and end in divorce (it did, in 1961). She would become unable to work at all, and would eventually commit suicide (she did, in 1962). Had we been told about conspiracy theories and Kennedy connections, we would simply have shrugged our shoulders. The pressure of just being Marilyn Monroe was already making each day a painful struggle for her, and the end of the story was inevitable.

While she was making *The Prince and the Showgirl*, Marilyn was often in great distress. Of course she was in an unfamiliar foreign country, but even those with whom she had chosen to surround herself were from a completely different world to her. Milton and Amy Greene, Lee and Paula Strasberg, Arthur Miller, Hedda Rosten, Arthur Jacobs and Irving Stein all came from a New York, Jewish, immigrant background which was the opposite of Marilyn's unstructured Californian upbringing. Not for her the possessive mother in the warm Bronx kitchen, giving a child a sense of its own worth, and the future confidence that goes with it. And yet, when she was in front of a camera, Marilyn radiated a joy and a vitality which made everyone else pale by comparison. No wonder we cannot forget her.

It was clear that *The Prince and the Showgirl* was not destined to be a big success at the box office. It was too 'stagy' and too claustrophobic. Nor would the film make much impact on the career of either of its two stars. Paradoxically, it was Olivier's perform-ance that was most affected by the problems on the set. Despite his unprintable comments about her inexperience and unprofessionalism, Marilyn had appeared in virtually the same number of films as he had (*The Prince and the Showgirl* was her twenty-fifth to his twenty-eighth), and her relationship with the camera was more intimate than his – Dame Sybil was right. Watching the film today, Marilyn appears happy and natural, while Olivier often looks stiff and awkward.

Marilyn's next film role, in *Some Like it Hot*, brought her great critical acclaim, but no relief from the problems of production. Many years after it was made I met the director, Billy Wilder, at a Hollywood party. Stuck for something to say to this fierce old Austrian, I murmured that I too had worked with Miss Monroe. 'Then you know the meaning of pure pain,' he growled, and stalked away. Yes – but of pure magic too.

Laurence Olivier did not forget his promise to take me with him. He had found a play which would give him the new lease of life he had been looking for. *The Entertainer* by John Osborne opened at the Royal Court Theatre on 10 April 1957, and is still consid-ered one of Olivier's greatest performances. I became his personal assistant, and also the Assistant Stage Manager at the Court. We took the play on tour and then to the Palace Theatre in the West End. Halfway through the run Joan Plowright took over the role created by Dorothy Tutin, and Olivier's marriage to Vivien Leigh finally collapsed. By this time I had accompanied Larry and Vivien on the Royal Shakespeare Theatre's tour of Europe with *Titus Andronicus*, but that is the subject of a different diary.

I never worked on another feature film, and in the film world you are either in or out. Consequently I never saw David Orton or Mr Perceval again; but I owe them both a debt of gratitude. I continued my friendship with Tony and Anne Bushell, and I often visited Larry in his dressing room wherever he happened to be performing. Vivien I saw up until the last week of her life in July 1967.

After Olivier went to Hollywood to make *Spartacus* in 1959 I was offered a job by Sidney Bernstein, Chairman of Granada Television. Once more I had high hopes, but I soon found myself back where I had started, as a trainee Assistant Floor Manager. Eventually I did become a producer and director – of documentary films on 'the Arts', of which I made over a hundred. It has been a rewarding and enjoyable career, and I never forgot the lessons I learned on *The Prince and the Showgirl*.

INDEX